THE ALASKA RIVER GUIDE

*Canoeing, Kayaking, and Rafting
in the Last Frontier*

Karen J█████

Alaska Northwest Books™
Anchorage • Seattle • Portland

To my parents, Emil and Gladys Jettmar, who led me to water and boats early in life, and encouraged me to follow my dreams

NOTE: In this book, I have tried to describe the rivers as accurately as possible. And yet features of Alaska's rivers can change due to weather or the impacts of civilization. If you encounter conditions that are different from those I've described here, or situations worth noting in relation to private property, access, or other issues, please contact me through the publisher so that I can consider your suggestions for future editions of this book.

Second printing 1997

Library of Congress Cataloging-in-Publication Data
Jettmar, Karen, 1951–
       The Alaska river guide : canoeing, kayaking, and rafting in the last frontier / by Karen Jettmar.
              p.   cm.
       Includes bibliographical references (p. 292) and index.
       ISBN 0-88240-430-X
       1. Canoes and canoeing—Alaska—Guidebooks. 2. Kayaking—Alaska—Guidebooks. 3. Rafting (Sports)—Alaska—Guidebooks. 4. Alaska—Guidebooks. I. Title
       GV776.A4J48   1993
       796.1'22—dc20   92-45250
                                                          CIP

Managing editor: Ellen Harkins Wheat
Editor: Don Graydon
Cover and book designer: Cameron Mason
Maps: Carol Palmer and Cameron Mason

All photographs are by the author except: pages 95, 120, 132, 141, 245, 259, 263, U.S. Fish and Wildlife Service; page 158, Patty Brown; page 183, U.S. Department of Interior; page 226, Kirk Hoessle; and page 303, Emil Jettmar.
Front cover photo: *Rafters on the Tatshenshini–Alsek River paddle past the St. Elias Mountains in Southeast Alaska.* Photo by Karen Jettmar.
Back cover photos: (Top) *Camping beside an arctic river.* (Middle) *Aufeis on a Northern river.* Photos by Karen Jettmar. (Bottom) *Author Karen Jettmar.* Photo by Maria Gladziszewski.

Alaska Northwest Books™
An imprint of Graphic Arts Center Publishing Company
Editorial office: 2208 NW Market St., Suite 300, Seattle, WA 98107
Catalog and order dept.: P.O. Box 10306, Portland, OR 97210
       800-452-3032

Printed on acid-free paper in the United States of America

"He learnt to swim and to row, and entered into the joy of running water; and with his ear to the reed-stems he caught, at intervals, something of what the wind went whispering so constantly among them."

—Kenneth Grahame
The Wind in the Willows

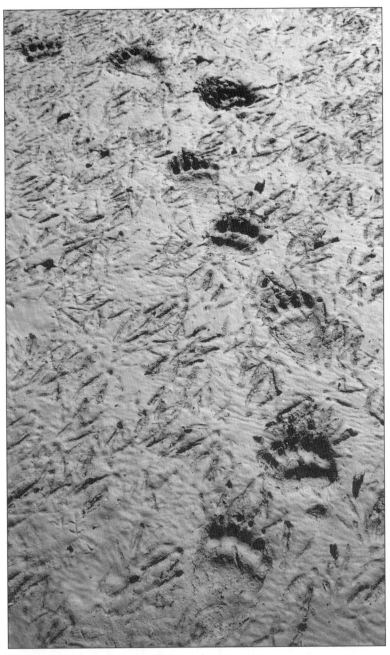

Bear and geese tracks in the river mud.

CONTENTS

ACKNOWLEDGMENTS

To Alaska's Native peoples, I wish to express my appreciation. For thousands of years they have lived beside the rivers, harvesting fish and wildlife, living in harmony with the land, and leaving little trace of their presence. I am also grateful to the explorers who came before me and recorded their observations, teaching us so much about the land and its inhabitants.

I wish to recognize the work of the people who were employed by the federal and state governments in the early 1970s and 1980s to float rivers and write river reports. I envy their experiences and am grateful for their observations, especially those of Jules Tileston and the folks at the Heritage Conservation and Recreation Service before it was disbanded. My gratitude goes to those working for the National Park Service, Bureau of Land Management, U.S. Fish and Wildlife Service, U.S. Forest Service, and the State of Alaska who have written about public lands in management plans, environmental impact statements, and Wild and Scenic River proposals and who are working to protect our precious wilderness and wild rivers. Bruce Talbot, Jim Hannah, Jay Wells, Alan Eliason, Page Spencer, and Patty Brown were especially helpful. The librarians at the U.S. Fish and Wildlife Service library and the Alaska Resources Library were very helpful, particularly Cathy Vitale, who had the uncanny ability to find resources I didn't even know I was looking for.

My thanks go to all the many friends, co-workers, and trip participants who have paddled wild rivers with me; to all the pilots who have landed me safely in places of incredible beauty; to Clarence Summers, for many years of encouragement; and to Kaci Cronkhite for her support while I led the dual life of guiding river trips and meeting book manuscript deadlines.

Finally, I am especially grateful to the people at Alaska Northwest Books: to Sara Juday for believing in me as a writer, to Marlene Blessing for encouraging my brainstorm of ideas and for accepting the project, and to Ellen Wheat, Cameron Mason, and Don Graydon for helping me transform it all into a beautiful book.

A LEGACY OF WILD RIVERS

The rich tapestry of Alaska is threaded together by 365,000 miles of waterways, from cascading mountain streams to meandering valley rivers, from the meltwaters of glaciers to broad rivers that empty into the sea. These waterways run deep in the fabric of Alaskan life, providing means of communication, nutrition, and transport for plants, animals, and people.

Thousands of years ago, many rivers were used by aboriginal peoples for passage between seacoast and Interior. Koyukon Athapaskan elders say that when the world was first created by the Great Raven, rivers flowed upstream on one side and downstream on the other. This made travel easy: no paddling was necessary. Raven, known as the Trickster, decided it was *too* easy, so he made the current flow only one way. From that time on, Natives poled up rivers in light boats to hunting and fishing camps, and seasonally they loaded skin or birchbark boats with dried fish or meat and floated down to their villages. The Native peoples of Alaska developed highly sophisticated cultures centered on the waterforms around them and the plants, animals, and landscapes associated with those waterways.

Foreign fur traders began arriving in the mid-1700s, followed by missionaries, prospectors, and geologists. These early explorers hired Natives to show them the way into this immense land, and they learned to use ancient Native methods of travel from watershed to watershed.

And so the land accepted the many migrations of people and is accepting them still. But the numbers of people now are greater, and their technology more intrusive. Some people look at rivers for their hydroelectric potential, while others prize them for the unspoiled wildlands they flow through. In a society that encourages exploitation and economic development while at the same time crying for protection of dwindling wild places, even maintaining the integrity of existing protected places is difficult. Our waterways are far from safe as they face such threats as poor forestry practices, chemical pollution, and petroleum exploration.

Even today, many of Alaska's rivers remain mysterious because they have been paddled so seldom. Alaska is so large it is commonly thought of as having six major regions, each with its own topographic and environmental features. The countless rivers offer a variety of experience not found in any other state in the nation. You can float through a suburban neighborhood on a stream that supports king salmon, or drive to the wilderness headwaters of the Chena River and, in two days, float into downtown Fairbanks. You can spend a weekend quietly paddling and portaging between lakes and lily pads on the Kenai Peninsula, or ride the silver-gray glacial meltwater of the Nenana River past tourists watching from Winnebagos as you disappear into the Nenana Gorge. You can follow an ancient Athapaskan trade route from the Yukon Territory to vast lake and oxbow country on the Yukon Flats, or glide over a seething mass of spawning salmon in a clearwater stream that empties into Bristol Bay. You can parallel the ancient path of great caribou migrations, from high in the mountains to the boreal forest, or eat ice from calving glaciers as you float down the Copper River to Cordova. All in the same day, you can paddle for hours in the sun wearing only shorts and a T-shirt, then don a hooded parka and wool gloves when a chilly wind whips up.

In this book, I profile a wide variety of rivers from all over Alaska, concentrating mainly on trips for intermediate boaters—those who have run Class I and II rivers with proficiency and who possess good wilderness camping skills. Some are good day trips; others involve major expedition planning. Most of the river trips described here are not high-speed experiences requiring helmets, wet suits, and sleek poly playboats—but several are. Some of the rivers are easily accessible by road and offer exciting whitewater runs (Gulkana River, Nenana River, Eagle River). On many of the rivers you can join tours, whether for an hour or for a month. I look at rivers as avenues to fine wilderness country and at boats as transportation rather than tools for surviving Class IV rapids.

In writing this guidebook I've tried to not steal away the elements of surprise and adventure that people seek on a wilderness trip. Alaska's remoteness and size still offer plenty of both. My goal has been to provide enough information to help you prepare for a trip, without spoiling your sense of discovery. At the same time, writing about an area inherently invites people to it and possibly makes it more popular. None of the rivers described in this guide is unknown, and some are already quite popular. The agencies that manage river areas can provide additional information on the places you plan to visit. You'll find a listing of land managers at the back of this book.

River ratings and other information in this book provide

guidance, but keep in mind that rivers are dynamic: they swell with snowmelt and rain, and they change course over time. For a particular river, use your best judgment in determining whether you have the boating and wilderness skills required. Factor in the river's remoteness and coldness, and the difficulty of being rescued, and then decide on the river for you.

Rivers are the stuff of memories, stories, and folklore. Once you float a river and enter "river time," you may never want to leave that dreamlike flow of life, especially in the endless daylight of the Northern summer. Alaska's rivers are for the weekend floater as well as for the bold adventurer. I hope that, in discovering Alaska's wild and free-flowing rivers, you will be struck with how precious they are and will become committed to their protection.

THE SPECIAL CHALLENGES OF ALASKA

There are few roads and relatively few people in Alaska. Distances from one region to another are immense—like traveling across several states in the Lower 48. In other regions of the United States, the national parks, forests, refuges, and other public lands are often surrounded by cities and smaller towns. These public lands are islands of wilderness bordered by civilization. It's the other way around in Alaska, where pockets of civilization are surrounded by wilderness. In Alaska, it is still possible to take a river trip and see no one.

Alaskan solitude comes at a price, of course. Part of your river adventure involves getting to the river. At times this can be difficult, on unpaved four-wheel drive roads or, more frequently, by air. Entire watersheds are essentially primitive, with few or no official landing strips. Flying within the state is expensive, whether it's via scheduled airline or on charter aircraft. Air charter rates range from $200 to $600 per hour, depending on the size of the plane. For example, the air charter cost from Anchorage to the Wood River Lakes System in Wood-Tikchik State Park runs $500 to $700 per person, whereas a trip to Alexander Creek costs about $100 per person. There are more than a hundred air charter companies, each with its own "territory" and fare schedule. Finding a charter operator who knows about the river you want to float takes time and effort. The yellow pages of Alaska phone books and the land management agencies listed in this book's river descriptions (and in the roster of land managers at the back of the book) are good places to obtain the names of charter airlines. On the other hand, Alaska's road system can take you to some wonderful wild rivers for a fraction of the cost.

Part of the challenge of running a river in Alaska is being prepared for fickle weather and unpredictable transportation. Fourteen days of canoeing on the Kobuk River may begin with four days of sitting in Kotzebue as you wait for acceptable flying weather. And at the end of your trip, a storm in Ambler could delay your flight out as you wait, knowing you were supposed to be back at work three days ago. If your party splits up for flying to a river, make sure each planeload is self-contained, with food, stove, fuel, and gear in case the other members of the group are delayed by weather.

Once your pilot drops you off, you're on your own. It's too late

Wilderness rivers offer solitude and intimacy with the environment.

to remember the pump for the raft or the repair kit that could patch a folding canoe chewed by a porcupine. The prevention of serious illness or injury becomes vital. You'll need to be more cautious about running heavy whitewater when you realize it's many miles to the nearest help instead of 100 yards to the nearest road.

Proper preparation is the key ingredient for a successful Alaskan river expedition. Do your homework. Read up on the river, and talk to as many knowledgeable people as you can before the trip. Do not go until you have paddling ability for the river you want to visit and skills to deal with an emergency. Every member of your group should have wilderness camping skills and be prepared to deal with adverse weather for long periods of time. And before a trip, undertake a program of physical conditioning. The rigors of the trip—paddling, rowing, hiking, fighting headwinds, hauling gear, portaging boats, setting up tents in foul weather—all take endurance. The more fit you are, the more you'll enjoy your trip.

Group or family members without much camping experience may need help throughout the trip during difficult conditions. Decisions need to be made with the least experienced group member in mind. When hunger, fatigue, or cold set in, know when to stop and make camp. Set realistic goals for travel and don't expect to cover a set number of miles every day. Weather can pin you down, throwing your schedule way off. Allow in your planning for bad-weather days. If the bad weather never materializes, you'll simply arrive at your pickup point ahead of schedule—far better than endangering your party by struggling to make it on time. Carry the essentials to survive at all times: at the very least, a Swiss Army knife, waterproof matches, a compass, maps, emergency food, raingear, extra clothing, signal mirror, space blanket, a candle, a hook, and some fishing line.

Most first-time visitors to Alaska leave it to commercial river guides and outfitters to plan their itinerary. There are dozens of rafting, kayaking, fishing, and backpacking companies. The ones owned and operated by Alaskans living in Alaska will likely be the most knowledgeable. The Alaska Wilderness Recreation and Tourism Association (P.O. Box 1353, Valdez, AK 99686), a nonprofit organization that works for ecologically responsible recreation and tourism, maintains a list of members who offer river guide services. Other sources of information include conservation organizations (see list at the back of this book). Federal and state land managers keep rosters of guides, outfitters, and pilots operating on public lands; each trip description in this book lists the appropriate land managers (see back of book for information sources). Ask about the experience of your guide, the safety equipment that will be brought on the trip, and the number of participants on a trip. Do your best to learn what you're getting into before you decide to go.

WHITEWATER
CLASSIFICATION

The difficulty ratings in this book are generally for average conditions. They do not take into consideration travel on rivers during the worst times, such as just after breakup (when ice first breaks up in the spring, causing a river to flow again, usually at flood stage), or after heavy rains, or on a long, hot sunny day when glacier melt can cause rivers to swell enormously. Also, ratings don't take into consideration the remoteness and coldness of some Alaskan rivers. As a rule of thumb, many people rate Alaskan rivers an extra class higher in difficulty in order to factor in the coldness and remoteness of the river. Unless a river is accessible by road, it should be considered remote.

Only boaters who are fully prepared to deal with wilderness conditions and emergencies should undertake river trips that are rated at the high end of their ability. Start on an easy river with no technical difficulties. There are easy rivers that traverse outstanding scenery and primitive wildlands. Before you embark on a fly-in trip, talk to your pilot about conditions. Have an alternative plan ready in case the river looks too difficult or if conditions render it unfloatable. Arctic rivers often don't open up as early in the season as expected, and boaters have found themselves stranded with low water or have had to haul boats and gear across aufeis (large areas of thick ice covering the riverbed) where the river has not yet broken a channel through.

Whitewater classifications rate river difficulties in six classes, from easiest to most difficult.

Class I: Easy. Flatwater to occasional rapids characterized by low, regular waves. Obstructions are easy to avoid. Best route is easily recognized and maneuvered. Suitable for open canoes, folding boats, and whitewater kayaks, and for inflatable canoes, kayaks, and rafts.

Class II: Medium. Frequent rapids characterized by high, regular waves up to 3 feet. Easy to medium chutes, ledges, or falls. Back eddies and differentiating currents are easily negotiated. Best route is generally easy to recognize and maneuver. Suitable for open canoes, folding boats, and whitewater kayaks, and for inflatable canoes, kayaks, and rafts.

Class III: Difficult. Numerous rapids with high, irregular waves, rollers, breakers, and back eddies, requiring complex maneuvering. Chutes, falls, and ledges are difficult. Spray cover is necessary for open boats. Scouting is mandatory. Suitable for decked canoes or canoes with spray skirts, whitewater kayaks, and inflatable kayaks and rafts. Kayakers should be proficient in Eskimo roll.

Class IV: Very difficult. Long, difficult sections of rapids with high, irregular waves, breakers, powerful back eddies, whirlpools, sharp bends, and constricted canyons. Chutes, falls, and ledges with powerful rollers and undertow. Best passage is difficult to recognize and difficult to run. Scouting from shore is mandatory. Rescue can be difficult. Suitable for whitewater kayaks, whitewater decked canoes, and rafts. Helmet and proficiency in Eskimo roll is mandatory in whitewater kayak.

Class V: Extremely difficult. Long sections of continuous violent rapids with very high, unavoidable irregular waves, breakers, haystacks, and powerful rollers. Very fast current with powerful whirlpools and boiling back eddies creates complicated routes that require scouting. Suitable for whitewater kayaks, whitewater decked canoes, and rafts. Helmet, hull flotation, and expert proficiency in Eskimo roll is mandatory in whitewater kayak.

Class VI: Highest level of difficulty. All whitewater Class V difficulties are intensified to the upper limit of skills and equipment. Nearly impossible, extremely dangerous, and runnable only under ideal conditions. Scouting from shore is mandatory. Suitable for whitewater kayaks, whitewater decked canoes, and rafts. Second boat party should be scouting from shore, ready to assist the party running the rapids.

See "Rivers Grouped by Level of Difficulty" at the back of the book for rivers categorized by whitewater classification.

TOPOGRAPHIC MAPS

Basic topographic features like mountains, hills, and lakes don't often change. But rivers change their courses—particularly where they discharge into the ocean, forming wide deltas and sloughs—and the topographic maps made in the 1950s and 1960s may be incorrect. Newer maps have mostly just been updated with land status changes; for example, national parks and refuges are shown. But only some of the newer maps in the scale 1:63,360 have the water features revised. Keep this in mind when floating; always bring a compass, and take bearings.

Topographic maps listed for each river in this book are in the 1:63,360 series. If you want the overall view of a river, buy the 1:250,000-scale maps. You can buy maps in the visitor contact stations of many of the national parks and wildlife refuges.

The best complete source for maps is United States Geological Survey (USGS) Map Sales, 101 12th Avenue, No. 12, Fairbanks, AK 99701 (907-456-0244). In Anchorage, USGS has a walk-in map store on the campus of Alaska Pacific University at 4230 University Drive (907-786-7011).

Maps are also available by mail from USGS Map Sales, Box 25286, Denver, CO 80225 (303-236-7477). To purchase Canadian maps, write to Canada Map Office, 615 Booth Street, Ottawa, Ontario, Canada K1A 0E9 (613-952-7000).

Contact the land managers listed for each river for more information. You may also want to write or visit one of the Alaska Public Lands Information Centers: Anchorage Public Lands Information Center, 605 West Fourth Avenue, Anchorage 99501; Tok Public Lands Information Center, Mile 1314, Alaska Highway, P.O. Box 359, Tok 99780; Fairbanks Public Lands Information Center, 250 Cushman Street, Suite 1A, Fairbanks 99701.

CHOOSING THE
RIGHT BOAT

Hard-shell canoes and kayaks are wonderful for road-accessible rivers. These rigid boats have an obvious disadvantage as wilderness craft in Alaska; they don't easily fit into small planes. The effort and expense to transport a boat to some locations can be more than the boat originally cost. For this reason, Alaskan paddlers who spend much time on rivers have more than one boat. Sometimes we use hard-shell boats, other times folding or inflatable boats.

The Federal Aviation Administration prohibits pilots from carrying boats strapped to floatplane pontoons if the plane is carrying passengers. Some pilots will transport hard-shell boats separately from passengers, either in planes large enough to take boats as cargo or strapped to the floats of a plane. Where this is not possible or practical, we use inflatable boats or folding boats (boats that come apart and fold up into a bag). Inflatable kayaks and canoes may be suitable on rivers that are too rocky or shallow for folding boats.

Hard-shell canoes. Advantages—Large carrying capacity, for taking large quantities of gear and food; nice for families and fishing. Disadvantages—Not suitable for heavy whitewater, except in the hands of experienced paddlers; expensive to transport to and from fly-in locations.

For two adults or for family canoeing, look for a canoe that is large enough to carry two adults plus one or two small children. A good choice is a 17-footer with a flat or slightly rounded bottom and sides at least 14 inches high and a total weight between 65 and 80 pounds. For solo canoeing, get a boat that is 15 to 16 feet long.

Most hard-shell canoes today are made of Kevlar, fiberglass, aluminum, or plastic (ABS or RAM X). Kevlar is one of the strongest and lightest materials available. Boats made of Kevlar are scratch-resistant, lightweight, strong—and more than twice as expensive as fiberglass models.

Canoes made of ABS, RAM X, or other plastics are the most durable. These boats can bend nearly in half around a boulder and spring back into shape. This pliability is also a plus in shallow rapids, where the boat bottom gives and slips off rocks. Unfortunately, these non-Kevlar boats are heavy.

Fiberglass boats are strong, fast in the water, and easy to repair. Design and handling characteristics vary with the boat manufacturer. In general, fiberglass boats are low maintenance.

Aluminum canoes are durable, stable—and noisy. It's difficult to paddle an aluminum boat silently, and paddles and rocks both clank on the aluminum. These boats require no maintenance, however, and they are usually the safest, most stable boats on the water. If they hit a rock broadside in a strong current, they will get bent. Reshaping a bent canoe may cause it to tear, but it can be mended.

Hard-shell kayaks. Advantages—Lightweight, easy to maneuver in the hands of a skilled paddler, can be taken in rougher water, sit low in the water and are relatively unaffected by wind; paddling is more efficient and responsive than in hard-shell canoes; good for groups in which each person wants to paddle an individual craft. (Two-person hard-shell kayaks are not generally recommended except on slow-moving Class I rivers.) Disadvantages—Difficult in shallow water, carry very little gear, expensive to transport to and from fly-in locations. River-touring kayaks and some sea kayaks designed for river touring are larger and can carry much more than whitewater kayaks; on some rivers they are ideal. Hard-shell kayaks are generally made from fiberglass, ABS plastic, or Kevlar.

Folding canoes and kayaks. Advantages—Transportable by car, plane, even the U.S. Postal Service; stable, easy to repair; carry medium amount of gear; some have built-in inflatable sponsons that prevent the boat from sinking even if it capsizes. Disadvantages— Not suitable for heavy whitewater; must take care that bottom is not damaged on rocks or gravel bars because a broach on a single rock can destroy a boat; animals, like porcupines and arctic ground squirrels, may chew on them. Unloaded folding canoes may be tippy and unstable.

Folding kayaks were developed in Germany, where people needed a portable boat that could be carried on trains. The Klepper Aerius, with a skin of canvas and Hypalon rubber over a frame of hardwood and aluminum, was the first folding kayak (and the only one on the market for many years). Kleppers are finely crafted, sturdy boats. Made in both one- and two-person models, they probably have descended more Alaskan rivers than any other type of kayak. Now there are several manufacturers of folding kayaks. Boats made by Nautiraid, Folbot, and Feathercraft have all been used successfully on Alaskan rivers. Though folding kayaks have been used

Assembling a folding Klepper kayak at the start of a river trip.

successfully on Class III rivers and even for a crossing of the Atlantic Ocean, they are best suited to Class I and II rivers and sea kayaking. Folding canoes made by Ally are suitable for Class I and II rivers.

Inflatable canoes. Advantages—Easily transportable by car, airplane, mail; easily inflated; fun to maneuver (respond very much like a rigid canoe); fairly easy to repair; carry medium amounts of gear. Disadvantages—Can be punctured on rocks; animals, like porcupines and arctic ground squirrels, may chew on them.

Metzeler boats made in Germany were the forerunner of inflatable canoes. These boats, now manufactured by Zodiac but still with the name Metzeler, are decent pack-in boats. Other excellent brands to look for are Grabner, made in Canada, and Eurocraft, made in Austria.

Inflatable kayaks. Advantages—Made of much more durable fabric than in the past; self-bailing models widely available; lightweight and easy to transport; highly maneuverable; one-person or two-person models; fairly easy to repair; can handle whitewater. Disadvantages—Animals, like porcupines and arctic ground squirrels, may chew on them; two-person model may not be large enough for two paddlers and gear for an extended wilderness trip.

Pioneered by the French and Germans, the inflatable kayak has been around since the 1960s. Many companies, such as Achilles,

Hyside, Aire, Riken, Momentum, Sevylor, Metzeler, and Northwest River Supplies, now make inflatable kayaks. Some, like the Metzeler, are still made in a traditional kayak shape. Most, however, are sled-shaped with an open cockpit, inflatable tubes, and a thwart, and can be paddled like kayaks or canoes. Be aware of the fabric used in making the boats. Light-gauge PVC (polyvinyl chloride) boats are not trustworthy on remote or whitewater rivers. Look for boats made of Hypalon, heavy-gauge PVC, or neoprene.

Inflatable rafts. Advantages—Can carry lots of gear; novice boaters can learn with experienced paddle captain, or novice boaters can be rowed without having to do any of the work of maneuvering the boat; can be safely taken in heavy whitewater in the hands of experienced boat handlers; can hold an entire family or group of friends; resilient and pliable but tough enough to absorb the shocks of banging and scraping against rocks; easy to repair. Disadvantages—High profile in the wind and therefore very slow when there are upriver winds; not streamlined and therefore slow-moving, a problem when the current is slow and you feel you're making little progress downriver.

There are many excellent inflatable rafts on the market, con-structed from lightweight and durable polymers, including PVC, PVC-coated Dacron, Trevira, Hypalon, and neoprene. Conventional rafts have flat, firm floors. Self-bailing models have an inflated floor with drain holes that send water back out of the raft. Self-bailers are heavier and bulkier than conventional rafts, but safer in heavy whitewater, where bailing is required. Some people prefer the firm floor for standing and stowing gear. Catarafts are rafts constructed of two inflated pontoons held rigidly with a frame between and atop them. The double tubes have a low center of gravity for greater sta-bility and increased flotation, allowing quicker response than con-ventional rafts. A Cataraft pivots and spins like a raft and pushes through heavy whitewater without stalling.

GEARING UP

Alaska's weather extremes and wilderness conditions can tax you and your gear to the maximum. It's important to dress properly and to carry sufficient food and equipment to respond to emergencies.

CLOTHING

Inner clothing should include long underwear, socks, and glove liners, all of polypropylene or other synthetic fibers known for their ability to wick moisture away from your body. Outer clothing should include synthetic pile (Polarfleece or Synchilla) and/or wool. Bring a nylon windbreaker because pile or wool garments alone, without wind protection, are often inadequate. Bring enough layers to stay warm, especially on a long trip. Temperatures can dip to freezing even in summer. Always bring at least one change of clothes in a waterproof float bag so that if you capsize or get wet, you have a dry set to wear. And don't forget that clothes should be comfortable.

Footwear

Footwear varies according to personal preference. On most trips, I wear knee-high rubber boots with wool socks and wool felt insoles. Alaskan waters are extremely cold and if you try to paddle in just a pair of running shoes or Aquasocks, your feet will get too cold. Even in rubber boots with insoles and two pairs of wool socks, feet can get cold. The water on glacial and arctic rivers may be just above freezing. The best knee-high boots are those that are 14 to 16 inches high and fit snugly around the ankle, both for support and for the flexibility they give you while hopping in and out of a boat or while hiking across wetlands after you're ashore. When made of neoprene, these boots remain supple in cold weather. Some people prefer to wear wet-suit booties inside running shoes or under a pair of river sandals. I find that the booties work fine on warm days, but on overcast days when I'm constantly in and out of the boat, my feet eventually freeze. It's not a good idea to wear hip boots; they will pull you under if you fall into the river.

Even with knee-high boots, feet often get wet. It's just one of those things that comes with jumping in and out of the water and pushing off gravel bars. Even when water fills a boot, though, it's surprising how warm your feet can stay, as long as you are wearing wool socks and wool felt insoles.

For exploring on land during your river trip, you'll probably want another pair of shoes. On wet days and when hiking on wet tundra or marshlands, I wear my neoprene boots (made by Servus or BF Goodrich). Some people like to wear a combination rubber and leather boot, like the Maine hunting shoe sold by L. L. Bean. With a leather lace-up upper and molded tread rubber bottom, such boots are great for variable conditions, including rock and scree slopes. Other people rely on a good sturdy pair of broken-in hiking shoes. Heavy lug-soled boots, especially all-leather types, are unnecessary and only add extra weight to your feet and gear. The leather gets wet and won't dry out, and heavy boots damage fragile tundra. On a river trip, especially when you won't be backpacking, choose the lightest shoe that offers support for your body weight. The lightweight, fast-drying, synthetic hiking shoes and boots available today are perfect for Alaska. For around camp, whether or not you bring hiking shoes, it's also nice to have a pair of old running shoes or a pair of river sandals that you can wear with socks. These can also be used for stream crossings.

It's important to remove your traveling boots once you're off the river for the day, to give your feet a chance to air out and to let the boots dry. Even if you don't get water inside the boots, they get clammy inside. I pull out the felt insoles and lay the boots on their sides, with the insoles alongside, in the sunniest place I can find.

Hand Protection

Some people get blisters from paddling or rowing boats and like to wear leather gloves. Others prefer light polypropylene liner gloves, wool gloves, or neoprene gloves if it is cold. I've also used liner gloves inside thick rubber gloves, the kind that cannery workers and fishermen use, but that combination is a bit too bulky. Hands are also subject to sunburn, so consider covering them with gloves or sunscreen for that reason alone. Bring a couple pairs of gloves. They will protect not only against cold, blisters, and sun, but also rain, insects, and heavy brush.

Head Protection

The sun in Alaska is intense: it's up for more than 20 hours in the summer and the ultraviolet rays are strong. On the water, the effects are greater yet. Sunglasses are essential, along with a brimmed hat—a baseball cap, crusher, or something similar. For cold weather, a wool cap or comparable pull-on hat is essential. Some people like to use a balaclava, which pulls down to cover the neck but leaves a face opening. You may also want to carry a mosquito head net or a mosquito-repellent mesh jacket with hood. I never travel anywhere in Alaska during the summer without a head net.

Raingear

Outdoor people in Alaska swear by their raingear. It *rains* here, especially in Southeast and Western Alaska. When it rains, it is also cold, so if you get wet, you're minutes away from hypothermia if you can't get into dry clothes. In Southeast and Southwest Alaska I usually carry Helly Hansen raingear consisting of heavy rubberized canvas bib overalls and a hooded jacket, gear designed for commercial fishermen. In other areas, I sometimes carry lighter weight raingear, but I always choose fabrics that are *waterproof* and strong enough not to tear easily. Gore-Tex may breathe, but it is a semi-permeable material so that eventually water passes through, especially if you are sitting in a boat all day. If your raingear does not breathe and causes you to sweat inside it, you can always dry it out. Your raingear should have a hood. It's nice to have tight-fitting material at the wrists (either elastic or a Velcro closure) to keep water from running down inside your sleeves. Specially designed whitewater paddling jackets are good. Strong, sturdy rain outfits are what you want—definitely no ponchos.

LIFE JACKETS

Some people think they are safe as long as they have life jackets (personal flotation devices) inside the boat. They're wrong. You need to wear them. It doesn't matter if the air temperature is 35 degrees or 85 degrees: if you fall in the water, you can drown. Each year in Alaska, canoes and other small boats capsize and people drown because they weren't wearing life jackets.

I consider a life jacket both essential safety equipment and essential clothing that helps me stay warm while in the boat. A life jacket should be worn at all times during travel on the water. Type III life jackets have a minimum buoyancy of 15.5 pounds and are designed for most recreational use. Type IV personal flotation devices are seat cushions or ring buoys; because they cannot be worn, they are basically useless on rivers except to sit on. Type V life jackets, with a minimum buoyancy of 22 pounds, are designed for heavy whitewater use.

A good life jacket should fit properly, be comfortable, and be specially designed for wearing while paddling. A good life jacket will not only keep your head afloat if you capsize but will also conserve body heat. Proper fit means that it feels snug around your body. If you wear a loose-fitting or unzipped life jacket and you go into the water, it will float up over your head or may come off. Life jackets are available in several sizes, including children's sizes, so finding one to fit you should be no problem. Closed-cell Ensolite vest-type life jackets, such as the ones made by Extrasport, are the most durable.

Life jackets can also serve as a sleeping pad. I have used two life jackets under my sleeping bag on many a trip when I didn't want to take up space in a small boat with a sleeping pad; the life jackets were a little lumpy, but it was better than having my bag on the cold ground.

Life jackets should always be worn *outside* your outside layer of clothing. If you are wearing a raincoat, the life jacket goes *over* it. Then if you go overboard, your clothing won't invert over your head and pull you down.

DRY SUITS AND WET SUITS

If you plan to paddle a Class III river in a whitewater kayak, you may want a dry suit. Dry suits are suits made of coated nylon or other synthetic fabric, with gusseted cuffs and neck and a waterproof zipper. In a dry suit you stay dry, except for the sweating inside. In cold conditions, they are ideal. At other times, they may be too hot.

Wet suits, on the other hand, can be downright miserable in Alaska, where the water and weather are often cold and clammy. Some people swear by them, but I can't imagine anything worse than having to don a wet wet suit on the fifth day of a river trip. The idea behind wet suits is that water is allowed into the suit, but the suit's neoprene material is supposed to prevent significant water movement over your skin. Your body warms the water, so you stay warm, though wet. If you're just going on a day trip, wet suits are fine, with a waterproof paddling jacket and pants on top and synthetic long underwear underneath—and your life jacket over all.

BASIC GEAR FOR EXPEDITION RIVER TRIPS

In packing for expedition river trips, don't omit essential items because of weight or space. Instead, examine each item and reduce it to its smallest bulk. For example, bring only a small amount of toothpaste instead of a family-size tube. Don't bring cast-iron pots or cases of beer if you're taking a small plane in and out of the river. Leave the lawn chairs and hardback novels at home. Every time you make or break camp, you have to carry everything you brought on the trip. Just making camp can take an hour, and after a day or two you'll wonder why you brought all that extra stuff. Leave out unnecessary items and bulky or heavy foods. If you plan to do much lining or portaging, you'll want to plan out your gear so that it is easy to carry. Waterproof bags with backpack straps, kitchen boxes with two handles for carrying, and 5-gallon plastic buckets with lids make life easier for you when portaging or when carrying gear up onto a gravel bar to camp.

Individual Gear List

Each person on an expedition should have the following items:

- sleeping bag
- sleeping pad
- space blanket (aluminized tarp designed to reflect heat; may also be used as an emergency signaling device)
- water bottle
- cook kit
- cup/spoon
- knife (recommend Swiss Army-type)
- lighter
- waterproof matches
- candle
- two full sets of warm clothes (polypropylene, pile, and wool)
- shorts and T-shirt
- rain jacket
- rain pants
- light nylon windbreaker
- warm jacket (pile or wool)
- wool hat
- wool gloves
- one or two bandannas
- insect repellent

- mosquito head net
- rubber boots (with wool felt insoles)
- wool socks (two pairs)
- athletic shoes or river sandals
- toothbrush/toothpaste
- sunscreen
- lip protection
- sunglasses (with cord to keep them snugly on your head)
- brimmed cap
- toilet paper
- waterproof bags for gear
- extra garbage bags for further waterproofing gear inside waterproof bags
- whistle
- personal items (fragrance-free), medications, first-aid supplies
- small stash of high-energy food for emergencies
- waterproof watch
- signal mirror
- optional—Book, hiking boots, journal, camera, binoculars, neoprene gloves, cayenne spray for use against bears, flashlight for late summer when days are shorter

Some comments on several of the items of the individual gear list that you should bring:

Sleeping bags—Never bring a down bag; if it gets wet, it is useless because it will not dry out. Synthetic bags will dry within a day.

Knife—A small sharp knife hanging on your belt, or in a pocket on your life jacket, may be essential if lines get entangled in an emergency.

Garbage bags and waterproof bags—Heavy-duty waterproof bags are usually excellent for keeping gear dry. If you don't have specially designed waterproof bags, stuff sacks and nylon duffel bags will work. Line the sacks with one or two garbage bags, place your clothing or gear inside, tie the garbage bags off tightly, and then close up the sack.

Expedition Group Gear List

Each expedition should have the following group gear, in addition to each person's individual gear:

- light tents with mosquito netting, vents, and rain fly (enough tents to accommodate everyone in your party)

- boat repair kit (see list of recommended contents below)
- boat pump for inflatable boats
- roll of duct tape
- paddle for each boater and one spare paddle
- life jacket for each boater
- two 30-foot 6mm nylon or braided polypropylene lines for lining and rescue (a throw bag can count for one of the lines)
- two carabiners
- sponge
- bailer
- first-aid kit
- topographic maps in see-through, watertight case
- compass
- stove and fuel
- stove repair kit
- waterproof matches in a waterproof container
- smoke flares
- 50 to 100 feet of 3mm nylon cord (for hanging food up in trees and for other uses)
- waterproof gear bags, with straps for carrying
- food for the number of days you expect to be out, plus an extra two to three days of food
- water containers
- water filter, water purification tablets, or enough fuel to boil all drinking water
- plastic trowel for burying human waste
- hook and line for emergency fishing
- tarp and lines to make a rain fly
- optional safety items—Gun; radio

Some comments on several of the group items:

Tarp—A tarp, either freestanding or used in conjunction with an overturned boat, can provide shelter from the elements. Many times I have turned a raft on its side and propped it up with paddles, then rigged a tarp to provide a windproof, rainproof shelter. The tarp also can be placed on wet ground under the tent as a ground cloth.

Throw bag—Although you can use a coiled rope as a throw line, a throw bag assures that you will always have a line that is free of tangles and kinks. The bow line is stuffed into a nylon bag which contains foam flotation and is closed with a drawstring. When you throw the bag, the line feeds out smoothly, without tangling. This is a worthwhile safety item.

Water filter—The water in Alaska is subject to contamination by giardia and other waterborne bugs. Don't risk drinking without filtering, boiling, or treating water.

Bailer—Depending on the size of your boat, you can use an empty detergent bottle, a 1-gallon bleach bottle with the bottom cut out, or a 5-gallon bucket with metal handle. Tie a short piece of line to the bailer, with a carabiner on the end so you can clip it to the boat. One time I foolishly paddled across Demarcation Bay in a folding kayak with neither a spray skirt nor bailer; I'd forgotten them both. I resorted to reaching into my day pack for a plastic bowl, which I used to bail furiously as a following sea sent waves crashing over the stern of my boat, eventually swamping it. Another lesson learned.

Boat repair kit. The repair kit you take for a weekend trip should be essentially the same as the one you take on a long trip. You need enough tools and parts to make a "broken" boat floatable and to patch a major rip or hole. The repair kit should include many of the following items, depending on whether you have an aluminum canoe, fiberglass or plastic canoe, folding canoe or kayak, or an inflatable boat of neoprene, Hypalon, PVC, or other fabrics:

- small file
- stitching awl
- awl punch
- small pliers
- five-minute epoxy
- assorted screws, nails, nuts, and bolts
- thin-gauge wire
- strip of soft leather
- strip of canvas
- large heavy-duty sewing needle
- heavy nylon or waxed thread
- patch material and glue recommended by boat manufacturer for repair of your boat
- Xylene, Gaco, or other appropriate thinner/cleaner/solvent
- sandpaper or emery cloth
- roller rasp
- scissors
- vise grips
- extra D-rings

- extra valves
- replacement parts for any breakable item
- Carboline or other adhesive recommended by boat manufacturer
- containers for mixing
- pencil
- extra webbing and rope straps

Kayaking Gear

Kayakers on an expedition need a few items in addition to the basic individual and group items already listed. These include a dry suit for each kayaker (for whitewater paddling) and a dry-suit repair kit. A helmet is recommended for kayakers on rivers rated Class III and above. A spray skirt for each kayak is essential for whitewater paddling. Bring an extra spray skirt along in case the first one rips.

Foam flotation is great for day kayak trips but impractical for longer trips because it takes up much-needed packing space. If you use watertight gear bags, the residual air trapped inside may be enough to keep the kayak afloat if you dump.

Stuffing all the group and individual gear into a hard-shell kayak can be a challenge, not to mention paddling with all this weight. Pack your boat with the heaviest gear in the bow. Practice paddling with a loaded boat before a long trip. Loaded kayaks respond much slower than empty boats. Folding kayaks hold much more gear, but still must be packed carefully so they don't lean to one side.

Canoeing Gear

With a canoe, you can carry more than in a kayak. One of the joys of canoe journeys is that it is possible to pack a couple months' worth of food and gear into the boat and be completely self-sufficient. Still, you want to keep your gear to a minimum, especially if you are flying in.

A canoe spray skirt is not necessary for Class I rivers, optional for Class II rivers, and essential for Class III rivers. Foam flotation is recommended for whitewater trips.

Rafting Gear

The Cadillac of river travel, a raft can get you and your friends into wild country and can carry the extra gear you may need to go hiking, climbing, or backpacking.

You'll want to be sure the raft has enough D-rings glued on to properly carry gear, with safety line tied through D-rings all around the top of tubes. The raft needs a bow and stern line, each at least 30 feet long.

Each raft needs a cargo platform or other method of suspending gear above the floor. Each raft also needs a tarp and lines, or a cargo net, to tie gear down on the boat. Whatever system you develop to suspend and tie down gear, be sure to keep gear off the floor of the raft, unless it is a self-bailing boat; otherwise, it can abrade or tear the boat's bottom. Gear must be securely tied down and in waterproof bags to prevent loss if the boat flips. Make sure there are no loose lines, which can entangle someone.

Each raft may have a frame and oar set-up. If you plan to do a fly-in trip with an oar frame, be sure the frame and components break down small enough to fit into the plane.

Day Trips

If you are going on a day trip, you won't need to bring everything that you take on an extended trip, but you still need to be prepared for an accident. Even on day trips, take all your basic boating equipment, plus a repair kit and rescue gear. Take a first-aid kit, matches and a fire starter, a knife, food, sunglasses, a throw bag (described earlier under expedition group gear), a life jacket, raingear or waterproof paddling jacket and pants, a tarp or space blanket, and a warm jacket. A day trip near a road is much different from a day trip in which you fly in by plane. Anytime you fly in to a place away from a road, assume that you are on an extended trip and prepare for all emergencies, including illness or injury. Prepare for the possibility of the pilot being late to pick you up because of weather.

SAFETY

River running is a safe sport if you take the proper precautions. The most important element in safe boating is to recognize your own limitations: accept that there are rivers you cannot run until you have the skill and experience to do them safely. Going on a river with an experienced guide may be one of the best ways to learn about Alaskan rivers. By going with someone who not only has the necessary river-running skills, but also knows wilderness survival, wilderness etiquette, and natural history, you may get more out of a trip than if you went on your own.

Some very basic tips: Practice your skills and know self-rescue techniques. Make sure at least one person (and ideally everyone) on the trip has taken classes in first aid and cardiopulmonary resuscitation (CPR). Don't be afraid to voice any fears you may have to other group members.

Before putting in on any river, go over safety, technique, and rescue methods as a group. Make sure everyone is comfortable with the difficulty of the river; find out if there are specific concerns or fears. Take no watercourse for granted, even if you have run it before. Portaging, lining (using a rope to guide a boat downstream from the shore), or simply bailing out of a bad situation are

Happy paddlers at the end of a 14-day arctic river trip.

all better than taking unnecessary risks.

Keep dry and warm and well-fed to avoid hypothermia. Always wear a life jacket. If your boat flips, stay with it if you can. If rain brings the water level up to a point where it is dangerous to travel, just stop and wait it out (after a day or two, rivers go back down to a manageable level). Paddle close to shore on lakes; if a high wind comes up, get off the water.

Always scout unfamiliar waters where there is a likelihood of rapids, sweepers (trees or logs hanging over or in the river), rocks, logjams, or other hazards. When running rapids, let only one boat go at a time, to help assure safety for the group. (If boats go together in a pack, they are too close to warn each other of upcoming hazards. And it's difficult to assist a boat that has just flipped when you are about to meet the same fate.)

If you plan to float whitewater rivers in a hard-shell kayak, learn to Eskimo roll. Practice it in a swimming pool. Learn to roll on both sides and practice rolling hundreds of times, until it becomes instinctive. Join a paddling group and you'll have others to practice with and accompany on paddling trips. When you're starting out in river running, go on trips with experienced boaters. Observe their techniques, listen to their stories, and heed their advice.

SOLO TRAVEL

Never run a river alone. If something happens to you, you're at the mercy of fate. But if two people are together, the other person can take care of the victim or try to get help. With three people, one person can stay with the sick or injured one, and the third person can go for help. On a challenging whitewater river in kayaks, three should be the minimum.

Although you shouldn't take a river trip alone, you *can* actually paddle alone without being alone. By traveling in your own canoe or kayak, you can have your own experiences with the water, getting a feel for the wind, waves, and current (while the others in your party are doing the same), and yet you have the group to fall back on if something goes wrong. It's also possible to travel as a group and take time out on the land to be alone. When you're on a river in separate boats, it's wise to stick fairly close together, however. Appoint one person as the leader—usually the person with the most expertise. If possible, have an equally experienced person as the sweep, or last boat.

Paddling with a partner is also a wonderful and challenging way

to travel. When two people have learned to coordinate their paddling in a canoe or kayak, movement can seem effortless. Two
people can certainly propel a boat faster than one.

COLD WATER

Alaska's waters are cold. Even in the summer, river temperatures range from the mid-30s on glacial rivers to the low 60s on
some Interior clearwater streams. Immersion in extremely cold
water can be incapacitating within seconds. Breathing is hard to
control and you can easily inhale water. Experts say that cold water
hitting the back of the throat can actually cause the heart to stop
beating. Hyperventilation causes the body to lose a great deal of
carbon dioxide, thus diminishing blood flow to the brain. Certain
muscles, especially those at the extremities, can go into spasm.
Falling into a glacial or northern river can have extreme conse-
quences. I've seen people fall in and not be able to help themselves.
Their bodies basically go limp in the cold water and they say later
that breathing was very difficult; they had the sensation of someone
standing on their chest. You really don't want to flip a boat on a
glacial river in Alaska.

AUFEIS AND CALVING GLACIERS

Many northern rivers have aufeis, sometimes called overflow
ice. As rivers begin freezing in the fall, they flow up and over the
new ice, creating layer upon layer of ice. By winter's end, these
layers may be more than 15 feet thick. Often covering extensive
areas of northern rivers, aufeis can block river channels or calve
into the river like icebergs. Other areas actually have glaciers that
reach into the rivers (the Copper and Alsek rivers, for example).
Glaciers and icebergs, so beautiful and intriguing, beckon exploration, but they can be very dangerous. They can rip a raft or folding
boat. Glaciers calve massive chunks of ice without warning.
Icebergs, which show only 20 percent of their bulk above the water,
can flip and break without warning. Keep a safe distance.

WEATHER

Weather during the ice-free river-running season varies throughout Alaska, and can even vary wildly within the same day. Be prepared for rain, high winds, heat, cold, sleet, and snow. In general,

areas with a maritime climate (Southeast Alaska, the coasts of the Gulf of Alaska and Bering Sea, and the Aleutian chain) have cool summer temperatures with heavy precipitation. In the Interior, the continental climate dominates, with warm, dry summers. In the transition area between the coast and the Interior, temperatures are warmer than those on the coast, and the rainfall is average. In the arctic, summer temperatures are generally cool, with low precipitation. Along the arctic coast it is often foggy or cloudy and the prevailing winds send cold air off the ice pack to the land.

Regardless of these general weather patterns, expect anything. One summer a group of us flew into an Arctic Slope river from the south, over the Continental Divide. The first planeload made it; those in the second planeload were stuck for a day and a half on a gravel bar where they were dropped by the pilot when clouds on the Divide closed in. Our group on the north side of the Divide experienced a storm that dumped several inches of snow during a mid-June night. Several days later, when we were all back together again, enjoying the river, the temperature was in the high 80s and we had stripped to shorts and T-shirts, with a liberal dose of mosquito repellent. On our last afternoon on the river, we went swimming in 90-degree weather. Moments later a wind came up, almost imploding our dome tents and creating a near-blinding sandstorm. In 10 minutes, the temperature plunged to 40 degrees, and we put on wool pants, sweaters, jackets, gloves, and hats.

Some regions in Alaska experience numerous williwaws— sudden gusts of wind that can reach speeds in excess of 100 miles per hour. A wind piles up on one side of a mountain and, without warning, spills over with tremendous force. On open lakes, particularly in the Bristol Bay region, many boats have run into trouble from wind-generated waves that appear seemingly out of nowhere. It's safer to paddle early in the day because the wind usually picks up in the afternoon.

HYPOTHERMIA

Preparation for river trips includes gaining a knowledge of hypothermia, the dangerous condition of having subnormal body temperature. Hypothermia occurs when exposure to cold causes a person's body to lose heat faster than it can be replaced, leading to the progressive mental and physical collapse that accompanies chilling of the body's inner core. Hypothermia can be caused by immersion in cold water, which cools the body 25 to 30 times faster than air of the same temperature. It can also be caused by exposure to rain, wind, or cold wet air, especially if you are inadequately clothed, ill, or exhausted. Alcohol consumption or old age can exacerbate the condition.

When you are exposed to cold air and don't have enough clothing, often you can exercise to stay warm and the body will adjust to maintain adequate temperatures in the vital organs. But if you must continue to exercise for a long time, your energy reserves will eventually exhaust themselves. The body then loses heat faster than it can produce it. The cold will begin to affect your ability to reason. As judgment and reasoning deteriorate, you enter the state of hypothermia. As your internal core temperature dips, you may lose use of fingers and hands. Violent and incapacitating shivering may be the first sign of hypothermia, but not always. Other symptoms may include confused thinking, shallow breathing, weak pulse, slurred speech, weakness, fatigue, drowsiness, and shivering that lessens or stops.

The best way to avoid hypothermia is to dress warmly and stay dry. Wet clothes lose 90 percent of their insulating value. Wool and high-tech pile, Polarfleece, and polypropylene garments lose less body heat than garments of cotton and other materials. The wind can be deadly. Even a slight breeze carries heat away from the body and pushes cold air under and through clothing. Other important strategies are to drink lots of fluids (three to five quarts daily) and to eat high-energy snacks and meals throughout the day. If you fall into the water, get ashore as quickly as possible. Carry waterproof matches or a lighter in your pocket so you can start a fire if necessary.

If you suspect that someone has hypothermia, immediately get that person out of wet clothing and into dry clothes and a sleeping bag. It may be best to put the person into a sleeping bag with someone else in order to absorb the healthy person's body heat. Do not rub or massage the victim's skin.

FILING A FLOAT PLAN

Before you leave on a trip, give some responsible person—a friend, relative, pilot, or someone else—the details of your planned trip. Better yet, copy the following form, fill it out, and give it to that person. If something happens and you don't show up when you're expected, someone will know where to begin looking. At the end of the trip, be sure to contact the person and close your float plan.

FLOAT PLAN

PARTY MEMBER	ADDRESS	PHONE	PERSON TO CONTACT IN EMERGENCY	PHONE

BOAT INFORMATION:

MAKE

TYPE

LENGTH

COLOR

VEHICLE INFORMATION (FOR ROAD-ACCESSIBLE RIVERS):

MAKE

MODEL/YEAR

COLOR

LICENSE

DATE, PLACE, AND TIME OF DEPARTURE

CHARTER AIR SERVICE USED

PHONE NUMBER AND PILOT

PUT-IN LOCATION

PLANNED TAKE-OUT LOCATION

ROUGH ITINERARY

PLANNED DATE AND TIME OF ARRIVAL AT TAKE-OUT

DATE/TIME TO CALL AIR TAXI/STATE TROOPER/LAND MANAGER/BEGIN SEARCH IF WE DON'T SHOW UP

SURVIVAL AND SAFETY EQUIPMENT ON TRIP

TRAVELING WITH CHILDREN

Why not take children on river trips? Children often have greater perception in nature than adults and may add a rich layer of experience to the trip. In a world in which wild places are increasingly threatened, children will be the ones to carry on the battle for protection and preservation. Taking a journey where travel is self-propelled and where teamwork and common goals are emphasized can be one of a child's greatest growth experiences. Even at an early age, children can be competent, contributing paddlers and partners.

Before taking children on a river trip, master the basics of canoeing and camping with kids. Take your children car-camping before you launch into a river trip. Start out with overnight car trips. Then try a basecamp trip near a lake, where you can use the boat but don't have to pack up your gear and set up a new camp each day. With a basecamp, you can take the watercraft out for a paddle, then return to the relative luxury of your site. Make sure your kids can swim and are Red Cross "water safe."

Once you have decided to take an overnight trip, no longer tied to a basecamp, the level of responsibility may increase dramatically. You have to think about finding a good place to put the tent, taking precautions against bears and other critters, and possible deteriorating weather. An overnighter is an entirely different experience from a day trip. You may want to paddle a lake or river where there are established campgrounds so you can feel safety in numbers or feel assured that you will have a flat tent-site and good water.

The land-management agencies named with each river trip in this book (and in the list of land managers at the back of the book) can provide information on campground locations and fees. Another option for your first overnighter might be to stay in a cabin. Alaska State Parks and the U.S. Forest Service have a number of cabins along lakes and rivers for public use by reservation, for a nominal fee. Cabins are usually reserved in January for the following summer, and the more popular cabins require early scheduling. The listed management agencies can also provide information on cabins.

In choosing a trip that includes children, try to decide what you and the kids would enjoy. Is your group interested in fishing? Do you think the group would enjoy leisurely or strenuous paddling? Do you want a remote wilderness experience where you are likely to see few or no other people? Would geological or natural history phenomena be especially interesting? Is the group interested in history? To help you select a trip, start with this book. Get USGS topographic maps. Read books on Alaska flora and fauna, anthropology, and history. Include nature essays, poetry, or fiction about the state. Talk to people who work in the national parks, refuges, or other areas that include the rivers you are interested in.

When purchasing, renting, or borrowing equipment, make sure the life jackets and paddles fit the children. Tents for families should be large enough to be comfortable, but still be lightweight. Fiberfill sleeping bags come in children's sizes. Have enough warm clothes for each family member; remember to plan for dressing in layers. Be prepared for wind and bad weather. Bring a tarp so you can construct a simple shelter using paddles and line to keep everyone comfortable. Be sure to bring head nets and insect repellent.

Bring some of the children's favorite foods along on the trip. During the trip, get children involved in food preparation: have them stir pancake mix or put raisins in the oatmeal. Take them berry-picking or fishing. If they catch a fish, teach them how to clean it and dispose of the offal. Try gathering a small amount of edible wild foods and share in their preparation. Learn how these foods were used by Native people in the past or how they are still utilized.

Fairbanks kids ready for a day trip on the Chena River.

Food gathering and preparation is a fun outdoor activity.

There are many other diversions for kids: camp chores, whittling, finding and identifying animal tracks, singing, keeping a diary, sketching, swimming, gold panning, and photography. I have friends who love to sit around in the evenings after a good day of paddling and read the poems of Robert Service. A book like Margaret Murie's *Two in the Far North* comes alive when it's read during a trip in which you float down an arctic river. Children's books about wild creatures are excellent on river trips. What better time to read Rick McIntyre's *Grizzly Cub* or Katy Main's *Baby Animals of the North*? A selection of naturalist guidebooks, along with binoculars and hand lenses, will increase your family's enjoyment and understanding of your surroundings. Good books to bring include *The Alaska-Yukon Wild Flowers Guide, Guide to the Birds of Alaska* (Robert Armstrong), and *Discovering Wild Plants* (Janice Schofield).

Just because you're in Alaska, don't assume that wildlife is crawling all over the place. In the Far North, the land's resources are thin and animals are not necessarily found in large concentrations except during migration. You may get a glimpse of a stately moose along a river or a brown bear sauntering up a gravel bar. But even if you don't, there's a world of activity and information in the tracks you find along rivers and streams. A wolf may have wandered along a gravel bar, following the tracks of a young caribou or moose. A river otter's tracks may lead up to the river and disappear where he dove into the water. Sometimes you can find otter slides leading down grassy banks into the water. The dragging tail of a beaver in a sandbar is very distinctive. Along rivers and streams, you'll find enough tracks to keep you busy for hours trying to identify the animals and figure out where they were going, how fast they were moving, how big they were, and how long ago they left the tracks. Carrying the *Peterson Field Guide to Animal Tracks* will help.

You can also learn much about an animal's food habits by examining the droppings, or scat, it has left behind. A large pile of steaming bear scat with red berries in it is an exciting sight.

Other clues to animals' movements exist in the brush and forest. You may find a tree that is used by bears as a scratch post. Claw marks and tufts of bear hair may cling to the tree. In the forest you can sometimes find bear trails that have been used for years. The bears step in the same track time after time, leaving deep depressions. Perhaps you'll spot antlers that have been chewed by porcupines, mice, voles, or shrews. You may discover the cross-hatch tooth marks where porcupines have chewed the bark off trees. Or you may find the pointed, gnawed stump of a tree downed by a beaver.

It's fun to keep a record in a journal or sketchbook of what you find in the wilds. The kids can draw animal tracks on paper, or even preserve them in plaster of paris. A huge brown-bear track preserved in plaster is a stunning memento of a trip. For this activity, bring along a couple cups of dry plaster of paris in a Ziploc bag. If you find a worthy track, mix the plaster with water and carefully pour the mixture into the track, deep enough to cover the track but not running over the sides. To prevent this, you can place a ring of thin cardboard around the track. After the plaster has hardened, wash off the sand, and you have a wildlife "trophy" to take home. (Before you try this activity, be sure you've followed all the proper safety procedures in bear country; see the accompanying list of precautions, titled "Traveling in Bear Country.")

Children can take photographs as another way to preserve memories of the trip. Children also enjoy following the route on a map. Make sure your own map-reading skills are sufficient before you leave on a trip. With a good trip description, topographic maps, and advice from people who have run the river before, you and your family can follow the river down, mile by mile, on the map, making notations where you encounter interesting features along the way. Sitting around the dinner table months or years later, you can look at the map and remember where you saw those 12-inch brown-bear tracks or where you found the beautiful waterfall cascading down a side canyon. A map is like a storybook. It unfolds before you as you read it, and you can re-read it later to experience the story all over again.

In the outdoors, we have an unusual opportunity for self-awareness and for understanding of each other. My deepest friendships have developed while in the wilderness. Taking children on a river trip gives both adults and children an occasion to expand their abilities and a chance for experiences together that form lifelong bonds and memories.

RESPECTING THE LAND AND ITS INHABITANTS

More and more people are seeking the silence and peace of wild places as a respite from urban living and as a way to learn about the natural world. With more people comes greater impact on the environment. The Chilikadrotna River, virtually pristine a quarter-century ago, now has a trash-strewn fire pit at every convenient gravel bar. There are few visual images worse than piles of human excrement and used toilet paper, as I found along the Kongakut River one summer. Increasing quantities of human waste in the wild is a great concern. Those of us who travel through the wilderness have a responsibility to respect and care for our precious wildlands. Following are a variety of important ways we can show this respect.

GROUP SIZE

In Alaska, where the ice-free season lasts only four to five months, vegetation grows slowly and the land is easily damaged by overuse. As the climate is harsh and demanding, so the land is delicate and slow to heal. Wherever tundra vegetation or delicate meadows dominate the landscape, particularly in the arctic, the land cannot withstand much human impact without plant cover being damaged or destroyed. To practice minimum-impact camping, group size on trips should be no more than six people. Larger groups increase human waste, noise, and garbage.

BEARS AND OTHER WILD ANIMALS

Rivers are food corridors and travel routes for animals of all kinds. As you travel on a river, try to manage your activities to avoid confrontation with animals. They are as surprised to see you as you are to see them. Keep a respectful distance from wildlife and observe them in silence. Don't stalk or pursue them or interfere with their activities. Use long telephoto lenses if you are photographing, and slowly retreat if wildlife appears disturbed by your presence. Animals spend most of their waking hours in the summer and fall building up fat reserves for the long winter. Interruptions in obtaining food could mean an animal will be unable to feed its young or will starve during the winter.

Bears are generally not a problem; people are the problem, when they encroach on bear country. Knowing a little bear ecology can help minimize your impact in bear territory. In Alaska, bears (both brown/grizzly and black) usually emerge from winter dens in April. May and early June are times of critical food shortage because the land is not yet producing much greenery. Other food for bears (including moose and caribou calves) doesn't appear until late May. Bears depend mainly on last year's roots and berries and on a few small mammals. Sows with cubs are especially stressed in the early season and are extremely territorial and protective.

By mid-June, life is good. In the north, there are lots of baby animals and the bears waste no time in hunting them down to eat. Salmon are beginning to migrate up the rivers and bears gather at strategic sites to catch fish. If you enter prime feeding territory, you can unwittingly disturb bears and other wildlife. Handle and store your own food to secure it from bears and other critters, such as the arctic ground squirrels that will bite through waterproof bags, duffels, and some solid plastic containers.

Give bears plenty of space. Their most important place to find food is the river, particularly along the mouths of tributaries where fish feed and congregate. Don't camp at tributary streams or along likely bear travel routes. I once camped near a narrow, constricted point in a river valley. A mountain hemmed the valley in, forcing wildlife to walk right by our camp or climb the mountain to get past us. We realized our mistake after the first bear approached, and we moved our camp as soon as we could. We realized that by putting the camp there, we were guilty of a subtle but real form of wildlife harassment.

Yes, the wilderness is bigger in Alaska than in the rest of the United States, but at northern latitudes the land is more fragile, the growing season shorter, and it takes big country to protect the fish, wildlife, and plants. A single grizzly requires more than 100 square miles of territory. The Porcupine caribou herd annually migrates thousands of miles through northeast Alaska and northwest Canada while nibbling lichens and sedges, plants which grow very slowly and if overgrazed would create havoc in arctic ecosystems. Depending on the time of year, caribou may require high-nutrient forage and ice-free calving grounds, mosquito-free coastal areas, or protected wintering grounds.

TRAVELING IN BEAR COUNTRY

You can take precautions in the wilderness to prevent surprise encounters with bears. Follow these common-sense procedures to avoid most negative experiences with bears:

- Hike in a group. Bear attacks occur most frequently with lone hikers.
- Hike in the open where possible. When hiking through dense vegetation, make plenty of noise, with talking and singing or a loud bell tied to your pack.
- Don't bring a dog. Dogs can attract bears and provoke attack.
- Be on the lookout for fresh signs of bear—tracks, scat, diggings, a carcass stashed by a bear for later consumption—and avoid these areas.
- Cook and store food and garbage away from camp in sturdy containers. In treeless country, store food downwind from camp, at least 200 feet away but close enough that you will hear if a bear gets into the food. Consider using bear-proof containers. These black polycarbonate cylinders, with recessed screw caps, are available at some camping supply stores and national parks. If there are trees, suspend food as high as you can (at least 12 feet off the ground). This tactic will work for brown/grizzly bears. Black bears can climb trees, but if the food bags are up high enough, the bears may not smell the food and won't be tempted to climb. A light sleeper in the group might sleep nearest to the food to guard it against marauders. If a bear goes after your food, try to run it off by shouting or banging pots.
- Clean dishes, pots and pans, and utensils thoroughly and store with food.
- Store toiletries, toothpaste, and any other aromatic personal items with food at night.
- If you catch fish, clean them on the river far from camp. After eating fish, dispose of fish wastes (bones, skin) in the river.
- Don't bring smelly foods like bacon and smoked fish on the trip.

- Keep food smells out of your tent. Consider wearing separate clothes for cooking and for sleeping, and wash your face and hands before bedding down for the night.
- Never camp in obvious bear-use areas or along bear trails.
- Leave the area if you come upon a bear that is feeding.
- Never approach a cub, or a sow with a cub. Sows are extremely protective of their young.
- Don't expect to outpaddle or outrun a bear; you can't.
- If a bear approaches, stay calm and do not run. Stand your ground and make yourself look as large as possible, and spread out your arms. Talk loudly to the bear, while acting submissive (hang your head and avoid eye contact). If you encounter a brown/grizzly bear in an area with big trees, back up slowly to a tree and climb it (grizzlies don't climb trees; black bears do). Because bears have poor eyesight, they often approach to see and smell and then, after they have identified you, run off. This approach is not a charge, but many bears have been shot needlessly because people assumed they were being charged. A faceful of cayenne pepper spray has deterred many an over-curious bear.
- If you are charged by a brown/grizzly bear, play dead by rolling up into a ball on the ground with your hands behind your neck and remain motionless. If you are attacked by a black bear, fight back vigorously, striking the bear with whatever is at hand.

DOGS

While a dog may be your best friend, it's hardly an asset on a river trip. Domestic dogs and wild animals are a poor mix. Dogs chase and sometimes kill birds and small mammals. A barking dog alarms wildlife, not only disrupting the animals' routines but also causing them to go into hiding, perhaps robbing you of the thrill of seeing them. Some dogs will chase bears, provoking attack, and could even lead a charging bear back to your camp.

Dogs can cause other problems on a trip. Their barking can diminish the solitude sought by you and other voyagers on the river. And their droppings are difficult to keep track of and dispose of properly. You can do the wilderness and your fellow travelers a favor by leaving pets at home.

HUMAN WASTE

In some areas in the Lower 48, river runners now carry out all solid human waste. If rivers in Alaska ever get to the point of requiring such action, it will demonstrate that the rivers' carrying capacity has been vastly exceeded and that fragile ecosystems are being trampled. Some rivers in Alaska are reaching that point, however, and land managers will have to make some serious decisions about protecting them.

On some popular rivers, outhouses or porta-potties have been provided at the put-ins and take-outs, outside wild-river corridors. This is a necessary consequence of the popularity of road-accessible rivers. Individual deposits of waste decompose much more rapidly than large concentrations. Therefore, group pit toilets are not recommended unless you are camping in an area for an extended period or you are at a trailhead. Locate your personal latrine at least 150 feet from any river, lake, creek, or marshy area to allow waste to decay without polluting groundwater. Create a small pit no more than 6 inches deep by first peeling away the surface layer of vegetation so that the plants are not destroyed, then digging out a bit more dirt. After use, cover waste with the dirt and replace the wedge of vegetation. Do not bury toilet paper because it takes a long time to decompose and may be dug up by animals. Carry the toilet paper out in a plastic bag to burn later, or burn it on the spot. Toilet paper may even be unnecessary when natural materials are available. Tampons should be carried out or burned. In fragile alpine tundra areas, defecate only where there are natural piles of talus (rock debris) or boulders. Burying waste in such a place, where there is little or no soil, may be impossible.

CAMPSITES

Choose campsites that put the least stress on the environment. Camping on gravel bars is the least destructive to plants. Along rivers, clearwater tributaries are inviting for campsites, but these areas are also among the most productive in terms of fish and wildlife resources, which a camp would disturb. Camp a few hundred yards away from the outlet of a tributary to leave a wide berth for animals. If you find lots of animal tracks, signifying a high-use wildlife area, move on to a different site. Be aware of nesting birds (often on the ground) and avoid camping nearby.

Some other basic campsite tips: Don't camp in one location for more than a few days unless it's already an established campsite.

Pitch tents in sand or gravel or under the forest canopy rather than on wildflower meadows or tundra. Leave the area as you found it. Don't leave telltale stone rings outlining where you pitched your tent. Avoid digging trenches, moving rocks, or cutting live plants or trees.

FIRES

The days of the social and cook campfire are over, in the interests of protecting the wilderness ecosystem. Fires should be avoided as much as possible and should not be built at all in areas above the treeline. *True minimum-impact camping avoids the use of fires completely.* Properly prepared recreationists have all the food, clothing, stoves, and fuel they need without having to deplete wood resources. Trees grow very slowly in the North.

Build a fire only in an emergency, and avoid building one anywhere except where there is abundant driftwood and then only in a fire pan, or on sand or gravel. If you do use a campfire, have water nearby to douse it when you're through. Be certain the ashes are cool and then scatter them into the current in the middle of the river so there is no trace of a fire before leaving the area. Don't ring a fire with rocks because this will permanently blacken them.

Campfires can spark forest fires, particularly in Alaska's Interior (or anywhere in dry years). The slow rate of decay in the forests and peat lands results in thick layers of vegetation that lie just beneath a thin layer of topsoil. If these layers catch fire, the peat can burn underground, even through the winter.

GARBAGE AND CLEANUP

Trash cleanup begins even before you leave home. In packing, remove all extra packaging on food items. Don't take anything in glass; transfer it to Ziploc bags or plastic containers with screw-top lids. Try to plan your meals so that you won't have leftovers.

On the trip, you may end up with meal leftovers. Save them to eat at the next meal, rather than polluting streams by tossing the leftovers in. Carry out all trash and garbage; burying trash invites animals to dig it up and to prowl around your camp.

Paper trash can be burned, but *never* burn plastic; it emits chlorofluorocarbons, the ozone-layer destroyers. Avoid burning aluminum foil, which shreds into small pieces invariably left behind to litter the land. Fresh vegetable wastes, like onion skins and carrot scrapings, can be burned or carried out.

By flattening your trash (candy wrappers, chocolate packets, bags, cans, boxes), you can end your wilderness trip with no more than a small bag of compressed trash. First thoroughly rinse cans and other containers to get rid of any odor. All trash should be put in a plastic bag, then placed inside a stuff sack, bucket with lid, ammo can, or waterproof bag. Store this trash with the food. Keep clean empty Ziploc bags in a separate spot from the trash. These can be taken home and used again.

Pour wash water (from dishes and personal washing) into a natural depression or on a gravel bar far from any body of clean water. Use only biodegradable soap—and as little as possible.

HUNTING AND FISHING

As visitors to wilderness, we hardly need rely upon the harvesting of resources for our own survival. Even with our high-tech clothing, equipment, and food, however, we may feel some underlying need to connect with the land by hunting or fishing. But local rural residents depend upon Alaska's limited resources, and each year these resources are more in demand by sport and trophy hunters, commercial and sport fishers, subsistence hunters and fishers, and poachers.

A recreational river user may consider a frying pan full of fish a vital part of his or her experience, but the subsistence user of that river often sees this as taking fish from the mouths of his family. Villagers have concerns that recreational users catch too many fish and drive away wildlife. One year on the Kobuk River, eighty-five people in seven planes flew in to sportfish, and they drove away the caribou and moose. Federal law gives preference in harvesting Alaska's fish and wildlife to subsistence users.

Sport hunting is allowed in national wildlife refuges and in national preserves, and on lands managed by the Forest Service, Bureau of Land Management, and the state. Rural residents are permitted to continue traditional subsistence activities in national wildlife refuges, national preserves, and in seven of the national parks. You may encounter villagers hunting, fishing, trapping, or berry picking, or cutting trees for firewood or house logs. Before you hunt or fish in Alaska, learn about the region and river you are visiting. While fish are abundant in some areas, fish in Northern rivers grow very slowly in the short summer season. The char you catch could be 25 years old. Instead of catching a panful of grayling,

Gwich'in Athapaskan women of the Arctic.

be thankful that they eat mosquito larvae. Consider limiting any fishing to catch-and-release.

WILDERNESS USES

Wilderness in Alaska must accommodate many different uses. The Alaska National Interest Lands Conservation Act of 1980 (ANILCA) allowed for continuance of traditional uses by traditional means. In addition, airplanes are allowed to land in many parks and refuges—on land or water—making practically the entire state accessible. There are more planes per capita in Alaska than in any other state. This makes it easy for people to get to wilderness, but also makes wilderness more vulnerable to abuse or overuse. Helicopters are prohibited in wilderness.

Motorized boats are not prohibited on most rivers, including those in wilderness areas. So you may find your "pristine wilderness experience" disrupted by the appearance of a powerboat. Both you and the powerboater may have the right to be there. On State Recreational Rivers, some sections are designated for motorless recreation on certain days and for powerboats on other days. Mining operations occur along some rivers. Most of these involve placer mining, a process that tears up the land.

CULTURAL AND NATURAL RESOURCES

When you float down an Alaskan river, you may be following travel and trade routes used by wildlife and Native people for thousands of years. You may find well-worn animal trails along rivers and streams. Signs of human travel and occupation also exist. Ancient rock cairns and fences, a spear point or scraper, depressions or rings of stones where once stood a dwelling, the crumbling walls of a trapper's cabin—all remind us that the wilderness we experience has felt the footsteps of others. It is illegal to excavate, remove, or destroy artifacts, or to disturb archaeological or historical sites on federal or state lands. It is imperative that we not disturb archaeological sites or remove artifacts from their natural setting. Taking an object from its place of repose destroys much of its value to everyone in helping to put together the story of Alaska's cultural heritage.

Natural features deserve the same respect. It's illegal in some national parks and wildlife refuges to take flowers, rocks, fossils, animal parts, or other natural features, except plants for eating or dead and down wood for firewood. Why the concern over these resources? Every rock, flower, and fossil is an integral part of the natural environment that we come to witness. More importantly, these resources have a use in the total ecological web. Caribou and moose antlers are eaten for their calcium by porcupines, voles, and other small animals. Animal parts break down over time and become nutrients for the soil. Wildflowers provide nectar for bees.

Rangers at Gates of the Arctic National Park showed they were serious about caring for their area in an incident from the early 1980s. They confiscated many caribou and moose antlers from recreationists returning to Bettles from the park. Soon there was a huge pile of antlers sitting in the town. One ranger loaded up a plane with antlers, flew over the park, and randomly distributed them back to the land.

PRIVATE PROPERTY

Private lands exist along most rivers. Even though a river may traverse a national park, refuge, or other protected lands, or be protected as a national wild and scenic river, the lands are not all publicly owned. Waterways and the lands up to the high water mark are considered public property in Alaska, and camping on gravel bars in any river corridor is all right. But make yourself aware of the location of private lands within a river corridor you plan to travel. Federal and state land management agencies have maps showing private lands. Lands surrounding villages are owned by Native corporations and permits may be required to use these areas. Contact the corporations whose lands you will be traveling through.

You may run across empty hunting and trapping cabins and tent camps, structures essential to the subsistence livelihood of rural Alaskans. Some of the structures may appear abandoned but most likely are not. They are used seasonally and their contents are vital to the people who own them. The general rule is to trespass only in an emergency.

NATIVE VILLAGE LIFE

When you enter a small rural village, your presence has a strong impact. Respecting people's privacy means not taking photographs of residents unless you have their permission. Elders especially may be offended by camera-toting tourists. You may find the pace of life in village Alaska markedly different from where you live, and you may not be able to obtain the goods and services you desire. If you hope to camp at a village that is on private land, officials of the Native village corporation or other village residents can fill you in on local rules. Many villages are "dry," banning sale or possession of alcohol. You can play it safe by not bringing alcohol into any village.

The traditional lifeways of the Aleut, Inupiat, Athapaskan,

Yup'ik, Tlingit, Haida, and Tsimshian may not be easily discernible now that boats with outboard motors have replaced Native kayaks and the roar of snowmachines has largely drowned out the bark of dog teams. But Native traditions are alive. People may wear John Deere caps and drive pickups, but they still have their own languages, their own customs, and deep awareness of the natural world.

In the villages, people rely on a subsistence-based economy and way of life. Hunting, gathering, and food preparation are an integral part of the culture, with families and households sharing the harvest. Going upriver to hunt caribou is just as important today, though hunters travel in a skiff with an outboard motor, as it was when boats were made of walrus or seal hide and sails were made of marine mammal intestines. As much as traditional foods satisfy nutritional needs, they also meet psychological and spiritual needs. Listen to the sounds of singing and dancing coming from the community hall during a potlatch or other special occasion. Observe the joy, ritual, and significance of the first harvest of fall, when caribou are brought into the village and shared with everyone. The descendants of Alaska's first peoples are using the land in a tradition carried on for millenia.

KEEPING ALASKA'S RIVERS FLOWING FREE

Development has hit many once-remote wilderness areas. Some of Alaska's rivers now share a corridor with the Trans-Alaska Pipeline or are overshadowed by the North Slope oilfield complex. Others have been dammed, diverted, and dirtied in search of placer gold. One river carries toxics leaching from the world's second-largest lead–zinc deposit. Fortunately for Alaska's free-flowing rivers, many development proposals have been delayed or stopped, either because of the harm they would do to the environment or simply because they would cost too much. But the pressure to develop continues.

Passage of the Alaska National Interest Lands Conservation Act (ANILCA) in 1980 was an action of immense importance for the cause of American conservation. "Never before have we seized the opportunity to preserve so much of America's national and cultural heritage on so grand a scale," remarked President Jimmy Carter as he signed the act. While the act has its flaws, it did set aside 104.3 million acres as national parks, wildlife refuges, wilderness areas, and other conservation units. The act also gave protection under the National Wild and Scenic Rivers Act to 25 Alaska rivers: 13 within national parks, 2 within Bureau of Land Management conservation areas, 6 in national wildlife refuges, and 4 on lands outside of federally designated conservation units. (See the list of protected rivers at the back of this book.)

Implementation of ANILCA and the Wild and Scenic Rivers Act has been slow, with neither federal nor state governments giving them adequate support. Alaska's wild rivers continue to be threatened by such activities as mining, hydroelectric projects, and private holdings within conservation lands. Recreationists also can degrade river areas. On the Kenai and Russian rivers, large numbers of people fishing have trampled bank vegetation and brought on erosion. On the Arctic Slope, large commercial river trips have damaged fragile tundra. River management in Alaska is generally improving, however, thanks in great measure to the federal Clean Water Act. Federal agencies are now required to monitor rivers more closely to protect biological, physical, archaelogical, aesthetic, historic, and scenic features.

Rivers need our support. Many more than 25 streams in Alaska deserve designation under the National Wild and Scenic Rivers Act. Conservation groups are working hard to protect the state's wild rivers. See the list at the back of this book for information on how to contact these organizations to learn more about their work.

ALASKA'S RIVERS

Six distinct river drainage regions define Alaska: the Arctic Slope, Northwest, Yukon, Southwest, Southcentral, and Southeast. Within these are 12 major river systems: the Colville, Noatak, Kobuk, Yukon, Tanana, Koyukuk, Kuskokwim, Copper, Susitna, Stikine, Taku, and Alsek. The rivers, drawing on vein-like tributaries that spread out over the land, eventually run to the sea.

The total runoff of a drainage depends on precipitation, temperature, elevation, existence of permafrost, vegetation, and size of the drainage, and any of these factors can cause wide fluctuation in daily and seasonal river flows. Many rivers experience severe flooding behind ice dams at spring breakup. Breakup on an Alaskan river is an event you are unlikely to ever forget. Weakened by warming temperatures and water beginning to flow beneath the ice, huge slabs of ice creak, groan, pop, and break apart, thundering with wild abandon as they scrape together, moving down the river. For many people, breakup is an annual ritual; there are even contests, like the Nenana River Ice Classic, in which thousands of people wager when the river will break up in spring. Paddling a river during the middle of the summer, you may be shocked to see high-water marks from spring breakup which are as much as 12 feet higher than the water you're in. Immediately after breakup, many rivers are unrunnable.

Alaskan rivers are either glacial or nonglacial. Most glacial rivers are in Southeast and Southcentral Alaska. They are characterized by a high sediment load, giving the water a milky color of brown, gray, or blue. Glacial valleys are U-shaped and generally very scenic, with glaciers and mountains and sometimes forests. Stream channels are often wide and braided, composed of sorted gravel and of boulders in all sizes. Glacial river water is always cold and silty because its source is active glaciers.

In Southeast Alaska, glacial rivers commonly carry entire trees to gravel bars and sharp turns, where they tangle together in huge piles. The water level of glacial rivers fluctuates dramatically depending on the temperature. On a sunny day, glacial melt can raise the water level as much as 3 feet, transforming a moderate Class II river into a raging Class III torrent. This is more often true of Interior glacial rivers than of the short glacial streams of Southeast Alaska, where the Gulf of Alaska and its maritime climate tend to reduce daily fluctuation. But on any glacial river, the course can become more difficult to run in late afternoon and early evening as snow and icemelt from tributaries feed into the main river.

Nonglacial rivers are typical of Northwest Alaska, the Arctic Slope, and parts of Interior Alaska, though many waterways in other regions are also nonglacial. These rivers are characterized by a clear blue or brownish color and a meandering nature. If their origins are mountain streams, the water is clear; waters originating in marshy lowlands and muskeg swamps display brown-tinted water. With rainfall, nonglacial rivers quickly become muddy and turbid. The current is often swift, and in forested areas sweepers are common. The banks of these rivers are more stable than along glacial streams. The water is not as cold as in glacial rivers—but it's never warm.

ARCTIC SLOPE

From watersheds amid the Brooks Range, rivers and streams flow northward through rugged peaks, treeless rolling foothills, and across the tundra wetlands of the arctic coastal plain, and enter the Chukchi or Beaufort seas. The Colville River dominates the region, its watershed draining 24,000 square miles. Breakup on rivers is in June, and rivers reach their peak flows at this time, scouring the banks by pushing ice down braided streams that flow through U-shaped glacial valleys.

The mountains end abruptly at the rolling arctic foothills, punctuated by arcuate (curved) ridges. On the arctic coastal plain, countless lakes thaw, providing vital habitat for migrating shorebirds and waterfowl. Treeless for the most part, except for a few river valleys where balsam poplar has found a northern niche in protected microclimates, the land is underlain by a continuous permafrost barrier. Here, just a few inches of summer-thawed soil and plants cover a layer of permanently frozen ground. The depth of the permafrost layer may be only a few feet to as much as nearly a mile. Summers are short, with continuous daylight.

The climate is cold and dry. The arctic slope is a desert, receiving just 7 inches of precipitation annually. Less than half of this occurs as summer rainfall—but when a big storm hits during a river trip, you may swear it has rained most of those inches at one time. Rivers rise dramatically before your eyes. Because of the permafrost, the land does not soak up much of the rain as it falls. Quickly, then, the water moves down every depression, every creeklet, from every height, to the main arteries heading toward the coast. Rivers rise and fall with unbelievable quickness.

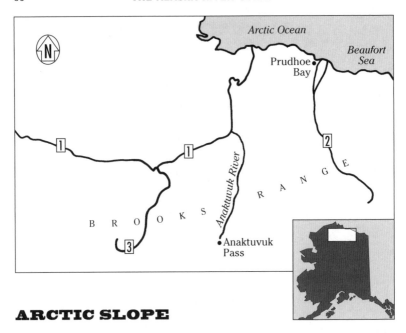

ARCTIC SLOPE

1 Colville River
2 Ivishak River
3 Killik River

1 COLVILLE RIVER

The Colville is the largest river draining the Arctic Slope of the Brooks Range and also is one of the most remote rivers in Alaska. It flows east out of the western end of the Brooks Range, then bends north to Harrison Bay on the Beaufort Sea 428 miles later, draining an area of 24,000 square miles.

For about 300 miles, the river traverses treeless arctic foothills and ridges. The lower river meanders over the arctic coastal plain, also treeless, which imparts a stunning sense of wide-open space. High cliffs along the river provide excellent habitat for raptors, and the Colville is one of the most productive peregrine falcon areas in Alaska. The lower Colville (the delta) continues to be a traditional fishing area for residents of Nuiqsut and Umiat.

The Colville area was originally inhabited by inland Nunamiut Eskimos, who lived in the Brooks Range along the upper reaches of the river and some of its tributaries, and Kuukpigmiut Eskimos, who inhabited the lower Colville. These groups hunted seal along the coast in spring or early summer, and spent fall and winter either fishing or up in the mountains hunting.

Between 1850 and 1890, sweeping changes were triggered by the whaling industry. The Nunamiut unwittingly hastened the depletion of caribou as a food source by shooting caribou for the whalers. With subsistence resources dwindling, and alcohol and disease making destructive inroads, many people abandoned their migratory patterns and moved into coastal settlements. When commercial whaling faded, fur trapping, particularly for arctic fox, became an important economic activity for the Natives, and the federal government instituted reindeer herding to replace dwindling caribou populations. Trading posts sprang up all along the coast. The village of Nuiqsut is a more recent creation, built in 1974 when 27 families from Barrow decided to move to the Colville Delta, where they had family ties.

The National Petroleum Reserve-Alaska, which encompasses the Colville River, is managed by the Bureau of Land Management. In the early 1920s, oil-stained sandstone was found in the foothills of the Brooks Range and along the arctic coast, and geologic, seismic, and drilling work was carried out between 1944 and 1953. Abandoned machinery, oil drums, and other detritus now litter the

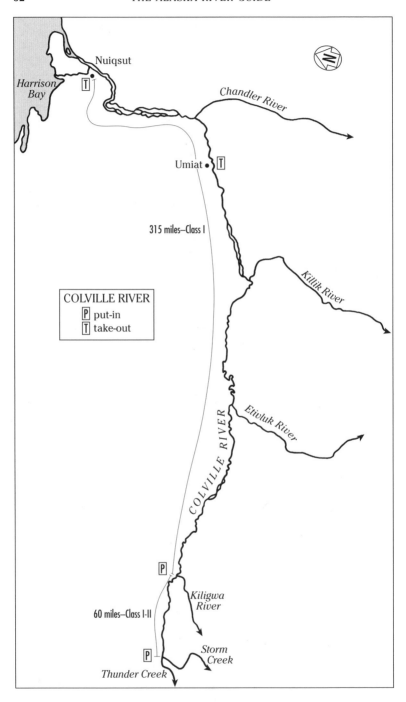

Nuiqsut

Harrison
Bay

Chandler River

Umiat

315 miles–Class I

COLVILLE RIVER
P put-in
T take-out

Killik River

Etivluk River

COLVILLE RIVER

Kiligwa
River

60 miles–Class I-II

Storm
Creek

Thunder Creek

tundra and part of the river. In 1980, an oil and gas leasing program began; about 558,000 acres are currently leased, but there are no actively producing wells.

Rating: Class I–II. Upper 60 miles, in vicinity of Thunder and Storm Creeks, is Class I–II; all the rest is fast Class I. It is not a difficult river, but due to its extreme remoteness, only experienced wilderness travelers should make the run.

Cautions: Upriver winds.

Trip length: 375 miles between Thunder Creek and Nuiqsut; allow 19 to 20 days. About 250 miles between Kiligwa River and Umiat; allow 14 to 15 days.

Season: June to mid-August.

Watercraft: Raft; canoe or kayak, preferably folding variety due to difficulty in transport of hard-shell boats. Use of a raft below Umiat is not advisable, due to upriver winds and tidal influence.

Access: In—Scheduled airline to Deadhorse (Prudhoe Bay), Kotzebue, or Bettles. Charter wheelplane to put-in on gravel bars in vicinity of Thunder Creek or Kiligwa River. Out—Take out at Umiat or continue to Nuiqsut. Then scheduled air service to Prudhoe Bay and on to Fairbanks or Anchorage.

Land manager: National Petroleum Reserve (Bureau of Land Management, Fairbanks); private; state. (See Land Managers section at back of book for address and phone information.)

Maps: Misheguk Mountain D–2, D–3; Utukok River A–1, A–2; Lookout Ridge A–4, A–5; Howard Pass D–1, D–2, D–3, D–4, D–5; Ikpikpuk River A–1, A–2, A–3, A–4, A–5; Killik River D–2, D–5; Umiat A–5, B–3, B–4, B–5, C–3, D–3; Harrison Bay A–2, A–3, B–1, B–2.

Fish: Arctic cisco, least cisco, broad whitefish, arctic grayling, humpback whitefish, arctic char, rainbow smelt, round whitefish, burbot. **Wildlife:** Caribou, grizzly bear, wolf, peregrine falcon, gyrfalcon, rough-legged hawk, golden eagle, yellow-billed loon.

2 IVISHAK RIVER

From headwaters on the north side of the Arctic Divide in the Philip Smith Mountains of the Brooks Range, the Ivishak flows north 95 miles to its confluence with the Sagavanirktok River. A large clearwater stream, the Ivishak begins in a narrow glaciated valley surrounded by peaks rising to almost 7,000 feet. Several of the small headwater streams that contribute to the Ivishak stem from relic Pleistocene glaciers hanging high in the valley. Porcupine Lake, east of the river in a glacial trough, is a natural reservoir for the upper river drainage. The river begins as a single channel, and as it flows north, it braids and increases in size, taking on the Echooka and Saviukviayak rivers as major tributaries and coursing through a broad floodplain.

Due to permafrost, water levels fluctuate daily, rising and falling dramatically with rainfall. Occasionally during dry spells in the summer, parts of the river may disappear beneath the broad gravel channel. Shallow and swift, the upper 12 miles of the river drop more than 100 feet per mile. Below here, the gradient averages 32 feet per mile. Tributary streams have steep gradients. The stream

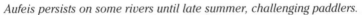

Aufeis persists on some rivers until late summer, challenging paddlers.

connecting Porcupine Lake to the Ivishak has an average gradient of 167 feet per mile.

The Ivishak flows entirely north of the treeline, so vistas along the entire river are excellent. Hiking is superb, especially in the upper river and headwaters areas.

The upper river corridor of the Ivishak is protected within the Arctic National Wildlife Refuge. The lower river includes some state-owned lands leased out for oil exploration and development. Some lands adjacent to the lower river are within the utility corridor for the Trans-Alaska Pipeline. The Bureau of Land Management has designated an Ivishak River Area of Critical Environmental Concern, but it protects only an 8-mile segment of the river. Many of the lands on the lower river are now vulnerable to development.

Rating: Swift Class I–II.
Cautions: Stream connecting Porcupine Lake to Ivishak River is extremely swift and shallow, with a narrow, winding watercourse 8 miles long. This section should be portaged or lined. Upper couple miles of the Ivishak are extremely steep. Aufeis exists along river; early in the season, channels may not be open through the ice.
Trip length: 88 miles from Porcupine Lake to confluence with

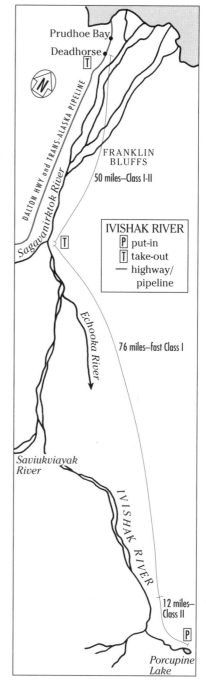

Prudhoe Bay

Deadhorse

DALTON HWY and TRANS-ALASKA PIPELINE

Sagavanirktok River

FRANKLIN BLUFFS

50 miles–Class I-II

IVISHAK RIVER
P put-in
T take-out
— highway/ pipeline

Echooka River

76 miles–fast Class I

Saviukviayak River

IVISHAK RIVER

12 miles– Class II

Porcupine Lake

Sagavanirktok River; allow 5 to 7 days. Allow another 3 days down
Sagavanirktok River to Deadhorse.

Season: Mid to late June through early August.

Watercraft: Raft; inflatable or folding kayak. Hard-shell boat not
recommended due to difficulty in transportation.

Access: In—Scheduled airline to Bettles, Fort Yukon, Deadhorse, or
Umiat. Put in on gravel bars in upper river by charter wheelplane, or
on Porcupine Lake by charter floatplane. Out—Take out on gravel
bar above confluence with Sagavanirktok by charter plane or continue down Sagavanirktok to Deadhorse and take scheduled air service to Fairbanks or Anchorage.

Land manager: Arctic National Wildlife Refuge; Bureau of Land
Management (Fairbanks). The Ivishak is a National Wild River. (See
Land Managers section at back of book for address and phone
information.)

Maps: Arctic C–5, D–5; Philip Smith Mountains C–1, D–1;
Sagavanirktok A–1, A–2, B–2, B–3.

Fish: Arctic char, arctic grayling, whitefish. **Wildlife:** Caribou, grizzly, Dall sheep, moose, wolf, wolverine, arctic fox, peregrine falcon,
gyrfalcon, golden eagle, rough-legged hawk.

3   # KILLIK RIVER

Rising amidst the massive peaks of the Endicott Mountains in the central Brooks Range, the Killik River flows northward through an open, treeless, glaciated valley for 135 miles, where it joins the Colville River. The Killik's classic U-shaped river valley has deep blue lakes, sand dunes, large lateral moraines, and rolling alpine tundra. Dramatic 6,000- to 7,000-foot peaks surround the headwaters. In the upper river the valley is about 2 miles wide and offers good hiking. As the river flows through the arctic foothills, the valley opens up, becoming 3 to 5 miles wide. Below Sunday Rapids, fossils are evident in rock outcroppings. The river becomes braided near its confluence with April Creek and remains braided, flowing across gravel flats that create aufeis in the winter.

Nunamiut Eskimos lived semi-nomadically in the region from the Anaktuvuk River west to the Killik River in the early 20th century. By the 1940s, they had moved either to the arctic coast or to Anaktuvuk Pass.

Rating: Class I–III. The river is swift Class I–II, except for one section of Class II–III rapids (Sunday Rapids) about 35 miles below confluence of the Killik with Easter creek.

Cautions: Upriver winds, especially on lower river; shallow water late in July.

Trip length: 105 miles from confluence of Easter Creek and the Killik River to the Colville River confluence; allow 7 to 10 days. Add another 3 days to paddle the Colville to Umiat.

Season: Late June to mid-August.

Watercraft: Raft; canoe; folding or inflatable kayak or canoe; be prepared to line or portage folding boats around Sunday Rapids.

Access: In—Scheduled airline from Fairbanks to Bettles. Or fly scheduled airline to Deadhorse, then on to Umiat. Put in at confluence of Easter Creek and the Killik by charter wheelplane, or put in at one of the larger lakes along the upper river by floatplane. Out— Take out at confluence with Colville River by charter plane or continue down the Colville to Umiat for scheduled service to Deadhorse and on to Fairbanks or Anchorage.

Land manager: Gates of the Arctic National Park and Preserve; National Petroleum Reserve (Bureau of Land Management,

Fairbanks); private (Native lands). (See Land Managers section at back of book for address and phone information.)

Maps: Killik River A–1, A–2, A–3, B–2, C–1, C–2; Ikpikpuk River A–2; Survey Pass D–3, D–4.

Fish: Arctic char, arctic grayling, whitefish, northern pike.

Wildlife: Caribou, wolf, wolverine, grizzly, Dall sheep, moose, waterfowl, peregrine falcon, white-fronted geese. The Western Arctic caribou herd uses the Killik River Valley as a migration route from the calving grounds on the Utukok and Colville rivers to winter range south of the Brooks Range.

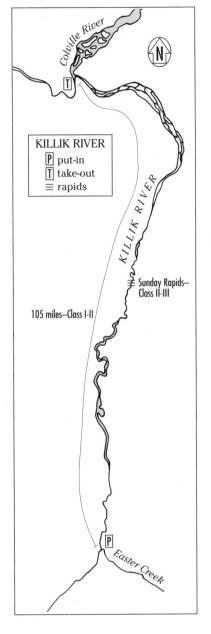

NORTHWEST ALASKA

The Seward Peninsula, with its small hills and marshy valleys, and the great deltas of the Noatak and Kobuk rivers form the nucleus of this region, along with the uplands, foothills, and head-water Brooks Range mountains (the DeLong, Baird, and Endicott mountains). The Noatak and Kobuk rivers drain almost 25,000 square miles. Sparse spruce forests occupy river bottomlands, and tundra vegetation covers hillsides and rolling plains throughout the region. Shallow lakes and tundra marshes are underlain by a layer of permafrost. On cutbank bluffs at bends on the rivers, it is some-times possible to observe permafrost ice wedges in the bank. The Unalakleet and Koyuk rivers drain southwest on the Seward Peninsula to enter Norton Sound.

The climate is transitional, so weather varies throughout the region. Annual precipitation averages 8 inches, except on the Seward Peninsula, where it averages 18 inches. Roughly half of this falls as rain in the summer months. Breakup on the rivers occurs in late May; by late October, streams are frozen again.

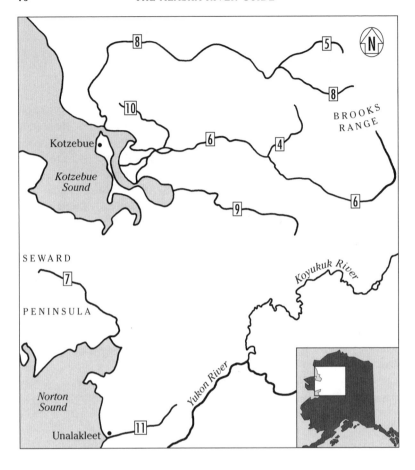

NORTHWEST ALASKA

4   AMBLER RIVER

Rising from the Schwatka Mountains of the Brooks Range at Nakmaktuak Pass, the Ambler River flows in a southwesterly direction for 80 miles to its confluence with the Kobuk River. Small and clear, the Ambler is a single channel for the first 15 miles from the confluence of two headwater forks, with many small rapids flowing over sharp rocks. The river passes through a narrow, constricted valley with steep mountains on the right bank. In its midsection, the forested valley broadens and the river is shallow and braided for about 35 miles before becoming a single channel once again a mile above Lake Anirak. From this point the Ambler meanders 30 miles through a broad floodplain to its confluence with the Kobuk at the Eskimo village of Ambler. (Refer to this book's entry on the Kobuk River if you wish to continue paddling to Kiana.)

The Ambler flows almost entirely through a forested region, except for its headwaters. The best hiking opportunities exist near the upper river, a primitive, remote area that is rarely visited.

Lieutenant G. M. Stoney led a U.S. Navy expedition up the Kobuk River in 1884–1885, exploring the western and central Brooks Range. The expedition sledded up the Ambler River in December 1885, and Stoney noted that the rapids did not freeze over. In the summer of 1898 more than a thousand prospectors ascended the Kobuk and scattered along the entire river. A mining camp and post office was established at Shungnak, 35 miles or so up the Kobuk from its junction with the Ambler. The Inupiat village of Ambler was established in 1958 when people from Shungnak and nearby Kobuk moved there to take advantage of the extensive spruce forests and abundant fish and wildlife.

Rating: Class I–II.
Cautions: Sweepers and numerous small rocky rapids with sharp, angular rocks on upper river. The 3-mile canyon in upper river is difficult at high water, particularly in a folding kayak.
Trip length: 80 miles from headwater forks to confluence with Kobuk River; allow 7 days.
Season: July and August.
Watercraft: Folding or inflatable canoe or kayak; small raft.
Access: In—Put in on gravel bar at confluence of headwater forks by

charter Supercub from Ambler. Out—Take out at Ambler or continue down Kobuk River to Kiana.

Land manager: Gates of the Arctic National Park and Preserve; NANA Regional Corporation; state. (See Land Managers section at back of book for address and phone information.)

Maps: Ambler River A–2, A–3, A–4, B–2, C–2.

Fish: Arctic grayling, arctic char, whitefish. **Wildlife:** Caribou, grizzly, moose, wolf, wolverine, fox, beaver, osprey, waterfowl.

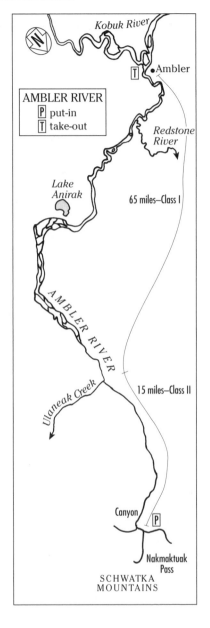

5   ANIUK RIVER

Beginning in the mountains northwest of lake-dotted Howard Pass, the Aniuk River flows southwesterly for 80 miles to its confluence with the Noatak River. A small clearwater stream spiked with rocky rapids, the Aniuk flows through a broad, sometimes marshy valley, with a gradient of less than 20 feet per mile. The watershed drains a thousand square miles. As an alternative starting point for a trip on the Noatak, the Aniuk traverses a rarely visited region of Noatak National Preserve. Entirely above treeline, the Aniuk begins in alpine tundra on the south side of the Brooks Range and traverses upland and wetland tundra habitats. Opportunities for observing wildlife are outstanding, as Howard Pass is a major migratory route and the vistas are expansive.

The Aniuk River was part of a traditional overland route to the Colville River. Eskimos used large portage boats in the spring, dragging them across the snow through a relatively gentle pass. The first non-Native to document a descent of the Aniuk was Philip S. Smith, who led a U.S. Geological Survey crew to the National Petroleum Reserve in 1925. After canoeing up the Etivluk River, his party

Subsistence fishers often dry fish along a river, then store it for winter use.

portaged to one of the Aniuk's tributaries and floated down the Aniuk to the Noatak.

Rating: Class II. A small, shallow river with rocky riffles.

Cautions: Shallow, rocky rapids.

Trip length: 80 miles to confluence with Noatak River; allow 4 to 6 days. For pickup at confluence of Noatak and Cutler rivers, continue downriver 20 miles; allow one extra day.

Season: Late June through August.

Watercraft: Canoe, kayak, or small raft.

Access: In—Scheduled air service from Fairbanks to Bettles; put in at one of the lakes in the upper river by charter floatplane from Bettles. Or arrange air charter to Aniuk River from Kotzebue. Out—Take out at confluence with Noatak River or other prearranged spot by charter floatplane. (See this book's entry on Noatak River.)

Land manager: Noatak National Preserve; NANA Regional Corporation. (See Land Managers section at back of book for address and phone information.)

Maps: Ambler River C–1, D–1, D–2, D–3, D–4, D–5, D–6; Howard Pass A–3, A–4, A–5.

Fish: Arctic char, arctic grayling, northern pike, whitefish,

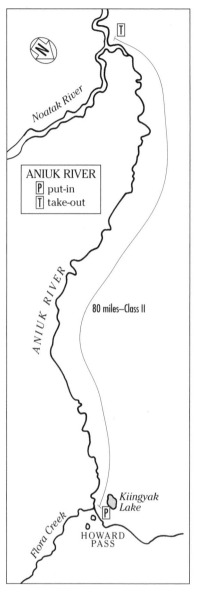

ANIUK RIVER
P put-in
T take-out

Noatak River

ANIUK RIVER

80 miles–Class II

Kiingyak Lake

HOWARD PASS

Flora Creek

chum salmon. **Wildlife:** Caribou, grizzly bear, Dall sheep, wolf, many migratory waterfowl.

6   KOBUK RIVER

From headwaters on the southern slopes of the Arrigetch Peaks, the Kobuk's 347-mile course lies north of and just about parallel to the Arctic Circle. This normally clearwater stream begins swiftly, flowing through tall forests of birch and white spruce for about 40 miles before joining an unnamed tributary originating at Walker Lake. Rarely is the upper 30 miles of the Kobuk floated; most trips begin at Walker Lake or below the Upper and Lower Kobuk River canyons. Below the confluence of the Kobuk with the Walker Lake tributary, the Kobuk flows into deep canyons, then becomes a broad channel that meanders through a wide forested valley. Moving from the headwaters to the coast, the forests become thinner and the trees stockier.

In the upper Kobuk (its name means "big river") and its tributaries, hiking opportunities are excellent. The trees are widely spaced and the forest floor forms a soft mat of lichens. The upper and middle regions are scenically spectacular. South of the river lie the wind-sculpted Kobuk Sand Dunes, covering more than 25 square miles, and beyond, the rounded hills of the Waring Mountains offer a contrast to the snow-capped peaks to the north. Downriver, willows create short, entangled, near-impenetrable jungle.

Below the Mauneluk River, the Kobuk's current slows and it forms huge oxbows. Near the coast, the river forms a wide delta at Hotham Inlet, with the current flowing at less than 3 miles per hour. Here it is joined by the smaller Selawik River, flowing out of the Lockwood Hills, and by the Noatak River, flowing out of bare, rugged mountains to the north. The combined waters of these three rivers form a channel 6 miles wide that opens into Kotzebue Sound and the Chukchi Sea.

The Kobuk has been a major trade and travel route for centuries. Natives continue to hunt, fish, and gather foods along the river. The people of the Kobuk, or the Kuvuungmiit, are Eskimo-speaking dwellers of the forest. The Kobuk people have apparently always traveled freely between the coast and the Interior. Formerly, they traveled in skin boats, or *umiaks,* often using dogs to help pull the boats upriver. Groups of families gathered to fish at favorite bends in the river or formed temporary winter settlements. At other times, small groups scattered for hunting and gathering.

With the establishment of trading posts, schools, and missions, four villages were founded along the Kobuk: Noorvik, Kiana, Shungnak, and Kobuk. Navy Lieutenants G. M. Stoney and John C. Cantwell were part of a U.S. government survey team sent up the Kobuk River Valley to its source in 1884. They used gas-powered boats as far up the river as Kobuk village, then took canoes all the way to Walker Lake in a quest for information about the region. Today motorized boats ply the lower 250 miles of the Kobuk when water levels are sufficient.

Rating: Class I below Lower Kobuk Canyon; Class IV–V rapids just below outlet of Walker Lake; Class II–IV rapids through Upper and Lower Kobuk canyons. **Cautions:** One-third of a mile of Class IV–V rapids is encountered less than a mile below the outlet of Walker Lake, with four major drops of several feet, boulders, haystacks, serious hydraulics, and no clear chutes. Portaging is essential. Pull out on the left side of the river as soon as you see the first boulder on the left. Fifty yards below here, the river bends to the left. Carry boats and gear one-third mile through the forest. Below the falls is a half-mile of Class II whitewater through rocks and riffles. Upper Kobuk Canyon (Class II–IV) is

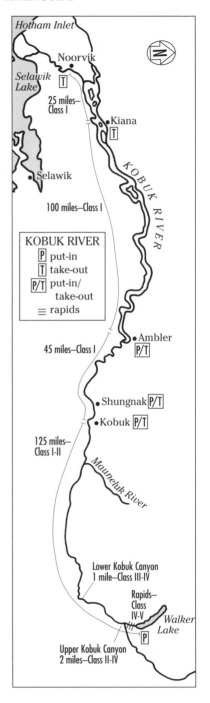

Hotham Inlet

Noorvik

Selawik Lake

T

25 miles–Class I

Kiana

T

Selawik

100 miles–Class I

KOBUK RIVER

P put-in
T take-out
P/T put-in/take-out
≡ rapids

K O B U K   R I V E R

45 miles–Class I

Ambler P/T

Shungnak P/T

Kobuk P/T

125 miles–Class I-II

Mauneluk River

Lower Kobuk Canyon
1 mile–Class III-IV

Rapids–Class IV-V

Walker Lake

P

Upper Kobuk Canyon
2 miles–Class II-IV

encountered about 10 miles below Walker Lake.

A canyon wall on the left and a huge boulder mid-river signify the canyon. Scout and/or line boats on the right for one-quarter mile. Lower Kobuk Canyon (Class III–IV) is about a mile long and is 18 miles below Upper Kobuk Canyon. This section can be lined on the right on a shale ledge; rock cliffs downriver of the ledge on the last section of rapids make for tricky lining conditions.

The lower canyon consists of three sections of rapids. The first is 150 yards long and consists of a chute with 2-foot standing waves and rock outcrops. The second section is a quarter-mile farther down the river and consists of two chutes, the second of which drops 5 to 6 feet with a big hydraulic at the end. The third section is one-third of a mile downriver and consists of two channels divided by an unbroken line of boulders. Within each channel are several drops within a stretch of about 100 yards. Conditions may change dramatically depending on water levels.

Trip length: 125 miles from Walker Lake to Kobuk village; allow 6 to 7 days. Or paddle all the way to Kiana or anywhere in between. From Walker Lake to Ambler is about 175 miles and takes about 10 to 14 days; from Walker Lake to Kiana is about 260 miles and takes 15 to 20 days.

Season: June through end of September.

Watercraft: Folding kayak or canoe, canoe, inflatable kayak.

Access: In—Scheduled air to Bettles or Ambler; put in by floatplane on Walker Lake. Out—Take out at Kobuk or any of the other villages along the Kobuk. All have scheduled air service to Bettles, Kotzebue, or Fairbanks.

Land manager: Kobuk Valley National Park; Gates of the Arctic National Park and Preserve; private; NANA Regional Corporation. The Kobuk is a National Wild River. (See Land Managers section at back of book for address and phone information.)

Maps: Survey Pass A–3; Hughes C–5, D–3, D–4, D–5, D–6; Shungnak D–1, D–2, D–3, D–4; Selawik D–3, D–4, D–5, D–6; Ambler River A–4, A–5, A–6, D–1, D–2, D–3, D–4; Baird Mountains A–1, A–2.

Fish: Arctic grayling, northern pike, whitefish, and arctic sheefish.

Wildlife: Caribou, grizzly and black bear, moose, beaver, and many forest mammals and birds. The Western Arctic caribou herd has several migration routes through the Kobuk River Valley.

7   KOYUK RIVER

Originating in the central upland of Northwest Alaska's Seward Peninsula, the Koyuk begins at an unnamed lake 140 miles northeast of Nome on the north side of the Bendeleben Mountains. The river flows for 150 miles, first in a generally easterly direction for 125 miles. Then, at the confluence with its East Fork, the river swings south, traversing tundra wetlands for 25 miles to the village of Koyuk on Norton Bay. The Koyuk drains about 2,000 square miles.

The uppermost 20 miles of the river are within Bering Land Bridge National Monument. Ridges and mountains to the north, east, and south form a horseshoe-shaped ring around the upper and middle Koyuk and range from 2,000 to over 3,000 feet in altitude. The Koyuk is a clear stream flowing across rolling tundra-covered hills and ridges, with land elevations along the river usually less than 50 feet except for occasional ridges rising over 100 feet. Below Knowles Creek, willows, spruce, and birch appear along the river and the domes of Granite Mountain and the Bendeleben and Darby mountains offer scenic vistas.

From its lake of origin to Caviar Creek, the Koyuk drops an average of 40 feet per mile. Downstream from its confluence with Caviar Creek, the Koyuk drops 33 feet per mile. Here the river is about 30 feet wide and 1 to 2 feet deep. About a half-mile below Knowles Creek, an unnamed tributary comes in from the south, almost doubling the Koyuk to about 60 feet wide and 2 to 4 feet deep. Downstream, the river gradually increases in width to over 250 feet, reaches a depth of 5 feet, and becomes a very slow-moving body of water.

The archaeological site of Iyatayak, south of Koyuk on Cape Denbigh, reveals evidence of humans inhabiting the region for the past 6,000 to 8,000 years. The village of Koyuk was first recorded by Lieutenant L. A. Zagoskin of the Imperial Russian Navy in the 1840s. But William Ennis of the Western Union Telegraph expedition in 1865 reported that Koyuk had been deserted for 13 years and that by that time most of the villagers had died, possibly from smallpox. The remaining Unalit Eskimos were joined by Malemute Eskimos when they began resettling the Koyuk/Norton Sound region around 1860, arriving from the Kobuk and Buckland regions to take advantage of the large caribou migration. About this same time, however,

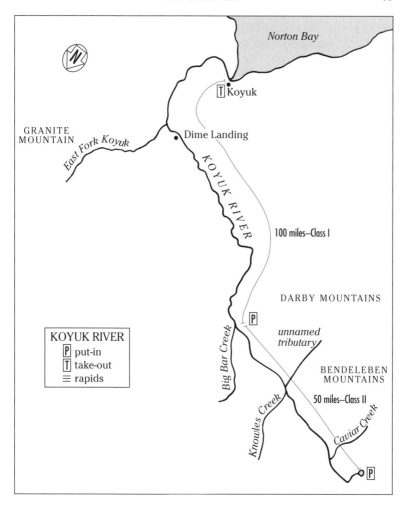

the caribou herds on the Seward Peninsula were declining.

After 1867, when Alaska was sold to the United States, the Koyuk region bustled with trade activity. The search for gold dramatically altered Eskimo lifeways as hordes of adventurers arrived. Mineral prospects along the Koyuk River never panned out, but several claims were filed on tributaries. A trading station was built at Koyuk in 1900 and two boomtowns, Dime Landing and Haycock, appeared upstream. Mining claims are currently worked near Haycock and in the Dime and First Chance creek areas. Koyuk today has primarily a subsistence economy. Residents hunt for moose and caribou in the upper river and hunt ducks, trap, fish, and collect berries and greens in the lower river. The sale and importation of alcoholic beverages is prohibited.

Rating: Class I–II. The river is Class II from headwaters to Big Bar Creek; Class I from Big Bar Creek to Koyuk. The Koyuk offers an easy flatwater float for families or novices from a point just upstream of Big Bar Creek to Koyuk. Above this point the river crosses numerous rocky ledges. A 4-mile stretch just upstream of Knowles Creek drops more than 75 feet per mile. Sufficient water for paddling in the area above Knowles Creek is usually present only through mid-June or temporarily after heavy summer rains.

Cautions: Four-mile section above Knowles Creek is swift and rocky.

Trip length: 100-150 miles; allow 7 days.

Season: Mid-to-late May to early September.

Watercraft: Medium to small raft, folding canoe or kayak, inflatable kayak.

Access: In—Scheduled air service from Nome to Koyuk. Put in by riverboat at a point just upstream of Big Bar Creek, above which numerous rocky ledges prevent easy travel. Or put in by floatplane on oxbow lakes along the middle and lower river area. Out—Take out at Koyuk.

Land manager: Bering Land Bridge National Preserve (upper 20 miles); state; Bureau of Land Management, Anchorage; Koyuk Native Corporation and Bering Straits Native Corporation. (See Land Managers section at back of book for address and phone information.)

Maps: Bendeleben B–1, B–2; Candle A–4, A–5, A–6; Norton Bay D–4, D–5.

Fish: Arctic char, arctic grayling, whitefish, northern pike, sheefish, chum and pink salmon. **Wildlife:** Grizzly and black bear, moose, wolverine, lynx, fox, Canada geese, and other waterfowl.

8   NOATAK RIVER

The Noatak provides an excellent wilderness expedition for intermediate boaters with backcountry skills. Entirely above the Arctic Circle, the Noatak drains the largest river basin in North America that is still virtually unaffected by human activities. From its headwaters on Mount Igikpak, the Noatak flows 396 miles from the mountains to the sea, arcing westward across the Western Arctic, then south along the DeLong Mountains to spill into Kotzebue Sound, after draining an area of 12,600 square miles.

The Noatak traverses six distinct regions: alpine tundra and mountains, the Noatak basin with its rounded mountains and vast tundra, the 65-mile-long Grand Canyon of the Noatak, the 7-mile-long Noatak Canyon, the plains and rolling Igichuk Hills, and the flat coastal delta.

The first 60-mile stretch of the Noatak courses through a narrow valley between mountains that rise thousands of feet within a couple miles of the river. The valley then widens, the mountains become distant, and a wetland tundra harbors many lakes and marshes. Below the Nimiuktuk River, the Noatak swings south into the Grand and Noatak canyons between the foothills and mountains of the DeLong and Baird ranges, confining itself in a single channel. Below Noatak Canyon, the river begins to braid; below Kelly River it becomes a tangle of braids. If you plan to take out at Noatak village, stay to the right well above the village or you will miss it. Below the village, the river is relatively confined as it flows to its mouth, where it spreads into a delta 15 miles across as it enters Kotzebue Sound.

Noatak means "passage to the Interior." Migratory peoples traversed the region seasonally, hunting wildlife, particularly along major caribou migration routes. The earliest inhabitants came from northern Asia more than 12,500 years ago. Modern Inupiat culture emerged, a culture that fully utilized marine resources, such as seal, walrus, and whale, and Interior resources like caribou and musk oxen.

Traditional Inupiat life began to change in 1850 with non-Native contact. An emphasis on fur trading and new technologies, and establishment of trading posts, schools, and post offices, changed patterns of movement and settlement. In 1908 the Friends Church established a federally supported mission school at what is now

Noatak village, and Eskimos embraced the Christian faith of the Friends. The culture of shamans, taboos, spirits, and the rich Inupiaq language was replaced by Western medicine, ceremony, the English language, and store-bought goods.

The first recorded non-Native exploration of the Noatak was in 1885 by S. B. McLenegan, who arrived aboard the revenue steamer *Corwin*. With a seaman, he traveled upriver to the Noatak headwaters in a 27-foot, three-hole, skin *baidarka* (Eskimo and Aleut kayak) that he acquired in Unalaska. The river was later mapped by C. E. Griffin of the U.S. Geological Survey in 1911. By 1915, the Inupiat had largely abandoned the upper Noatak, moving permanently to villages. Inupiat camps still exist, however, and historic trails within the river corridor are still used for travel, hunting, and fishing.

The Noatak basin is designated an International Biosphere Reserve. Under this United Nations scientific program, the area's ecological and genetic components are monitored to establish baseline data for measuring changes in other ecosystems worldwide. Information is also being collected on sustainable uses of natural resources by the Inupiat and other Natives who have lived off the land for thousands of years.

Rating: Class I–II, with 8 to 10 miles of Class II water below Douglas Creek and a Class II ledge just above Noatak Canyon. At certain water levels, boaters can encounter 3-foot standing waves in the Grand Canyon of the Noatak.

Cautions: At low water, the river is rocky, with many shallow gravel bars. Strong upriver winds can prevent downstream progress at times. Sweepers and submerged masses of sod are a hazard on the lower river. The water level in the Noatak changes dramatically during spring breakup and after rainfall, when it can rise several feet in a few hours.

Trip length: 347 miles or less; 7 days to 3 weeks. Allow 10 days to paddle from headwater lakes to Cutler River; 16 to 18 days from headwater lakes to Noatak village.

Season: June through September.

Watercraft: All.

Access: In—Scheduled air from Fairbanks to Bettles or Kotzebue; put in at one of the lakes in the upper river by charter floatplane from Bettles or Kotzebue. Out—Take out at prearranged spot by floatplane or wheelplane, or float to Noatak village. You can also float all the way to the mouth of the Noatak for pickup by boat or

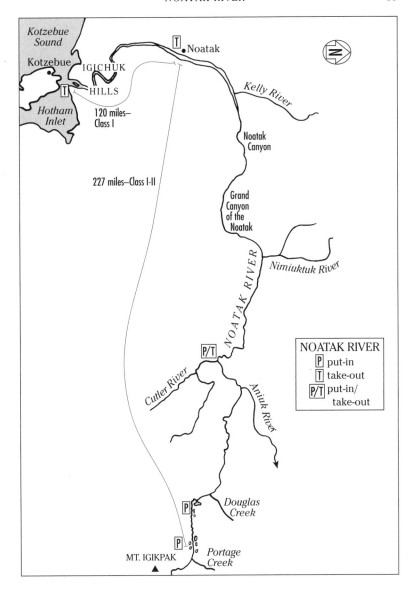

plane. Or you can continue on, paddling across a portion of Kotzebue Sound to Kotzebue. But beware: high winds are notorious on the Sound and can capsize boats. Do not attempt to cross except when conditions are very calm, early in the morning. Crossing should be made only in a sleek boat, such as a folding kayak, and *not* in a raft.

The Upper Noatak weaves through a vast tundra basin.

Land manager: Gates of the Arctic National Park and Preserve; Noatak National Preserve; NANA Regional Corporation; private. The Noatak is a National Wild River. (See Land Managers section at back of book for address and phone information.)

Maps: Survey Pass C–5, C–6; Ambler River C–1, D–1, D–2, D–3, D–4, D–5, D–6; Howard Pass A–3, A–4, A–5; Misheguk Mountain A–1, A–2, A–3, A–4, A–5; Baird Mountains D–3, D–4, D–5, D–6; Noatak A–1, A–2, B–1, B–2, B–3, C–1, C–2, C–3, D–1, D–2; Kotzebue D–1, D–2.

Fish: Arctic char, arctic grayling, northern pike, whitefish, chum salmon. **Wildlife:** Caribou, grizzly bear, Dall sheep, wolf, peregrine falcon, migratory waterfowl. The Western Arctic caribou herd, numbering 200,000 animals, crosses the Noatak during migration.

9   SELAWIK RIVER

From its headwaters in the Zane Hills, the Selawik River gathers water from the surrounding Kobuk lowlands and flows between the Kiliovilik Range and the Purcell Mountains and out onto the flats of Selawik National Wildlife Refuge. The upper river offers views of the mountains to the north and south. Downriver, the country flattens out and the river travels over miles and miles of rich wetlands, teeming with bird life. The river meanders slowly for over 200 miles to Selawik Lake, which drains into Hotham Inlet and then into Kotzebue Sound and the Chukchi Sea. The current decreases drastically on the lower river (below the Kugarak River), where the Selawik becomes a single channel up to 125 feet wide. On the lower river, traveling in the early morning or late evening is usually best for avoiding upriver winds.

The Inupiat culture which developed around the Selawik River centered on hunting of seals, walrus, other marine mammals, waterfowl, fish, and caribou. Eskimos living upriver waited for spring breakup, then rode the high water down to the coast in umiaks. Lieutenant L. A. Zagoskin of the Imperial Russian Navy first reported the village of Selawik in the 1840s. At that time, people lived in sod houses. U.S. Navy Lieutenants G. M. Stoney and John C. Cantwell explored the Selawik in 1884, learning that Natives reached the Yukon River by ascending the Selawik nearly to its headwaters and then descending the Koyukuk River system. Around the turn of the century, prospectors strayed from the golden beaches of Nome to the Selawik region in search of gold, but these efforts proved to be unsuccessful.

Ownership of large areas within Selawik National Wildlife Refuge, especially along the river, has been conveyed to Native corporations and individuals. There are private cabins and tent camps.

Rating: Easy Class I.
Cautions: Along the upper 50 to 70 miles are numerous sweepers, clumps of eroded streambank, and boulders. On the lower 25 miles beware of strong head winds, which create choppy 1- to 2-foot-high standing waves.
Trip length: 207 miles; allow 14 to 16 days from headwaters to Selawik.

Season: Late June to early September.

Watercraft: Hard-shell, folding, or inflatable canoe or kayak.

Access: In—Scheduled airline to Kotzebue from Anchorage or Fairbanks. Fly on charter floatplane and put in on small lakes in upper river, or fly on charter wheelplane and land on gravel bar in vicinity of Shiniliaok Creek. Out—Take out at Selawik and fly on scheduled air service to Kotzebue.

Land manager: Selawik National Wildlife Refuge; NANA Regional Corporation. The Selawik is a National Wild River. (See Land Managers section at back of book for address and phone information.)

Maps: Shungnak B–2, B–3, B–4, B–5, B–6, C–2, C–3, C–5; Selawik B–1, C–1, C–2, C–3.

Fish: Arctic char, arctic grayling, northern pike, sheefish, burbot.

Wildlife: Caribou, grizzly and black bear, moose, wolf, wolverine, waterfowl, shorebirds, raptors.

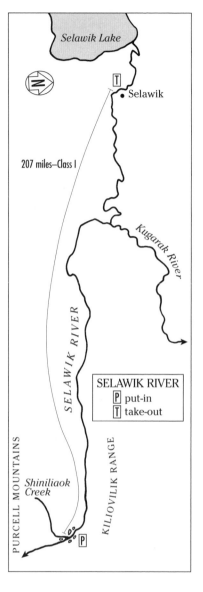

10   SQUIRREL RIVER

The Squirrel is a readily accessible arctic river traversing varied scenery, with outstanding hiking. This is a good family trip for experienced wilderness travelers. Originating in the Baird Mountains of the Brooks Range, the Squirrel River flows southeasterly for about 95 miles through a broad mountain-flanked valley forested with spruce, birch, aspen, and balsam poplar and enters the Kobuk River just upstream of the village of Kiana.

Excellent hiking is available in the headwaters, where the Baird Mountains rise 2,500 to 4,500 feet in elevation. Crystal-clear, yet emerald green in hue, the river traverses a range of northern ecosystems: alpine terrain, forested valleys, and expansive arctic tundra. The river braids over an extensive gravel floodplain, then forms a single channel as it flows past the Kiana Hills. Below the Kiana Hills, the lower river traverses open tundra, with the Kallarichuk Hills visible to the northeast.

The Squirrel drops from its headwaters elevation of 750 feet to less than 100 feet in 95 miles. Most of the gradient occurs in the first 15 miles, where the average drop is 40 feet per mile. Even with this relatively steep gradient, there are no notable rapids. However, the upper 10 miles are not easily accessible or easily floated. The last 85 miles of the river has an average gradient of just 2 feet per mile.

The Squirrel is a small river, ranging in width from 15 feet, at a point 10 miles from its headwaters, to 200 feet at its confluence with the Kobuk River. The Squirrel and its tributaries drain an area of about 1,600 square miles. After the first of August, the Squirrel may be too shallow to float in a folding kayak much farther up than several miles above the North Fork. If there is rain, the entire river can be floated easily. Without rain, the river can drop visibly overnight (up to several inches).

The Squirrel River was utilized in the past by Natives portaging between the Kobuk Valley and Noatak Valley. By 1910, the lower few miles of the river and an adjacent wagon road were used to get to placer gold mines on Klery Creek.

Rating: Class I. There are no notable rapids, nor are there any obstacles for the paddler.
Cautions: Bears.

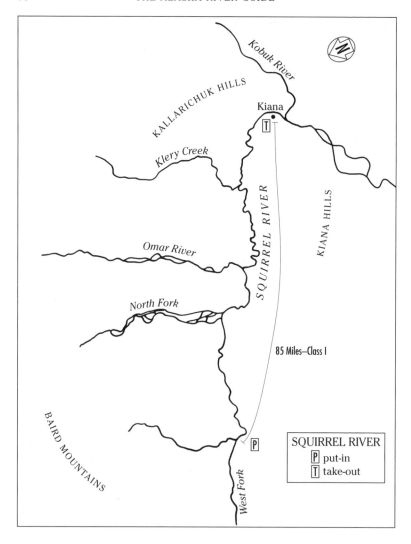

Trip length: 85 miles; allow 5 to 7 days.

Season: Mid-June to early August.

Watercraft: Kayak, canoe, or small raft. Transportation of hard-shell boats is difficult, so is not recommended.

Access: In—Scheduled airline to Kotzebue, then scheduled airline to Kiana, then fly on charter wheelplane to gravel bars on upper Squirrel River. Or take charter wheelplane from Kotzebue to upper Squirrel. Out—Take out at Kiana and take scheduled airline to Kotzebue, then scheduled airline on to Fairbanks or Anchorage.

Land manager: Bureau of Land Management, Anchorage; NANA Regional Corporation; state. (See Land Managers section at back of book for address and phone information.)
Maps: Baird Mountains A–3, A–4, A–5, B–5, B–6; Selawik D–3.
Fish: Arctic grayling, northern pike, whitefish, burbot, chum and pink salmon. **Wildlife:** Grizzly and black bear, moose, wolf, wolverine, lynx, beaver, river otter, osprey, golden eagle, sandhill crane, migratory waterfowl.

Porcupines leave toothmarks on shrubs—and occasionally on boats.

11   UNALAKLEET RIVER

Beginning in the Kaltag Mountains, the Unalakleet River flows 90 miles in a southwesterly direction to Norton Sound, just south of the village of Unalakleet. A clear, quiet, braided river, the Unalakleet flows through the Nulato Hills, a region forested in spruce and willow. Hiking is excellent in the vicinity of Old Woman Mountain and other mountains paralleling the area, where the vegetation is alpine tundra.

Leaving the Nulato Hills, the river meanders through muskeg spruce in the low coastal region before reaching the village. There are no rapids and the water consists of fast-moving riffles and pools and slow meandering sections. The Iditarod Trail passes along part of the river, and there are several cabins and historic mail sites. It's possible to hike part of the Iditarod Trail.

Old Woman River is a significant tributary, with a volume at least as great as that of the Unalakleet where they join. The Unalakleet receives heavy summer use by subsistence fishers; there is also a commercial arctic char fishery. Berry picking, beginning in midsummer, is excellent.

Unalakleet, or its Eskimo name Ounakalik, means "place where the east wind blows." Archaeologists have uncovered house pits in the area that date back to 200 B.C. Lieutenant L. A. Zagoskin of the Imperial Russian Navy was the first non-Native to report on the area, after the Russian American Company established a trading post at St. Michaels in 1833 and in Unalakleet a few years later. Vigorous trade existed between coastal Eskimos and Interior Indians across the Kaltag Portage, since the Unalakleet River provided the shortest route between Norton Sound and the Yukon River.

Remains of old settlements lie scattered from the mouth of the Unalakleet to its headwaters. In 1898, reindeer herders arrived from Lapland to establish reindeer herds. One old fishing camp on the river is still known locally as Naplathlasit, meaning "where the Lapp herders were," and some of their descendants still live in Unalakleet. By the beginning of the 20th century, gold prospectors had flooded the Seward Peninsula and many traveled over the Kaltag Portage. Later the U.S. Army Signal Corps constructed the Washington–Alaska Military Cable and Telegraph System, with cabins and lines along the Unalakleet River; soon after, mail routes were established.

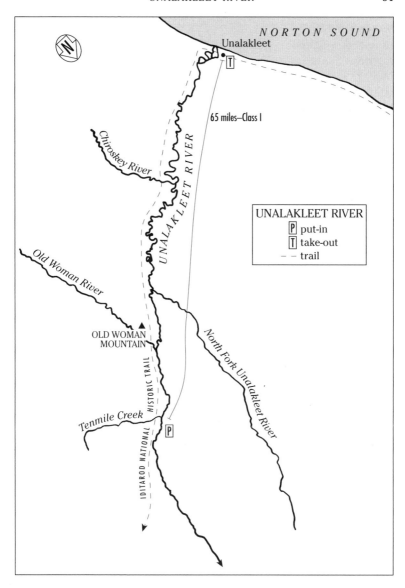

Rating: Class I.

Cautions: Many snags, sweepers, and sharp turns, especially in the braided area above Old Woman River and below the North Fork.

Trip length: 65 miles; allow 6 days from Tenmile Creek to Unalakleet.

Season: June through mid-September.

Watercraft: All.

Access: In—Scheduled airline to Nome. Put in by charter Supercub to gravel bar in upper river. Or take scheduled airline from Nome to Unalakleet and hire local resident to take you upstream by motorboat to Tenmile River. Out—Take out at Unalakleet.

Land manager: Bureau of Land Management, Anchorage; Unalakleet Native Corporation. The Unalakleet is a National Wild and Scenic River. (See Land Managers section at back of book for address and phone information.)

Maps: Norton Sound A–1, A–2; Unalakleet D–2, D–3, D–4.

Fish: Arctic grayling, king, coho, and sockeye salmon, Dolly Varden.

Wildlife: Caribou, grizzly, wolf, wolverine, fox, beaver, marten, bald eagle; abundant waterfowl, shorebirds, and raptors.

YUKON REGION

The Yukon River, draining 35 percent of Alaska's land mass, forms the nucleus of this region. Rising in Canada, the Yukon flows north-northwest to the U.S. border. From the border, the Yukon arcs across Alaska, finally emptying into the Bering Sea more than 1,400 miles later. Large tributaries—the Porcupine, Tanana, and Koyukuk—add volume and width to the Yukon.

The region is especially valuable for the extensive river flats in the Lower Yukon region which have formed over thousands of years, leaving behind oxbows, sloughs, marshes, and a myriad of lakes and marshlands teeming with wildlife. Forests, too, are extensive, and forest fires are common in the summer—some burning underground for years, fueled by centuries-old layers of peat. Rivers in this region are generally nonglacial, relatively slow-moving, and meandering. Ice exists underground along rivers as permafrost.

The climate is continental, so summers are hot and dry and winters are very cold. Fort Yukon has recorded a high temperature of 100 degrees Fahrenheit. Arctic Village has reported temperatures as low as minus 78 degrees. The average annual precipitation is 10 to 12 inches in the uplands and 6 inches on the Yukon Flats.

Breakup on rivers begins in late April or May, with peak flow in May; freezeup occurs in October. Flooding of the lowlands is an annual occurrence, and villages along the Yukon and other rivers often suffer major damage as a result of ice damming the rivers at breakup.

YUKON REGION

12 Alatna River
13 Anvik River
14 Beaver Creek
15 Birch Creek
16 Black River
17 Charley River
18 Chatanika River
19 Chena River
20 Delta River
21 Fortymile River
22 John River

23 Middle Fork Koyukuk River
24 North Fork Koyukuk River
25 Melozitna River
26 Nenana River
27 Nowitna River
28 Porcupine River
29 Sheenjek River
30 Tinayguk River
31 Wild River

12   ALATNA RIVER

The Alatna is a good river for a family with some Alaska river experience, a family that is prepared with the skills to live and travel in a pristine, remote region. Rising from lakes in the Central Brooks Range, the Alatna flows more than 180 miles through the Endicott Mountains, the Helpmejack Hills, and the Alatna Hills in a southeasterly direction to its confluence with the Koyukuk River at Kanuti Flats. The river begins in alpine tundra where the scenery is dominated by mountains, including the Arrigetch Peaks, and descends through dense spruce forests to lowland flats dotted with lakes.

The Alatna is entirely within designated wilderness in Gates of the Arctic National Park and offers an outstanding wilderness experience. Hiking opportunities, particularly in the upper half of the river, are excellent. The upper 25 miles of the river, from headwater lakes, is shallow and rocky, often requiring lining of boats for several miles. Just above Ram Creek is a short section of Class II–plus to Class III rapids, which can be lined or portaged. The next 22-mile

Permafrost may be visible in cliffs and cutbanks along Northern rivers.

portion is shallow and swift, with sweepers. From Circle Lake, near Arrigetch Creek, the river deepens and mellows, meandering slowly enough to allow you to thoroughly enjoy the scenery.

The Alatna River was mapped in 1909 by Philip Smith, who found a dramatic outcropping of granite mountains with "sensational needlelike peaks extending for six or eight miles in a horseshoe around the gushing creek which rose in the glacier." The Eskimos called these mountains Arrigetch, which means "fingers of the hand extended."

When Robert Marshall arrived in the central Brooks Range in 1929, there were two villages at the mouth of the Alatna River: Alatna and Allakaket, on opposite sides of the river. Two cultures, the Kuvuungmiit Eskimos and the Koyukukhotana Athapaskans, came together here to trade goods. The Eskimos lived in Alatna, on the river's north bank, and the Indians in Allakaket, on the south side. These two villages still exist. In 1929, each village had a store. Allakaket had an Episcopal mission that had been founded in 1906 by Archdeacon Hudson Stuck, who in 1913 led the first ascent of Mount McKinley.

Rating: Class I–II, with one section of Class II–III rapids which can be lined or portaged.
Cautions: Rapids just above

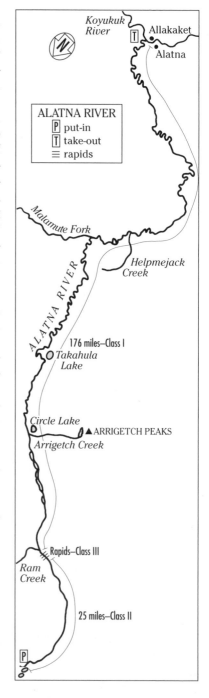

Koyukuk River

Allakaket

Alatna

ALATNA RIVER
P put-in
T take-out
≡ rapids

Malamute Fork

ALATNA RIVER

Helpmejack Creek

176 miles–Class I
Takahula Lake

Circle Lake
▲ ARRIGETCH PEAKS
Arrigetch Creek

Rapids–Class III
Ram Creek

25 miles–Class II

P

Ram Creek; sweepers; black bears.

Trip length: 184 miles from headwater lakes to Allakaket; allow 9 days. 137 miles from Circle Lake to Allakaket; allow 7 days. Or shorter trips with floatplane pickup in the Helpmejack Hills. For a longer trip, continue down the Koyukuk River.

Season: June through September.

Watercraft: Canoe, folding kayak, inflatable kayak. Raft is OK, but slow on lower river.

Access: In—Put in at headwater lakes by floatplane from Bettles or Fairbanks for 184-mile float to Allakaket; put in at Circle Lake by floatplane for 137-mile Class I float to Allakaket. A put-in at Takahula Lake is also possible. Out—For a shorter trip, take out by floatplane at Malamute Fork, Helpmejack Creek, or other location agreed upon by charter pilot. Or take out at Allakaket and fly on scheduled air service to Bettles or Fairbanks.

Land manager: Gates of the Arctic National Park and Preserve. The Alatna is a National Wild River. (See Land Managers section at back of book for address and phone information.)

Maps: Survey Pass A–1, A–2, B–2, C2, C–3, C–4, C–5, D–5; Hughes C–1, D–1; Bettles C–6.

Fish: Arctic char, arctic grayling. **Wildlife:** Caribou, grizzly and black bear, Dall sheep, moose, wolf, wolverine, migratory waterfowl.

13 ANVIK RIVER

The Anvik is a fine family float, with good hiking in the upper region and limited hiking outside the river corridor on the lower river due to extensive birch and spruce forests. Beginning in the rolling Nulato Hills, the Anvik River flows southerly for 141 miles, joining the Yukon River 1.5 miles below the village of Anvik. A clear-water river in the Middle Yukon region, the river flows through alpine tundra and forested hills as it winds its way down to the Yukon.

Occupied by Ingalik Athapaskans for centuries, the Anvik River Valley and the Middle Yukon region supplied people with a variety of wild game, fish, berries, and other plants. The first Europeans to penetrate the Middle Yukon were Russians. Andrei Glazanov left St. Michaels, a trading post at the mouth of the Yukon, in 1833 to develop trade networks with Natives upriver and found several hundred people living in Anvik. In 1887, Episcopal missionary John Wright Chapman established the Christ Church mission and an orphanage across the river from Anvik.

While missionaries scrambled to stake their religious claims on Native settlements, prospectors poured into the Yukon and staked claims for gold. Anvik served as a wood refueling stop for stern-wheelers along the route to the Klondike gold fields. Today, Anvik is a small subsistence village of less than 100 people. Every other year, Anvik is a checkpoint on the Iditarod Trail Sled Dog Race.

Rating: Class I.
Cautions: Sweepers.
Trip length: 121 miles from McDonald Creek to Anvik; allow 7 days.
Season: June through September.
Watercraft: All.
Access: In—Scheduled airline to Anvik, St. Marys, or Grayling, from Fairbanks or Anchorage. Put in at headwaters by floatplane or riverboat or on gravel bars by wheelplane in vicinity of McDonald Creek, or take a riverboat from Anvik. Out—Anvik.
Land manager: Bureau of Land Management, Anchorage; Ingalik Native Corporation. (See Land Managers section at back of book for address and phone information.)
Maps: Holy Cross C–3, C–4, D–4; Unalakleet A–4, B–3, B–4.

Fish: Arctic char, arctic grayling, northern pike, sheefish, king, coho, pink, and chum salmon (one of the largest runs in the world), rainbow trout. **Wildlife:** Grizzly and black bear, moose, wolf, beaver, marten, waterfowl.

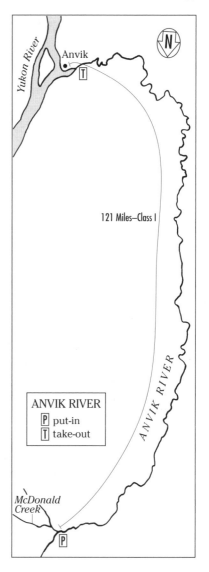

14   BEAVER CREEK

Beaver Creek offers an excellent family or novice float and is one of the few road-accessible streams in Alaska designated as a Wild and Scenic River. Originating at the confluence of Bear and Champion creeks in White Mountains National Recreation Area, Beaver Creek is a shallow, moderately swift clearwater stream flowing through rolling hills and the jagged peaks of the White Mountains before slowing and meandering through the Yukon Flats to the Yukon River. The White Mountains form a dramatic backdrop for the first 127 miles.

A trip down Beaver Creek begins on Nome Creek, usually with a day or two of difficult paddling and lining of boats over shallow riffles in a narrow twisting channel 5 to 20 feet wide, with numerous sweepers. Beginning at Beaver Creek at River Mile 6, the paddling is leisurely and it is possible to easily travel 10 to 15 miles a day. The river becomes 75 to 150 feet wide and is 2 to 4 feet deep, with an average gradient of 8 feet per mile all the way to Victoria Creek. As the river flows into Yukon Flats National Wildlife Refuge, its gradient decreases to less than 2 feet per mile. The depth increases, as well as the width, and broad gravel bars appear more frequently. The river becomes somewhat turbid in the lower section.

Vegetation in the river corridor is determined by permafrost patterns. Poorly drained areas are dominated by sedges, low shrubs, and stunted black spruce; elsewhere, you will find spruce, white birch, balsam poplar, and aspen. The region forms an outstanding mosaic of green vegetation, trees, dramatic limestone peaks, colorful exposed rock cliffs, and meandering river.

Rating: Class I.
Cautions: Sweepers.
Trip length: 303 miles on Nome and Beaver Creeks to the Yukon, plus an additional 96 miles on the Yukon to the Yukon River bridge on the Dalton Highway. Allow 1 to 3 weeks, depending on how much of the river you wish to float. Allow 7 to 8 days between Nome Creek put-in and Victoria Creek (127 miles). Allow another 8 to 14 days to continue another 272 miles through Yukon Flats National Wildlife Refuge to the Yukon River bridge on the Dalton Highway.
Season: May through September.

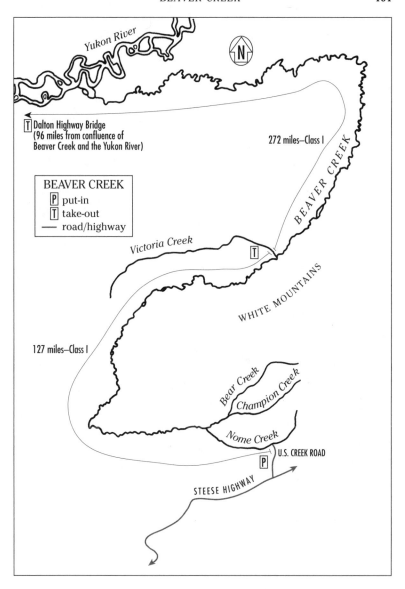

Watercraft: All.

Access: In—Take Steese Highway from Fairbanks to Mile 57.3 and turn left on U.S. Creek Road to Nome Creek. Put in on Nome Creek. Out—For 127-mile float, take out by charter wheelplane on gravel bars in vicinity of Victoria Creek or by charter floatplane in quiet stretches below the creek. If paddling the entire river, take out at

Whether plain or fancy, lunchtime on the river is always a treat.

the Yukon River bridge on the Dalton Highway.

Land manager: Bureau of Land Management, Fairbanks; Yukon Flats National Wildlife Refuge. Beaver Creek, from the confluence of Bear and Champion creeks to River Mile 127, is a National Wild and Scenic River. (See Land Managers section at back of book for address and phone information.)

Maps: Livengood B–1, B–2, C–1, C–2, D–1; Circle B–6, C–6, D–5, D–6.

Fish: Arctic char, arctic grayling, northern pike, whitefish, sheefish, burbot, slimy sculpin, long-nose sucker. **Wildlife:** Caribou, grizzly and black bear, Dall sheep, moose, wolf, lynx, beaver, peregrine falcon, golden eagle, bald eagle.

BIRCH CREEK

15

A designated National Wild and Scenic River accessible by road at both the put-in and take-out, Birch Creek is an attractive float for people who would like a wild-river experience without the expense of flying into a roadless area. This is an exciting family rafting trip for experienced wilderness campers who also have boating experience or for intermediate canoeists and kayakers.

From headwater creeks issuing from Mastodon Dome, Birch Creek flows swiftly through upland plateaus, forested valleys, rolling hills, and low mountains. Nearing the marshy lowlands of Yukon Flats National Wildlife Refuge, the river slows and meanders. It joins the Yukon River after flowing for 344 miles.

A moderately swift, shallow stream, Birch Creek begins a mile above its confluence with Twelvemile Creek. For the first 9 miles, the stream is narrow, winding, and sometimes shallow. It may be necessary to drag boats through shallow riffles in this section. For the next 24 miles (up to Mile 33) between Harrington Fork and Clums Fork, the stream widens and increases its depth to an average of 2 to 6 feet. Short rapids and exposed gravel bars characterize the stream.

For its first 113 miles, the stream's average gradient is 13 feet per mile. The gradient gradually lessens and by Mile 126 is less than 2 feet per mile, while the water depth increases to 8 feet. At the Birch Creek bridge on the Steese Highway (River Mile 126; Highway Mile 147), the National Wild and Scenic River designation ends. Birch Creek continues another 218 miles across the Yukon Flats before its confluence with the Yukon River. Especially scenic in its upper reaches, views of cliffs and bedrock outcrops stand out against green vegetation on low rolling hills—black spruce and muskeg woodlands contrasting with birch and aspen uplands.

Very little indication of early Native use of Birch Creek has been found, but it is certain that Gwich'in and Han Athapaskans used the region. Caribou were hunted in the flats near Medicine Lake until the mid-1960s, when the herd began to decline greatly in number. Beaver have been trapped in the flats and lakes near Birch Creek and whitefish have been netted in Birch Creek and Medicine Lake since 1900.

Gold was discovered by non-Natives in 1893, leading to

formation of the Circle Mining District. Many mining claims still exist along tributaries of Birch Creek. Improvements in mining technology and a rise in the price of gold created a surge in mining activity in tributaries of Birch Creek into the 1980s. Following complaints of environmental degradation from recreationists, environmentalists, and Native subsistence users, and legal action by the Sierra Club, the Bureau of Land Management stiffened its regulation of mining.

Rating: Class I–II, with several Class III rapids.
Cautions: Upper 9 miles often require lining.
Trip length: 126 miles from Twelvemile Creek to Birch Creek bridge at Mile 147 Steese Highway; allow 7 to 10 days. Trip may be extended all the way to the Yukon River, another 218 miles; allow an additional 10 days.
Season: May through September.
Watercraft: All.

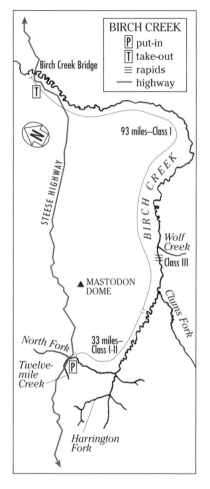

Access: In—Put in at Mile 94.5 on the Steese Highway. Line boat down Twelvemile Creek 1,000 feet to its confluence with Birch Creek. Out—Take out at Mile 147 Steese Highway.
Land manager: Bureau of Land Management, Fairbanks; private. The first 126 miles of Birch Creek is designated a National Wild and Scenic River. (See Land Managers section at back of book for address and phone information.)
Maps: Circle A–3, A–4, B–1, B–2, B–3, B–4, C–1.
Fish: Arctic grayling, northern pike, whitefish. **Wildlife:** Caribou, grizzly and black bear, moose, lynx, small forest mammals, migratory waterfowl.

16   BLACK RIVER

From its origins on the Porcupine River Flats of the Yukon Territory, the Black River flows 255 miles through rolling and low-land forests of spruce, hardwoods, and willow, joining the Porcupine River about 16 miles northwest of Fort Yukon. Very little topographic relief presents itself, though the river has cut an ancient swath through the Yukon Flats, with numerous bluffs and high banks. The upper river flows at a moderate pace (3 to 4 miles per hour); below Salmon Fork, it slows, widens, and meanders through high bluffs. Below Chalkyitsik the river widens and slows even more, and high banks limit the view of the surrounding forest.

Overall, the river is confined and somewhat unchanging in terms of topography and vegetation. There are remains of old cabins along the river, particularly up the shallow slough to the site of Old Salmon Village. Rich in wildlife that are prized for their fur, the Black River region is known as "the cradle of the lynx."

One of the most notable non-Native ascents of the Black River came in 1911 when a Canadian attaché to an American surveying party took the *Aurora,* a specially constructed boat with a 24-horsepower engine driving a stern paddle wheel, up the river, pushing a 40-foot barge. The boat made it 200 miles upriver before being halted by shallow water.

The most extensive chronicle of 20th-century use of the Black River area is Evelyn Berglund Shore's *Born on Snowshoes.* In 1928, when she was a child, her family settled the area to trap. For many years, they spent the winter running trap lines and the spring trapping beaver and skinning wolves. In early summer they would make a quick float trip down to Fort Yukon for supplies, then motor and pole back up the river. The fall was spent woodcutting, meat cutting, berry picking, and toboggan-making.

The people of the Black River, Gwich'in Athapaskans living in Chalkyitsik about 70 miles upstream from the Porcupine, continue to use the Black as a travel route. They possess intimate knowledge of the riffles and bends in the river and continue to make regular trips to Fort Yukon or up the river for hunting, trapping, and gathering firewood.

Rating: Flatwater Class I river. The Black River affords a remote, little-traveled float through the Yukon Flats.

Cautions: Upstream winds on the lower river create whitecaps and can impede progress or cause capsizing.

Trip length: For 150-mile-plus trip, allow 10 days between Birch Lake and Chalkyitsik. For 260-mile trip, allow 14 to 16 days between Birch Lake and Fort Yukon, via the Black, Porcupine, and Sucker rivers.

Season: June through September. (Above Chalkyitsik the river may be too shallow to float after early July.)

Watercraft: Hard-shell canoe or kayak, folding canoe or kayak.

Access: In—Take scheduled air service from Fairbanks to Fort Yukon. Put in by floatplane from Fort Yukon to Birch Lake or other small lakes or on the river between Grayling Fork and Salmon Fork. Out—Take out at Chalkyitsik and take scheduled air service to Fort Yukon, or take out by floatplane from Black or Porcupine rivers. For 260-mile trip, take out on Sucker River after paddling 3 miles upriver to a road which leads a short distance to Fort Yukon.

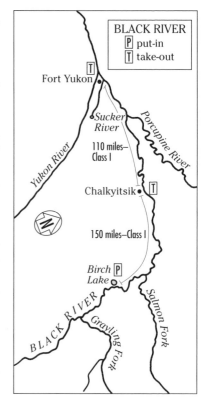

Land manager: Yukon Flats National Wildlife Refuge; Chalkyitsik Native Corporation. (See Land Managers section at back of book for address and phone information.)

Maps: Black River A–3, B–3, B–4, C–4, C–5, C–6; Fort Yukon C–1, C–2, C–3.

Fish: Arctic grayling, northern pike, whitefish, sheefish, chum salmon. **Wildlife:** Grizzly and black bear, moose, wolverine, lynx, waterfowl.

17 CHARLEY RIVER AND YUKON RIVER

For the advanced rafter, canoeist, or kayaker, the Charley offers many miles of whitewater challenges in a remote, seldom-visited wilderness. Known for its exceptional clarity, the Charley rises in the Tanana Hills, flowing from headwaters about 4,000 feet above sea level and descending at an average gradient of 31 feet per mile to meet the Yukon at 700 feet above sea level. With an average current of 4 to 6 miles per hour, the Charley is never dull over the course of its 88 miles.

During high water, usually late May to July, the upper two-thirds of the river is lively and challenging. High water occurs at breakup and when there are rainstorms. Water levels rise dramatically within hours. At low water levels, exposed gravel bars and boulders require vigilant maneuvering and scouting as you thread through whitewater rapids.

The river cuts through high plateau tundra and valleys untouched by glaciation and mostly free of human imprint, traversing low rugged mountains and passing high steep bluffs, all clothed with a mosaic of vegetation—willow and alder thickets, white spruce, and cottonwood stands along the river; boggy wetlands with stunted black spruce; upland spruce, birch, and aspen; and finally the open tundra sweeping upward to scree slopes and granite pinnacles.

Hiking opportunities are good in the upper river corridor and the scenery throughout the preserve is superb. Along the river, you'll pass historic old camps and cabin sites of trappers and prospectors. The Charley enters the Yukon and loses itself in this broad, silty river. Along the Yukon to the town of Circle, paddlers may encounter fish camps with fish wheels or nets in the river, or fish drying on racks.

Archaeological evidence indicates that the Charley River region may have been occupied as early as 27,000 years ago. The Yukon and Charley river corridor was unglaciated during the Wisconsin Ice Age and is close to the hypothesized ice-free corridor connecting Pleistocene Alaska with the contiguous 48 states. Thus the area has a potential for answering questions relative to early man in the New World. Han Athapaskans inhabited the region in historic times, living in scattered villages for up to seven months a year and

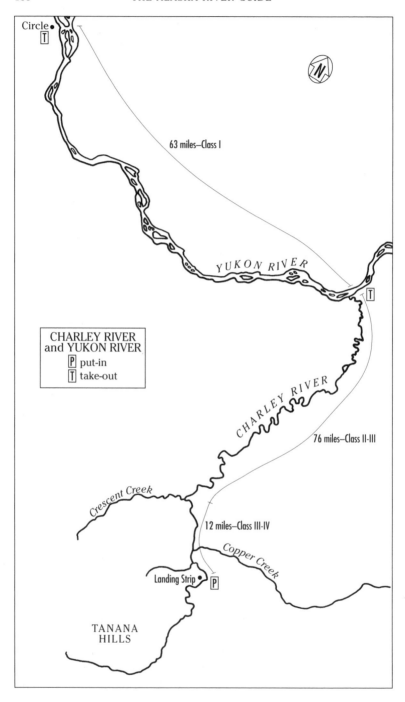

Circle

63 miles—Class I

YUKON RIVER

CHARLEY RIVER
and YUKON RIVER
P put-in
T take-out

CHARLEY RIVER

76 miles—Class II-III

Crescent Creek

12 miles—Class III-IV

Copper Creek

Landing Strip P

TANANA
HILLS

N

hunting, fishing, or gathering the rest of the year.

Native life changed with the arrival of outsiders. First fur trading and then the boom-bust cycles of gold rushes eroded traditional culture as the Han replaced birchbark pots and root baskets with cast-iron skillets, and replaced birchbark canoes, pole homes, and caribou clothing with flat-bottomed boats, log cabins, and mackinaws. Some items, like the repeating rifle and the fish wheel, brought radical changes in subsistence hunting and fishing techniques.

Rating: Class II–IV. The Charley is largely Class II with many Class III rapids. Class III–IV rapids between the upper Charley airstrip and the confluence of the Charley River with Crescent Creek may be lined or portaged. The Charley has boulder-strewn rock gardens with a swift current.

Cautions: Swift current; rapids; sweepers; exposed rocks and low water late in the season (September); rapidly rising river levels during storms.

Trip length: 88 miles on Charley River to confluence with Yukon River; allow 4 days. 63 additional miles on the Yukon to Circle; allow 3 extra days.

Season: Late May to early September.

Watercraft: All. Inflatable boats are easiest to transport in.

Access: In—From Fairbanks or Tok, or from Eagle on the Taylor Highway, put in by small charter aircraft on the primitive upper Charley landing strip, about 7 miles south of Copper Creek on the west side of the Charley. While helicopter landings are prohibited in designated wilderness in Alaska, it may be possible to obtain a special use permit from the National Park Service (Yukon-Charley Rivers National Preserve) for a helicopter landing at the confluence of Crescent Creek and the Charley River. Out—Take out at confluence with Yukon River or anywhere on the Yukon by motorboat or floatplane, or paddle all the way to Circle.

Land manager: Yukon-Charley Rivers National Preserve. The Charley is a National Wild River. (See Land Managers section at back of book for address and phone information.)

Maps: Charley River A–4, A–5, B–4, B–5, B–6; Circle D–1; Eagle C–6, D–5, D–6.

Fish: Arctic grayling, northern pike, sheefish; king, coho, and chum salmon. **Wildlife:** Caribou (calving grounds of the Fortymile caribou herd), Dall sheep, grizzly and black bear, wolf; prime breeding areas for peregrine falcon, bald eagle, osprey.

18 CHATANIKA RIVER

The Chatanika is a great river for a one-day family outing or a five- to seven-day trip. With headwaters in the rolling hills north of Fairbanks, the Chatanika River flows west-southwest 128 miles through spruce and birch forests to its confluence with the Tolovana River. A clearwater stream, the Chatanika courses mostly through a mature U-shaped valley, with low hills surrounding the valley and with mountains in the distance. The lower river traverses Minto Flats, an area covered with many small, clear lakes.

The Elliott Highway crosses the river at midpoint and the Steese Highway crosses and parallels the upper reaches of the river. There are state and Bureau of Land Management roadside campgrounds and waysides along the river. The historic Fairbanks-to-Circle gold trail follows the upper Chatanika, and some cabins may be found along the river near the town of Chatanika. While not a remote wilderness trip, the Chatanika offers an excellent recreational experience, with good wildlife viewing and a bit of gold mining history.

Thousands of gold miners and fortune seekers came to the Chatanika River just after the turn of the century, and the mining settlement of Chatanika was established in 1904. The river was important because of its access to gold deposits and because, via the Tolovana River, it emptied into the Tanana River and thus was part of a navigable waterway between the Interior and the Bering Sea.

Rating: Class I.
Cautions: Sweepers; logjams.
Trip length: 128 miles or less, depending on put-in location; 60 miles from Sourdough Creek to the Elliott Highway bridge, allow 3 to 4 days; less from other put-in locations. For a longer trip, continue past the Elliott Highway bridge to Minto Flats on the Tolovana River and to the Tanana River for take-out at Manley Hot Springs—an added distance of about 75 miles; allow an extra 3 to 4 days.
Season: June through September.
Watercraft: All.
Access: In—Drive the Steese Highway north of Fairbanks to Mile 60 (Sourdough Creek bridge). Another possibility is Mile 53 (Cripple Creek bridge and BLM campground; follow side road near

campground entrance to boat launch site). Other possible put-in locations include: Long Creek bridge at Mile 45; Chatanika River bridge at Mile 39. Out—Take out at the bridge on the Elliott Highway at Mile 11, or continue to Manley Hot Springs on the Tanana River.

Land manager: Bureau of Land Management, Fairbanks; Upper Chatanika River State Recreation Area; Lower Chatanika State Recreation Site; private. (See Land Managers section at back of book for address and phone information.)

Maps: Circle A–6, B–5, B–6; Livengood A–1, A–2, A–3, A–4, A–5, A–6; Fairbanks D–4, D–6.

Fish: Arctic grayling, northern pike, sheefish. **Wildlife:** Caribou, brown and black bear, Dall sheep, migratory waterfowl.

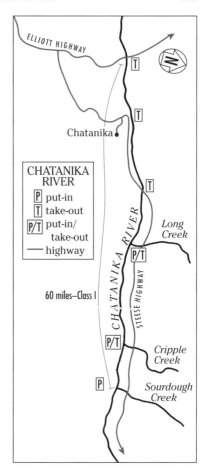

19   CHENA RIVER

Beginning in low mountains of eastern Alaska, the Chena is a subarctic clearwater river which flows westerly for 141 miles to its confluence with the Tanana River near Fairbanks. Draining about 1,980 square miles, the Chena cuts through forested mountains and hills and traverses muskeg and scrub thickets.

The upper 100 miles of the river are generally clear, though this has not always been the case. The Chena is typical of many Alaskan subarctic rivers that in the past were polluted by gold mining activities, which have now been drastically curtailed. Unfortunately, the lower reaches of the river, particularly the lower 30 miles, are polluted by domestic and industrial wastes from Fairbanks. Still, boaters in Fairbanks love the accessibility of the Chena, which is the most popular and intensively utilized sportfishing river in Interior Alaska.

Like the nearby Chatanika River, the Chena was visited by gold miners at the turn of the century and also was part of the navigable waterway between the Interior and the Bering Sea. The first building in Fairbanks was a log cabin trading post built on the Chena in 1901

The Chena River is popular for a leisurely 4-hour or 4-day float.

by adventurer and con man E. T. Barnette. Felix Pedro discovered gold on the Little Chena River tributary of Fairbanks Creek and the gold rush was on. Since the early days of mining, Fairbanks has developed into the state's second largest city, the home of the University of Alaska, and the trading center for all of Interior Alaska.

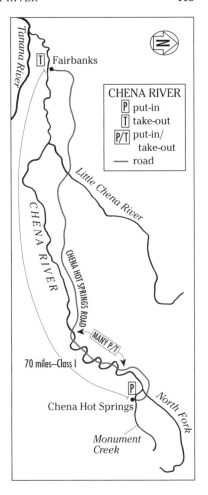

Rating: Class I.

Cautions: Sweepers; logjams; braided channel just above confluence with Little Chena.

Trip length: 70 miles from Chena Hot Springs to Fairbanks; allow 2 to 4 days.

Season: June through September.

Watercraft: All.

Access: In—Drive Chena Hot Springs Road to Chena Hot Springs and put in on the river. Other possible put-in or take-out locations: Chena Hot Springs Road, Mile 40; Chena Slough (take Badger, Peede, and Persinger roads). Out—Take out at Wendell Street bridge in Fairbanks, or other locations within or below the city.

Land manager: Alaska Division of Parks; state; private. (See Land Managers section at back of book for address and phone information.)

Maps: Circle A–5; Big Delta D–5, D–6; Fairbanks D–1, D–2.

Fish: Arctic grayling, northern pike, round whitefish, humpback whitefish, northern pike, sheefish, burbot, king and chum salmon, least cisco. The Chena River and its tributaries once supported the largest recreational arctic grayling fishery in the world. Overfishing reduced the grayling population drastically, so that now all catches must be released. **Wildlife:** Moose, beaver, muskrat, migratory waterfowl.

20   DELTA RIVER

The Delta is a small river flowing north out of Lower Tangle Lake through the highly scenic Amphitheater Mountains into the foothills of the Alaska Range. Beginning as a 16-mile string of clearwater lakes, the river flows for 22 miles before becoming cloudy with glacial silt. The scenery changes from open tundra to spruce and aspen forest as the valley widens. Vistas of 13,700-foot Mount Hayes and the rugged peaks and glaciers of the Alaska Range are outstanding.

This is a popular float with intermediate boaters because of its road access and its length (it can be done in a three-day weekend). It's also popular with expert boaters because of the challenging whitewater at Black Rapids. Beginning at the boat launch at the Tangle Lakes campground, paddle through four of the Tangle Lakes, which are connected by shallow channels of moving water. During low water levels, lining canoes and rafts may be necessary for short distances.

The first 1.25 miles of river are shallow, rocky Class II water. Two miles below Tangle Lakes, the river makes a 90-degree eastward bend and enters a half-mile canyon, 600 feet wide and 100 feet high, with Class V waterfalls. Portage around the falls on a half-mile maintained trail on the right. The trail is divided into two sections, with a pond crossing after the first quarter mile. Just below the portage are another couple miles of shallow, rocky Class III rapids. Wrecked and abandoned canoes offer a warning to the wary. Run these on the left or line boats along the right.

Below the rapids, the next 12 miles offer easy Class I water. At the confluence of Eureka Creek with the Delta, the river becomes cold, silty glacier water. Past and present gold mining claims exist in the vicinity of Eureka Creek. The last 7 miles to the recommended take-out at Mile 212.5 on Richardson Highway are braided, swift, and shallow Class II, with numerous channels and gravel bars. The take-out is marked with signs on the right just below the river's confluence with Phelan Creek.

The next 20 miles, from Ann Creek to One Mile Creek, is known as the Black Rapids. The river becomes very swift and braided Class III and becomes Class IV in the upriver of Black Rapids Glacier. Portage around this section is recommended, putting in again

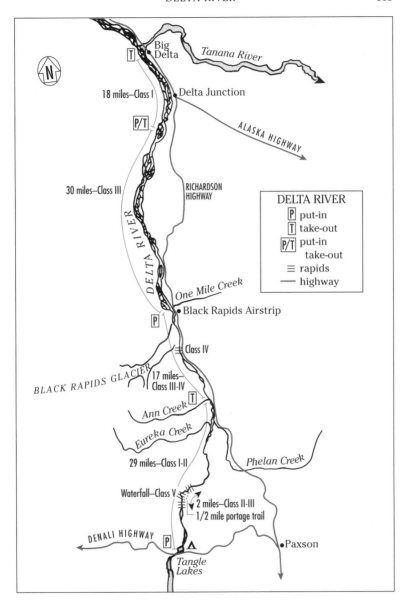

around Mile 229. The next 30 miles are Class III with very fast glacial water moving through braided channels. The last 18 miles to the town of Big Delta, at the confluence of the Delta and Tanana rivers, are Class I–II.

Native habitation of the Tangle Lakes-Delta River region goes back 10,000 years. The Delta River was first mapped during the Klondike gold rush by the U.S. Army under the command of Captain Edwin F. Glenn, who led his party down the Delta to the Tanana just before the turn of the century. By 1902, prospectors established placer mines on nearby Rainy Creek. The Valdez-Fairbanks Trail, completed in the early 1900s, ran through the middle and lower Delta River Valley. It was improved in 1923 to accommodate automobiles.

Rating: Class I–V. See description above for details.

Cautions: Sweepers, canoe fragments wrapped around rocks, bears, cold and wet weather, high winds. Only experts should attempt to run Black Rapids (Class IV–V) below Mile 229 on Richardson Highway.

Trip length: 29 miles to Mile 212.5 Richardson Highway; 114 miles to Big Delta; allow 2 to 4 days.

Season: Early June to mid-September, depending on ice breakup and precipitation.

Watercraft: Canoe, kayak or 12- to 14-foot raft.

Access: In—Drive on the Denali Highway to Mile 21 and put in at Tangle Lakes Campground. Out—Take out at one of many spots along the Richardson Highway. Recommended is Mile 212.5 Richardson Highway or at Mile 229 across from Ann Creek. Taking out at Mile 212.5 requires a 49-mile vehicle shuttle; floating to Mile 229 requires an 82-mile vehicle shuttle. For full trip to the Delta's confluence with the Tanana, take out at Big Delta.

Land manager: Bureau of Land Management, Anchorage. The Delta is a National Wild, Scenic, and Recreational River. (See Land Managers section at back of book for address and phone information.)

Maps: Mount Hayes A–4, A–5, B–4, C–4, D–4; Big Delta A–4.

Fish: Arctic grayling, northern pike, lake trout. **Wildlife:** Bison herd in the vicinity of Black Rapids glacier, moose, caribou, bear, wolf, waterfowl, gyrfalcon, rough-legged hawk.

21   FORTYMILE RIVER

Spreading like fingers on a hand across the southern side of the Upper Yukon Valley, the five forks of the Fortymile River begin as numerous small, clear headwater streams. A major tributary of the Yukon River, the Fortymile flows generally northeasterly to empty into the Yukon in Canada. The Fortymile and its tributaries drain approximately 6,600 square miles of the Yukon–Tanana Uplands. The Fortymile offers mining history, scenic country, and a road-accessible river trip.

The North Fork of the Fortymile is formed by the confluence of Slate and Independence creeks, which flow from 5,000-foot mountains in the Yukon–Tanana Uplands. The North Fork flows east, then south, and after the Middle Fork empties into it, flows southeasterly to its confluence with the South Fork, for a total distance of 55 miles. Average gradient of the North Fork is 10 feet per mile.

Immediately below the Middle Fork confluence, Class II rapids begin on the North Fork, followed by The Chute, a Class III rapid. The river straightens out from a turn to the right as you approach The Chute. This section can be portaged on either side of the river. Below The Chute, two significant streams enter the river on the right. The second of these, Hutchinson Creek, is about 10 miles below The Chute. From this point, stay on the right side of the river as it bends to the left.

Before the river turns back to the right, stop to scout the Class V rapid at The Kink, about 3 miles below the mouth of Hutchinson Creek. The Kink drops 18 feet in a short series of 3- to 4-foot drops with big recirculating hydraulics, making it rarely runnable, particularly in canoes. The portage is usually made over the bedrock shelf on the right bank. At high water, use the trail on the higher shelf. In general, the North Fork becomes easier to paddle as the volume of flow decreases in late July and August.

The Middle Fork begins in a small, flat valley, with small, meandering headwater streams feeding into it. Flowing 78 miles, the Middle Fork drops an average of 16 feet per mile, coursing over small sets of rapids confined to a single channel. After 41 miles, the river meanders through flat marshes and then enters a narrow, forested valley. Bald Eagle Rapids, Class III, just above the confluence of the Middle and North forks, is run on either side of the large rock in the middle of the river.

The South Fork is formed by the merging of Mosquito and Dennison forks and flows east for 4 miles, then turns sharply and flows north for 23 miles to its confluence with the North Fork. Virtually all of the South Fork has placer mining claims on it. If you have an aversion to suction dredges, underwater mining, and environmental destruction, you may want to avoid this unscenic section.

Below the confluence of the North and South forks, the Fortymile has two more major rapids. Class III Deadman's Riffle is about 15 miles below the Fortymile bridge and can be portaged on the right side of the river. Canyon Rapids is in Canada, below the confluence with Bruin Creek. Generally Class III, it is lined or portaged on the right.

Mosquito Fork rises on a 4,000-foot ridge and flows east and then southeast for 140 miles to Mosquito Flats, then northeast around Taylor Mountain before turning southeast to merge with the Dennison Fork. From its upper reaches to a point about 85 miles above its mouth, the Mosquito Fork flows in a wide valley between unnamed mountains over 4,000 feet high and crosses Mosquito Flats, a tangle of swampy lakes and sloughs.

The flats widen in places to 14 miles across. Mosquito Fork drops 23 feet per mile in its upper 55 miles, then only 8 feet per mile once it reaches the Flats. This section is floatable only during times of high water.

Dennison Fork starts from a 2,500-foot slope, then flows 76 miles northeasterly, then northerly, to merge with Mosquito Fork. In its upper reaches, Dennison Fork traverses a broad, swampy basin, dropping less than 10 feet per mile. West Fork joins Dennison Fork 17 miles above the mouth and the river widens, with numerous small rapids in its lower section.

The Fortymile River region cradled the Interior's early Athapaskan culture for centuries before becoming the center of the area's earliest gold mining activity. In 1881, two Yukoners, named Bates and Harper, found ore on the North Fork of the Fortymile. In 1886, prospectors Howard Franklin and Micky O'Brien discovered gold on the South Fork. The resulting Franklin Gulch Strike of 1887 began the Fortymile Gold Rush, and soon the communities of Jack Wade, Chicken, Franklin, and Steele Creek were established.

The boomtown of Fortymile, at the mouth of the river, was named for its distance from Fort Reliance, just downstream from Dawson City on the Yukon River. The boomtown lasted just 10 years. When gold was discovered on the Klondike River in 1895,

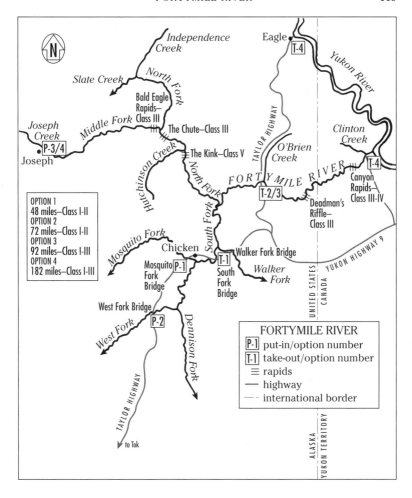

Fortymile emptied out as people moved on to Dawson. Today all that remains is a church, a few cabins, and an old store used as an overnight stop for river travelers.

A historic and hydrologic feature of the river is The Kink. Originally the name of a sharp bend in the North Fork of the Fortymile River, it now refers to a channel that was blasted 100 feet through a ridge that formed the neck in the bend. The 1904 blast diverted the river so that an area of riverbed nearly 3 miles long would be left dry for mining. The original channel was 15 feet wide, but by the 1970s it had eroded to 50 feet. The Kink is now on the National Register of Historic Places to signify a major engineering feat of its time. It is part of the Class V rapid on the North Fork.

Ospreys nest in the cliffs or tall trees along the Fortymile River.

Rating: Class I–V. This river is best suited to experienced paddlers because of the increasing difficulty of the rapids, and the need to portage, line, or run the whitewater.

Cautions: Rapids; sweepers; losing your way on the river. In this rugged country the river winds around bends in ways that make the bends look a lot like each other. Keep track of your way on the map as you descend the river; you may become disoriented and fail to recognize upcoming rapids. Carry maps and a compass.

Trip length: Anywhere from an afternoon to 10 days.

Option 1: Mosquito Fork bridge to South Fork bridge; 48 miles; allow 2 to 3 days. Only at times of high water is it possible to float this section. Put in at the Mosquito Fork bridge, Mile 64.3 on the Taylor Highway. Take out at South Fork bridge, Mile 75.3 Taylor Highway.

Option 2: South Fork Fortymile River; West Fork bridge to O'Brien Creek; 72 miles; allow 3 to 4 days. Put in at the West Fork bridge, Mile 49.3 on the Taylor Highway. Carry boat 20 yards to the river. Take out at Mile 112.4 Taylor Highway.

Option 3: Middle Fork and North Fork Fortymile River; Joseph to O'Brien Creek; 92 miles; allow 4 or 5 days. Fly by charter wheelplane to Joseph from Tok. The gravel airstrip is rough and narrow and requires local knowledge for landing. Follow a 50-yard trail at the eastern end of the runway to the river. Take out at O'Brien Creek (Fortymile bridge) at Mile 112.4 Taylor Highway.

Option 4: Middle Fork and North Fork Fortymile and Yukon River; Joseph to Eagle; 182 miles; allow 7 to 9 days. Fly by charter wheelplane to Joseph from Tok. Travel the river past O'Brien Creek and the Taylor Highway, into Canada's Yukon Territory and past Clinton Creek bridge, and enter the Yukon River. Then paddle all the way to Eagle. Eagle is at Mile 161 on the Taylor Highway, so you can drive to other population centers in Alaska from here, or you can take scheduled flights to Fairbanks. A shorter alternative is to take out at the Clinton Creek bridge in the Yukon Territory, where there is an old asbestos mine. This take-out is accessible via spur road off Yukon Highway 9, about 30 miles from the border.

Season: Late May through September.

Watercraft: Raft; hard-shell or inflatable kayak. Open canoes can make it but you'll have to portage some rapids.

Access: Highest road-access point is at Mile 49.3 Taylor Highway (the West Fork bridge; campground and long-term parking). Other access points on the Taylor Highway are Mile 64.3 (Mosquito Fork bridge; boat launch ramp and parking); Mile 74 (boat ramp and parking); Mile 75.3 (South Fork bridge); Mile 82.1 (near Walker Fork bridge; campground); Mile 112.4 (Fortymile bridge); and Mile 161 (the town of Eagle). For up-to-date river information, contact Chicken Field Station, Mile 68.2 Taylor Highway, Chicken, AK 99732.

Land manager: Bureau of Land Management, Fairbanks. The Fortymile is a National Wild, Scenic, and Recreational River. (See Land Managers section at back of book for address and phone information.)

Maps: Eagle A–2, A–3, B–1, B–2, B–3, B–4, B–5, B–6, C–1, C–3, D–1; Tanacross D–2, D–3.

Fish: Arctic grayling, northern pike; king, coho, and chum salmon.

Wildlife: Caribou, grizzly and black bear, moose, wolf, wolverine, fox, beaver, osprey, peregrine falcon.

22 JOHN RIVER

Beginning on the south side of the Arctic Divide in the Central Brooks Range, the John River flows 145 miles through alpine tundra and forested valleys. From its headwaters on Soakpak Mountain, it flows south through Anaktuvuk Pass, an important migration route for the Western Arctic caribou herd. The scenery is outstanding throughout the entire river valley, with the jagged peaks of the Endicott Mountains rising from the spruce-covered valley. There are many tempting side valleys and tributaries to explore and you could easily spend a couple weeks in the watershed, hiking and floating. At Anaktuvuk Pass, the river is at 2,200 feet in elevation. Where it empties into the Koyukuk River about 5 miles downriver from Bettles, the elevation is less than 600 feet.

The John River was named for John Bremner, who joined U.S. Army Lieutenant Henry T. Allen on his journey up the Copper River in 1885. Bremner went as far as the Koyukuk with Allen and then stayed on to prospect for gold in 1886 and 1887. Prospectors called the river Old Johns River or Johns River before it was officially mapped as John River. Gordon Bettles opened a trading post at the mouth of the John River in 1898 and the settlement that grew up around the store was named after him.

Rating: Class I–III. Upper river is Class II–III, depending on water levels, with a couple swift whitewater stretches in the first 5 miles. The upper river should be attempted only by experienced paddlers with solid wilderness skills. The rest of the river is swift Class II, slowing to Class I in the last 53 miles. The lower 53 miles, from Sixtymile Creek, make a nice family float to the confluence with the Koyukuk.
Cautions: Swift current and a few eddies on upper river at high water; lining boats may be difficult. At low water, river may be too shallow to float above Hunt Fork Lake.
Trip length: 135 miles from Anaktuvuk Pass to Bettles; allow 7 days. 100 miles from Hunt Fork Lake to Bettles; allow 5 to 6 days. 54 miles from mouth of Sixtymile Creek to Bettles; allow 3 to 4 days. About 60 miles from mouth of John River to Allakaket; allow 2 to 3 days.
Season: June through September.
Watercraft: Canoe, kayak, or small raft.

Access: In—If floating upper river, take scheduled airline to Anaktuvuk Pass from Fairbanks. Portage boat to the river and line boat down through the first 5 miles of swift water and rapids. If floating lower 100 miles, take scheduled airline to Bettles from Fairbanks, then charter floatplane to Hunt Fork Lake. If floating lower 53 miles, take charter wheelplane to landing strip near confluence of Sixty-mile Creek and Allen River. Out—Take out on Koyukuk River at Bettles, after lining boats upriver 4 miles. As an alternative, get picked up by charter floatplane at mouth of the John River, or float downriver to village of Allakaket.

Land manager: Gates of the Arctic National Park and Preserve; Nunamiut Corporation. The John is a National Wild River. (See Land Managers section at back of book for address and phone information.)

Maps: Wiseman A–4, B–4, B–5, C–5, D–5; Bettles D–4; Chandler Lake A–4.

Fish: Arctic grayling, whitefish, burbot, chum salmon. **Wildlife:** Caribou, grizzly and black bear, Dall sheep, moose, wolf, wolverine, migratory waterfowl.

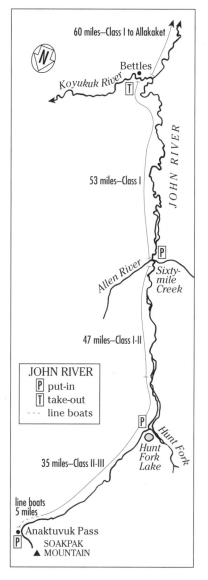

60 miles–Class I to Allakaket

Bettles

Koyukuk River

JOHN RIVER

53 miles–Class I

Allen River

Sixty-mile Creek

47 miles–Class I-II

JOHN RIVER
P put-in
T take-out
--- line boats

Hunt Fork

Hunt Fork Lake

35 miles–Class II-III

line boats 5 miles

Anaktuvuk Pass
SOAKPAK
▲ MOUNTAIN

23 MIDDLE FORK KOYUKUK RIVER

The Middle Fork Koyukuk offers an interesting journey through historic gold mining country, on a river that is accessible by road. The trip is suitable for families well-practiced in wilderness camping.

From beginnings in limestone mountains on the south side of the Arctic Divide, the headwaters of two rivers, the Bettles and the Dietrich, meet to become the Middle Fork Koyukuk about 30 miles south of the Arctic Divide. Where the 3- to 4-mile-wide glacial valleys of the Bettles and the Dietrich meet to form the Middle Fork, the gray limestone peaks of Wiehl Mountain and Sukakpak Mountain rise precipitously above low hills.

The Middle Fork is a gentle river, dropping less than 200 feet from the Dietrich-Bettles confluence to its confluence with the North Fork Koyukuk 68 miles later. It flows in a braided fashion through a relatively wide valley, with boreal forests covering its banks and rolling hills which give way to alpine tundra-covered mountain slopes and flat, plateau-like benches. The mountains tower above. Moving southward, the mountains are eventually left behind and the river becomes a single channel, traversing boreal forests of black and white spruce, birch, and aspen to Bettles and Allakaket.

The region now encompassing Gates of the Arctic National Park was once the hunting grounds of aboriginal Athapaskans and Eskimos. The first white men to enter the Koyukuk River drainage north of the Arctic Circle were U.S. Army Lieutenant Henry T. Allen and Private Fred Fickett, who traveled 2,200 miles up the Yukon, Koyukuk, and John rivers in 1885.

With the discovery of gold on the Klondike, 80,000 men and women stampeded north. After all the good claims were taken on the Klondike and Dawson, some of the prospectors found their way to the Koyukuk. Trading posts and riverboats appeared. At the height of gold mining in the upper Koyukuk, population, gold production, and the number of prostitutes reached simultaneous peaks. In 1902, the population of the area was 350, including 10 prostitutes, and $200,000 in gold was taken out. Coldfoot had one gambling establishment, two roadhouses, two stores, and seven saloons. In 1915, the area's population was 300, including 14 prostitutes, and $290,000 in gold was taken. Today, prospectors continue to scour the rivers for gold. Private lands, often related to gold mining, exist in Wiseman, Nolan, Coldfoot, and Tramway Bar. Farther downriver are private Native allotments.

Rating: Class I.

Cautions: Upper 20 miles has many bridge abutments across the river; black and grizzly bears.

Trip length: 80 miles from confluence of Dietrich and Bettles rivers to the town of Bettles; allow 5 days. 140 miles from Dietrich-Bettles confluence to Allakaket; allow 7 days.

Season: Mid-June through September.

Watercraft: All.

Access: In—Drive Dalton Highway (Pipeline Haul Road) to about Mile 208 and put in near beginning of Middle Fork. Or fly on scheduled air service to Wiseman and put in on the river. Or fly on charter wheelplane to Dietrich airstrip and put in near beginning of Middle Fork. Out—Take out at Bettles or Allakaket and fly to Fairbanks on scheduled airline.

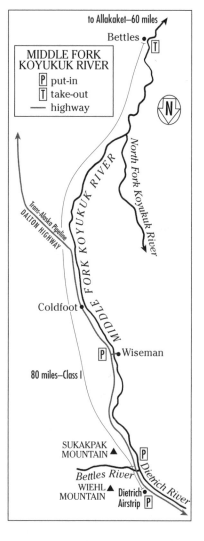

Land manager: Bureau of Land Management, Fairbanks; Gates of the Arctic National Park and Preserve; Kanuti National Wildlife Refuge; Doyon Ltd. (See Land Managers section at back of book for address and phone information.)

Maps: Bettles C–4, C–5, C–6, D–3, D–4; Chandalar C–6; Wiseman A–1, A–2, A–3, B–1.

Fish: Arctic grayling, whitefish, and burbot. **Wildlife:** Grizzly and black bear, Dall sheep, moose, wolf, wolverine, fox, migratory waterfowl.

24 NORTH FORK KOYUKUK RIVER

The North Fork offers an excellent family float for experienced wilderness travelers. From its headwaters on the Continental Divide in the Endicott Mountains, the North Fork flows south for 102 miles through broad, glacially carved valleys beside the Endicott Mountains in the Central Brooks Range.

A clearwater river, the North Fork begins as a trickle and flows south through dramatic peaks, picking up water from small creeks and tributaries. Mount Doonerak, which Robert Marshall described as the "Matterhorn of the Koyukuk," towers precipitously above. Below Doonerak there is usually sufficient water to launch a boat. From Bombardment Creek the river flows west a few miles, where it is joined by Ernie Creek, then continues south through the "Gates of the Arctic," named by Marshall in 1929. Boreal Mountain and Frigid Crags form stupendous walls on either side of the valley.

The river braids, then becomes a single channel near Redstar Creek. The route is all Class I, except for Squaw Rapids, a mile of Class II water near the confluence with Glacier River. Below here, it is an easy float. The North Fork joins the Middle Fork about 30 miles above Bettles.

Robert Marshall, a forester sent to explore the upper Koyukuk River drainage and across the divide in the Endicott Mountains between 1929 and 1939, discovered a huge expanse of wild mountain country virtually untrammeled by humans. Moved by the immensity and power of this wilderness, he suggested that all of Alaska from the Brooks Range to the Arctic Ocean be preserved as wilderness. Before protective measures could be taken, bounty hunters pursued wolves to near extinction in the Arctic, Eskimos settled permanently at Anaktuvuk Pass, and oil was discovered in Prudhoe Bay. The Trans-Alaska Pipeline was built and, while Marshall's vision did not come to pass, today we have an 8.4-million-acre national park—Gates of the Arctic—to protect the Central Brooks Range.

Rating: Class I, with shallow gravel bars and a few sharp turns, and one set of Class II rapids near Glacier River.
Cautions: Sweepers in mid to lower reaches; grizzly and black bear. High water from heavy rainfall can quickly turn Class I water into swift Class II water.

Trip length: 90 miles from Bombardment Creek to Bettles; allow 6 days. 60 miles from Redstar Creek to Bettles; allow 5 days.

Season: June through September.

Watercraft: All.

Access: In—Scheduled airline from Fairbanks to Bettles. Put in by chartered wheelplane to Bombardment Creek or by float-plane to lakes near mouth of Redstar Creek. Out—Take out at Bettles.

Land manager: Gates of the Arctic National Park and Preserve. The North Fork Koyukuk is a National Wild River. (See Land Managers section at back of book for address and phone information.)

Maps: Wiseman A–2, A–3, B–2, C–2, D–1, D–2; Bettles D–3, D–4; Chandler Lake A–1.

Fish: Arctic grayling, northern pike, whitefish. **Wildlife:** Grizzly and black bear, Dall sheep, wolf, fox, waterfowl.

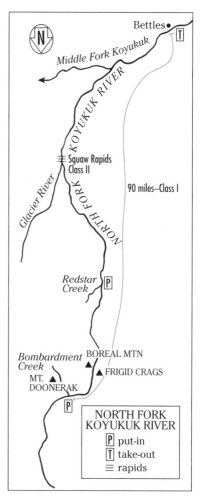

25 MELOZITNA RIVER

The Melozitna provides an excellent float for a family or for those who want to take a long trip in a remote, rarely traveled region of abundant wildlife where you're likely to encounter few or no other people. The Melozitna flows out of the Ray Mountains and meanders in a southwesterly direction for 270 miles before entering the Yukon River opposite the village of Ruby. Clear and free-flowing, the river is slow and winding, except for the lowest section where it flows through a canyon.

The landscape in the upper region is flat and boggy with low brush. There are occasional vistas of the Kokrines Hills to the southeast. The middle portion flows through a bottomland forest of white spruce, balsam poplar, and paper birch. Between Wolf and Big creeks comes a gradual transition to more open vistas and occasional rocky bluffs along the river. The lower river flows through an upland forest of black spruce and paper birch. Numerous bluffs and hills adjoin the middle and lower portions. The lower river culminates in a 10-mile canyon with a series of rapids over the course of about 4 miles which may require portaging, depending on water levels. These rapids limit motorized boat travel up the river, so the region is essentially primitive wilderness.

A village or seasonal camp at the mouth of the Melozitna River showed a population of 30 during the 1880 census, but the camp has been abandoned for many decades. There are no known cabins on the river. Some superstition about the area may have prevented past Native use of the river drainage. Today, the river is used by residents of Ruby for hunting, trapping, and fishing.

Rating: Class I–IV. The river is Class I except for about 4 miles of Class II–IV in the Melozitna Canyon on the lower river.
Cautions: High populations of grizzly bears in the middle section; black bears in lower section. An arduous portage may be necessary around the Melozitna Canyon rapids.
Trip length: 270 miles from Norseman Lake to Ruby; recommend 15 days.
Season: June through September.
Watercraft: All. Be prepared for lots of slow-moving water if you use a raft.

Access: In—Scheduled air service to Ruby (220 miles west of Fairbanks) or Galena from Fairbanks, then charter floatplane to headwaters at Norseman Lake. Or charter floatplane from Fairbanks to Norseman Lake. Out—Take out at Ruby and fly by scheduled air service back to Fairbanks.

Land manager: Bureau of Land Management, Anchorage (upper and middle 176 miles); state (77 miles surrounding middle river); Doyon and Dineega Native corporations (lower 77 miles). Nowitna National Wildlife Refuge adjoins and overlays the Melozitna River for 6 river miles above the mouth. (See Land Managers section at back of book for address and phone information.)

Maps: Melozitna A–4, A–5, B–3, B–4, C–1, C–2, C–3; Ruby C–5, C–6, D–5, D–6; Tanana C–6, D–6.

Fish: Arctic grayling, northern pike, king and chum salmon, Dolly Varden. **Wildlife:** Caribou, grizzly and black bear, moose, migratory waterfowl.

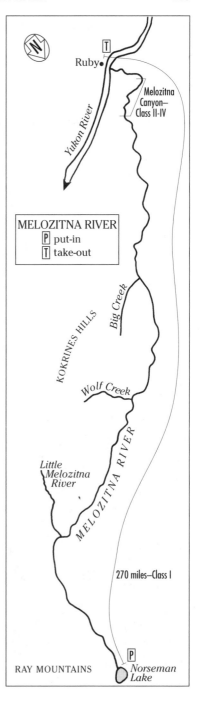

26   NENANA RIVER

Beginning on Nenana Glacier at an elevation of 3,200 feet in the vicinity of Broad Pass in the Alaska Range, the Nenana River flows north 140 miles to empty into the Tanana River. Draining about 3,920 square miles, the river is swift and cold. Braided in some sections, especially the lower 30 miles, it also cuts through incised canyons where turbulent and dangerous whitewater thrill the experienced paddler.

The Nenana Gorge, between McKinley Village Lodge and 10 miles below Healy, is Class IV whitewater. Only for expert boaters, this section of the Nenana River is one of the most popular and accessible difficult whitewater rivers in Alaska. Commercial raft companies conduct trips on this section of the river outside of Denali National Park and Preserve. The Alaska organization, Knik Canoers and Kayakers, offers a detailed description of the rapids in the gorge.

Alfred Brooks of the U.S. Geological Survey followed the Tanana River to its mouth in 1899. The Athapaskans he encountered were

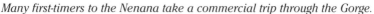

Many first-timers to the Nenana take a commercial trip through the Gorge.

busily catching and curing salmon, and he noted settlements at the mouths of the Nenana and Toklat rivers. Illnesses brought by traders and prospectors apparently had taken their toll. He found that, "Certain diseases seem to be quite prevalent among them, and the population is probably decreasing. . . . In the region traveled by us, old trails, blazes, and camps gave strong evidence that the region had been once more thickly populated."

Rating: Class I–IV. The section between McKinley Village Lodge and 10 miles below Healy—the Nenana Gorge—is Class IV. Flowing through an incised canyon with big holes, major hydraulics, and up to 10-foot standing waves, it is suitable only for expert boaters. Anyone who has not paddled the Nenana Gorge, regardless of experience, should go with experienced boaters who have done this section. The rest of the river between the Denali Highway and Nenana is Class I–II and is suitable for intermediate boaters. Beginners should not attempt paddling or rowing any of the Nenana because of its swift, cold, silty water and its large volume. Go first with those who are experienced.

Cautions: Cold, swift glacial water; Class IV Nenana Gorge.

Trip length: 38 miles from

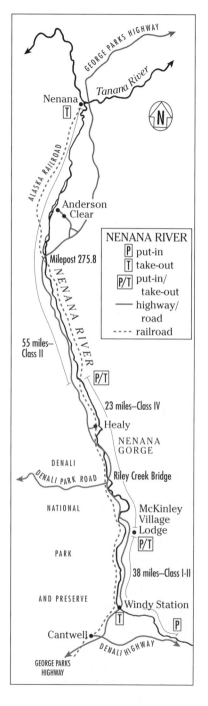

NENANA RIVER

P put-in

T take-out

P/T put-in/take-out

— highway/road

---- railroad

Denali Highway to McKinley Village Lodge (Mile 231.1 on George Parks Highway); allow 2 days. 23 miles from McKinley Village Lodge to 10 miles below Healy (Nenana Gorge); allow 4 hours. 65 miles from Healy to the town of Nenana; allow 2 to 3 days. For trip in its entirety, allow 5 days.

Season: June through September.

Watercraft: Hard-shell kayak, raft. For experienced boaters, canoe is suitable between Denali Highway and McKinley Village Lodge.

Access: In—Drive the Denali Highway from Cantwell and put in at Mile 18. Out—For 20-mile Class I float, take out at Alaska Railroad-Windy Station. North of Cantwell, the Nenana River parallels the George Parks Highway, providing several other convenient road access points between highway miles 215 and 231.1. For 38-mile Class I-II float, take out at Denali Grizzly Bear Campground or at McKinley Village (Mile 231.1). It is also possible to take out at the bridge over the Nenana at Mile 238 George Parks Highway, or at Healy (Mile 248.8), the Rex bridge (Mile 275.8), or Nenana (Mile 304.5). To bypass the Class IV Nenana Gorge, pull out at McKinley Village, then drive to a point about 10 miles below Healy and put in again and paddle to Nenana.

Land manager: Bureau of Land Management; Denali National Park and Preserve; private; state. (See Land Managers section at back of book for address and phone information.)

Maps: Fairbanks A–5, B–5, C–5; Healy B–3, B–4, C–4, D–4, D–5.

Fish: Arctic grayling, chum salmon. **Wildlife:** Caribou, grizzly bear, Dall sheep, moose, fox, waterfowl.

A trapper cabin on the Nowitna. (See next page.)

27   NOWITNA RIVER

Rising in the Kuskokwim Mountains, the Nowitna River flows northward for nearly 300 miles and enters the Yukon River about 45 miles northeast of Ruby. A medium-size, meandering nonglacial stream, the Nowitna traverses a remote, primitive area. Flowing swiftly, with occasional whitewater, the river travels through rolling hills, canyons, broad valleys, and flats on its northward journey. Black and white spruce, hardwoods, and shrubs characterize the vegetation throughout the river corridor. From headwaters to mouth, the river drops from 1,000 feet above sea level to 150 feet, and is generally wide and deep.

Known locally as the Novi, the river follows a rather serpentine course, except for the section from Mastodon Creek to 10 miles below the confluence with Big Mud River in which the river straightens and picks up speed. Whitewater stretches exist in this section as the river cuts through Nowitna Canyon. Below Big Mud River, the Nowitna meanders all the way to its confluence with the Yukon.

In the Nowitna region, Ingalik people found a rich supply of fish and wildlife. Birchbark canoes were used on the rivers and streams for travel, hunting, and fishing. Russians first penetrated the region in 1834. Lieutenant L. A. Zagoskin of the Russian Navy investigated Native trade routes up the Yukon to the Nowitna River. With the late-19th-century gold rush, an extensive woodcutting industry developed along the lower Nowitna to fuel steamboats. Gold was discovered on Ruby Creek in 1907 near the present location of Ruby. The Ruby Roadhouse, built in 1911 to accommodate prospectors, is now listed on the National Register of Historic Places. Although it was prospected, gold was never found on the Nowitna.

Rating: Class I, with a few Class II rapids in vicinity of Nowitna Canyon.
Cautions: Upriver winds, particularly in the lower river; black bears.
Trip length: 245 miles from Meadow Creek to confluence with Yukon River; allow 12 to 14 days; 290 miles from Meadow Creek to Ruby; allow 14 to 16 days.
Season: Mid-May through September.
Watercraft: All.
Access: In—Scheduled airline to Galena or Ruby. Charter floatplane

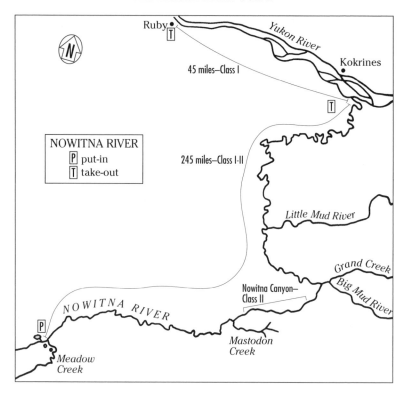

Ruby

Yukon River

Kokrines

45 miles—Class I

NOWITNA RIVER
P put-in
T take-out

245 miles—Class I-II

Little Mud River

Grand Creek

Big Mud River

Nowitna Canyon—
Class II

NOWITNA RIVER

Mastodon
Creek

Meadow
Creek

to upper river in vicinity of Meadow Creek, or to lakes alongside the river. It is possible to land on gravel bars in the river corridor, but only after water levels have gone down late in summer. Check with pilots. Out—Take out above confluence with Yukon by floatplane or by riverboat out of Ruby, or continue downriver to Ruby.

Land manager: Koyukuk/Nowitna National Wildlife Refuge; state. The Nowitna is a National Wild River. (See Land Managers section at back of book for address and phone information.)

Maps: Ruby A–2, A–3, A–4, B–2, B–3, C–3, C–4, C–5, D–3, D–4, D–5; Medfra C–4, C–5, D–4.

Fish: Arctic grayling, northern pike, sheefish, burbot, king and coho salmon, longnose sucker. **Wildlife:** Caribou, grizzly and black bear, moose, wolf, wolverine, waterfowl.

28   PORCUPINE RIVER

The Porcupine offers an excellent novice river trip for those experienced in remote wilderness travel and is an ideal river for a family expedition. One of the largest tributaries of the Yukon River, the Porcupine drains 46,000 square miles in Canada and Alaska.

Beginning in the Ogilvie Mountains in Canada's Yukon Territory, the river flows northeast and then west about 300 miles to the U.S. border, then southwest more than 200 miles to its mouth at the Yukon River at Fort Yukon. Starting at the U.S.-Canada border is a 40-mile segment with nearly continuous cliffs that rise between 250 and 500 feet above the river. Red Gate, a colorful, vertically walled canyon, marks the lower end of Upper Rampart Canyon. From here for a distance of about 35 miles, the river flows through low hills and lowlands and the river gradient slows considerably. After passing the Coleen River, the Porcupine enters Lower Rampart Canyon, 15 miles of limestone cliffs up to 60 feet high.

Below the canyons the Porcupine is a meandering watercourse with numerous loops, bends, and channels flowing through a marshy floodplain with thousands of lakes, oxbows, and sloughs as it crosses Yukon Flats National Wildlife Refuge. The region is heavily forested with spruce, commonly with boglike terrain. The portion of the river traversing northeastern Alaska has an average gradient of 1 to 2 feet per mile. During periods of high water, Class I conditions can rapidly turn into Class II water in confined canyons. Because of its remoteness and lack of roads, the area is basically untouched by recent development in the arctic. An 1871 treaty with Great Britain protects the international navigability of the river, so you will see barge and boat traffic.

The Porcupine River and its tributaries are the traditional home of the Gwich'in Athapaskans, who have hunted, fished, and trapped for thousands of years in a harsh, isolated environment. The wealth of fur from beaver, fox, marten, and lynx were known only to the Gwich'in until the early 1800s. In 1842, Englishman John Bell of the Hudson's Bay Company became the first white man to travel down the Porcupine River, discovering what the Natives knew all along—that the Porcupine River provided a natural trade route into the Yukon River Valley. Hudson's Bay Company established a trading post at the confluence of the Yukon and Porcupine rivers.

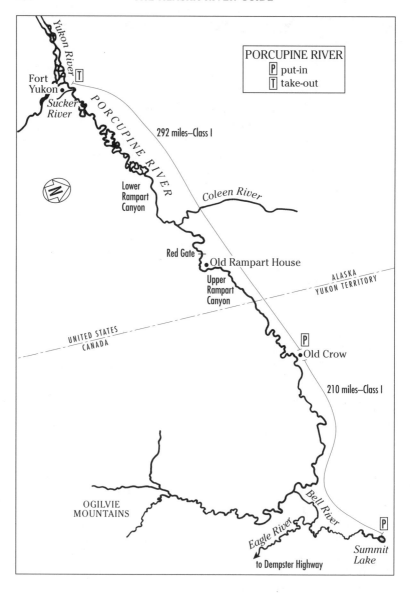

Voyagers in the Yukon Territory regularly paddled freight up the Rat River to a 9-mile portage over the Richardson Mountains, then down the Bell River to the headwaters of the Porcupine. Thirty-foot-long "Yukon boats" carried trading goods downriver past Gwich'in villages to Fort Yukon, where beads, cloth, metal tools, and trinkets were traded to the Gwich'in for furs. It then took three and a

Grave markers of Hudson's Bay Company pioneers in Fort Yukon.

half years for the furs to reach London via the river and lake route to Canada's Hudson Bay.

Today, some people still maintain trap lines in the area. Except for a few cabins on private lands along the river, the region is primitive and undisturbed. The site of Rampart House, just inside the Canadian border, still has the remains of three-story structures that were used by the Hudson's Bay Company after it moved from Fort Yukon up the Porcupine in 1887. Old Crow, in Canada, is the only permanent settlement on the river today.

Rating: Class I.

Cautions: Fast current through Upper Rampart and Lower Rampart canyons, which begin just above New Rampart in Yukon Territory.

Trip length: 292 miles from Old Crow to Fort Yukon; allow 10 to 14 days. For a longer trip, start from the upper Porcupine, the Bell River, or Eagle River bridge; an additional distance of more than 200 miles; allow at least 7 days to reach Old Crow.

Season: June through late September.

Watercraft: Canoe, kayak, or raft, with raft being the least recommended craft due to upriver winds.

Access: In—Scheduled airline to Whitehorse or Dawson, or drive to either of these towns. Take scheduled airline to Old Crow. For longer trip, take air charter to upper Porcupine or to Summit Lake on the Bell River. The Bell River is fast Class I, with no major hazards. The Porcupine is also accessible by road via the Dempster Highway at a point 270 river miles above the U.S.-Canada border. Put in at the Eagle River bridge at Mile 373 on the Dempster Highway, about 6 miles north of the Eagle Plains Lodge, float to the

Bell River and then to the Porcupine, passing Old Crow. Out—Take out at Fort Yukon by paddling 3 miles up the Sucker River from its confluence with the Porcupine River to a road. Start looking for the Sucker River when you reach Homebrew Island. (If you follow the Porcupine all the way to its confluence with the Yukon, you'll end up 2 miles downriver from Fort Yukon, so it's best to paddle up the Sucker River.) From Fort Yukon, fly scheduled airline to Fairbanks.

Land manager: Northern Yukon National Park (Canada); Arctic National Wildlife Refuge; Yukon Flats National Wildlife Refuge; Doyon Ltd., Gwitchyaa Zhee, and Chalkyitsik Native corporations; state. (See Land Managers section at back of book for address and phone information.)

Maps: Black River D–4, D–5, D–6; Coleen A–1, A–2, A–3, A–4, A–5, A–6; Fort Yukon C–1, C–2, C–3, D–1. Canadian maps (1:50,000): Bell River 116 P; Old Crow 116 O–N.

Fish: Arctic grayling, whitefish, northern pike, sheefish, burbot. The Porcupine River is believed to be among the most important fall chum salmon producing rivers in the Yukon River system. For this reason, no commercial salmon fishing is allowed on the Porcupine.

Wildlife: Moose, grizzly and black bear, caribou, beaver, lynx, fox, marten, wolf, peregrine falcon, Harlan's hawk, goshawk, golden eagle, osprey.

29   SHEENJEK RIVER

Traversing a vast wilderness just south of the Arctic Divide, the Sheenjek offers an opportunity to experience several arctic ecosystems while paddling through a wild, remote region. The Sheenjek begins as a swift mountain stream, rising from glaciers on the southern flanks of the eastern Brooks Range, and flows south for more than 240 miles before emptying into the Porcupine River 40 miles above Fort Yukon. The river cuts through precipitous mountains and alpine tundra, along a steep, shallow, braided channel with numerous rapids, riffles, and boulders in its upper reaches. The high peaks of the Romanzof Mountains rise dramatically from the valley floor. Hiking opportunities are excellent. Although the Sheenjek has glacial origins, it is generally clear water (due to its many clearwater tributaries), except after breakup and summer rains. Aufeis often covers the upper river until late summer.

In the vicinity of Double Mountain, the Sheenjek Valley widens, and scattered stands of white spruce appear. Below Double Mountain, the river is confined largely to a single channel and courses through an area of lakes and muskeg meadows, among them Last (Ambresvajun) and Lobo (Kuirzinjik) lakes. The current slows considerably and, below Lobo Lake, the river becomes wide and flat, flowing in well-defined channels through small islands for 20 miles. The surrounding country offers rolling hills with occasional peaks in the distance. The tundra gives way to boreal forest and the Sheenjek Valley is covered with spruce, cottonwood, willow, and birch, with extensive open meadows.

The gradient increases as the river narrows and picks up speed again, splitting into braided channels and oxbows with broad gravel bars. Below the Koness River, the Sheenjek slows, flowing sluggishly through the lake-dotted Yukon Flats. The lower river is tranquil and wide, with cutbanks and large meandering oxbows. Opportunities for observing wildlife along the river are excellent.

The Sheenjek was a major north-south travel and trade route between Gwich'in Athapaskans and Eskimos because it was a natural travel route over the Arctic Divide. Hudson's Bay Company established a major trading post at Fort Yukon in 1847. Sheenjek Village, 120 miles up the Sheenjek from Fort Yukon, was home to several families in the 1930s and '40s, but the village is now abandoned. Trapping remains a significant activity along the lower Sheenjek River, with other subsistence activities such as fishing with set nets and hunting.

Rating: Class I–II. Upper river is mostly Class II, while river is Class I below the Koness River. At normal river levels, the Sheenjek is suitable for experienced intermediate paddlers; at high water (just after rainstorms), the river can reach flood conditions very quickly, and swift, turbid water can make maneuvering difficult. Submerged sweepers have impaled folding boats.

Cautions: Aufeis and extremely shallow, braided channels on the upper river; sweepers; bears in late summer and early fall along the lower Sheenjek.

Trip length: 20 miles from upper gravel bar in vicinity of Double Mountain to Last (Ambresvajun) Lake; 2 days. 18 miles from Last Lake to Lobo (Kuirzinjik) Lake; 1 to 2 days. About 90 miles from Lobo Lake to Koness River; 4 to 5 days. About 120 miles from Koness River to confluence with Porcupine River; 5 to 8 days. 40 miles from confluence to Fort Yukon; 2 to 3 days. Total trip from upper gravel bar to Fort Yukon via Porcupine and Sucker rivers is about 288 miles; allow 14 to 18 days. (Also see this book's entry on the Porcupine River.)

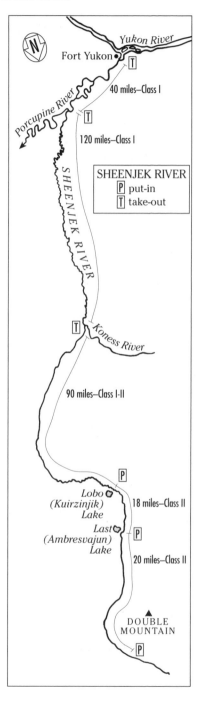

Meandering oxbows on the Sheenjek create sandbars ideal for camping.

Season: June to late September.

Watercraft: All.

Access: In—Charter floatplane to Last Lake or Lobo Lake from Fort Yukon, Arctic Village, or Fairbanks. Or put in by charter wheelplane on gravel landing area in vicinity of Double Mountain near the pass leading to the Kongakut River. Out—Take out on gravel bar near Koness River by charter wheelplane or float down to Porcupine River for floatplane pickup. Or float to Fort Yukon on the Porcupine River (see entry on Porcupine River).

Land manager: Sheenjek National Wild River; Arctic National Wildlife Refuge; Yukon Flats National Wildlife Refuge; Gwitchyaa Zhee Corporation; state. The Sheenjek is a National Wild River. (See Land Managers section at back of book for address and phone information.)

Maps: Table Mountain A–4, B–4, B–5, C–5, D–5; Coleen C–6, D–5, D–6; Christian A–1, B–1, C–1; Fort Yukon C–2, C–3, D–1, D–2.

Fish: Arctic grayling, northern pike, whitefish, king, coho, and chum salmon. **Wildlife:** Caribou, grizzly and black bear, Dall sheep, moose, wolf, lynx, beaver, migratory waterfowl. The Yukon Flats surrounding the lower Sheenjek provide some of the finest waterfowl nesting habitat in North America.

30 TINAYGUK RIVER

The Tinayguk (the word means "moose" in Inupiaq) is the largest tributary of the North Fork of the Koyukuk River. Rising from melting snows on several 6,000- to 7,000-foot peaks on the south slope of the Endicott Mountains, the 44-mile-long Tinayguk flows west and then south to its confluence with the North Fork Koyukuk. Coursing almost entirely through mountainous topography, the river and its surroundings are incredibly scenic. This mountain valley is one of the best examples of the unique geology of the Brooks Range, with its glaciated U-shaped valleys. Boreal spruce forest extends halfway up the river valley.

For its first 15 miles, the Tinayguk flows west against the jagged peaks of the Arctic Divide, beginning at an elevation of 3,000 feet. The first 12 miles drop 80 feet per mile. The current is swift, the water clear. For the last 32 miles, the river drops an average of 25 feet per mile to its confluence with the North Fork, at an elevation of 1,200 feet. There are several large rapids in the extreme head-waters. Farther down, occasional boulders and rocks create intermittent whitewater over most of the river. The Tinayguk is a small, single-channeled river, no more than a couple feet deep and 20 to 30 yards wide. For the experienced whitewater boater, well-versed in remote wilderness camping, the Tinayguk offers an outstanding opportunity for hiking and floating.

The first non-Native to explore the upper Tinayguk was Ernie Johnson, a Swede who came to America when he was 16 and joined the gold stampede in 1904, but eventually spent most of his time hunting and trapping. When Robert Marshall met him in 1929, Johnson was "the most famous trapper on the North Fork Koyukuk." Marshall teamed up with Johnson to explore the upper reaches of Brooks Range valleys, and Johnson told him, "I like it among these ruggedy mountains better than anywhere in the world."

Rating: Class II–III. Upper 15 miles is Class III; lower 29 miles is Class II and occasional Class III.
Cautions: Swift current, shallow water, rapids.
Trip length: 40 miles on Tinayguk; allow at least 4 days to float and to explore the valley; allow another 4 days to float the North Fork Koyukuk into Bettles, about 80 miles downriver. Total trip: 120 river

miles; allow 8 days.

Season: Late June to late August.

Watercraft: Small raft; inflatable canoe or kayak.

Access: In—Scheduled airline from Fairbanks to Bettles. Put in by chartered wheelplane to gravel bars on upper river; or to avoid difficult sections in the upper river, begin at confluence of Savioyuk Creek. Out—Take out at Bettles on Koyukuk River.

Land manager: Gates of the Arctic National Park and Preserve. The Tinayguk is a National Wild River. (See Land Managers section at back of book for address and phone information.)

Maps: Wiseman C–3, D–3, D–4; Bettles D–3, D–4.

Fish: Arctic char, arctic grayling. **Wildlife:** Dall sheep, grizzly and black bear, wolf, wolverine, porcupine, ptarmigan.

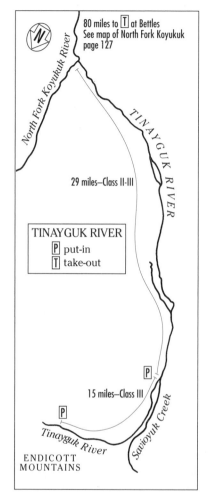

80 miles to T at Bettles
See map of North Fork Koyukuk
page 127

North Fork Koyukuk River

TINAYGUK RIVER

29 miles—Class II-III

TINAYGUK RIVER
P put-in
T take-out

15 miles—Class III

Savioyuk Creek

Tinayguk River

ENDICOTT
MOUNTAINS

31   **WILD RIVER**

The Wild River provides an ideal family float for intermediate boaters with wilderness skills. The river flows from Wild Lake, a long, deep, narrow lake in the Central Brooks Range, sitting in a broad U-shaped valley just south of the northern treeline. Sand beaches and white spruce forest make up the lake's 6-mile shoreline, and dramatic peaks rise above it. Upper slopes are covered with alpine tundra and the hiking is superb. There are some private cabins at the lake. Robert Marshall, visiting Wild Lake in 1931, said it reminded him of Lake Placid in New York, with its steep mountains rising from the shoreline, but Wild Lake had "no thickly clustered camps nor noisy powerboats."

The Wild River, small and beautifully clear, flows south from Wild Lake for 63 miles, emptying into the Koyukuk River just above Bettles. The upper reaches move swiftly; then the river slows to a meandering stream. Traversing the northern boreal forest typical of the Koyukuk region and Gates of the Arctic National Park, the Wild River is probably the most easily accessible trip in the park, and a highly scenic one at that.

Flat Creek, a tributary of the Wild River, was the scene of a gold

Lining boats is customary in folding kayaks to avoid rocks and shallows.

rush in 1913–1915. An interesting assortment of miners settled on Spring Creek and around Wild Lake by 1930, including Germans, Norwegians, Natives, and the only African American in the Koyukuk region.

Rating: Class I, with a few Class II rocky riffles that can be lined.
Cautions: Black bears; shallow water after early July.
Trip length: 63 miles; allow 6 days.
Season: June to early July.
Watercraft: All.
Access: In—Fly to Bettles on scheduled airline from Fairbanks. Fly to Wild Lake by charter floatplane. There is also a small wheelplane airstrip on Flat Creek. Out—Take out on Koyukuk River at Bettles.
Land manager: Gates of the Arctic National Park and Preserve; private. (See Land Managers section at back of book for address and phone information.)
Maps: Bettles D–3, D–4; Wiseman A–3, B–3, B–4, C–4.
Fish: Arctic grayling, northern pike, lake trout. **Wildlife:** Dall sheep, grizzly and black bear, moose, fox, beaver, marten, waterfowl.

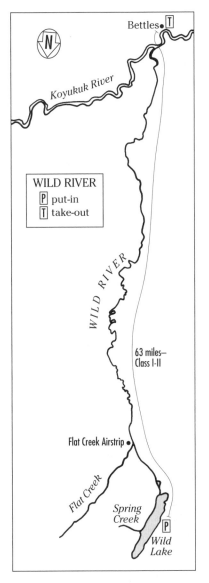

SOUTHWEST ALASKA

The Southwest region centers on the Kuskokwim River. Draining 43,600 miles, it flows through a wide, flat valley forested in spruce and hardwoods, with low, rolling hills rising abruptly throughout its course. Its many tributaries—Stony, Holitna, South Fork, and Swift Fork, to name a few—flow northward from headwaters in the Aleutian and Alaska ranges to the foothills of the Kuskokwim Mountains and to a confluence with the main stem of the Kuskokwim. Heading in mountain glaciers, rivers coming off the Alaska Range are long, silty, and braided, while rivers rising in the Kuskokwim Mountains are fast and meandering.

The other major river systems in this region are the Kvichak and Nushagak. Together they drain 21,800 square miles. These rivers and their tributaries originate in two great mountain systems north and west of Bristol Bay. The jagged Ahklun Mountains, rising between 2,000 and 5,000 feet, together with the Aleutian Range and the Nushagak-Big River Hills, give birth to shallow clear streams that drain mostly through incised bedrock gorges. The glacially scoured Wood River-Tikchik Lakes district is a showpiece of the region. These rivers and streams are the nursery for the most productive sockeye salmon fishery in the world.

The climate varies in this region. The coastal areas are maritime-influenced, while in the interior portion, the climate is continental. Annual precipitation varies from 12 to 24 inches. Breakup on rivers occurs in early May, with peak runoff in June. The rivers freeze up again in November. Discontinous permafrost exists in small pockets south of the Kuskokwim River; the permafrost is continuous north of the Kuskokwim.

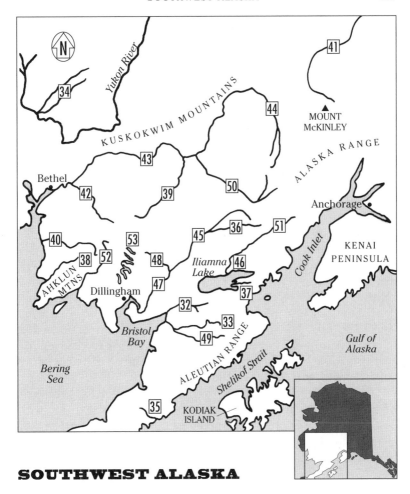

SOUTHWEST ALASKA

32 Alagnak River and Nonvianuk River
33 American Creek
34 Andreafsky River and East Fork Andreafsky River
35 Aniakchak River
36 Chilikadrotna River
37 Copper River
38 Goodnews River
39 Holitna River
40 Kanektok River
41 Kantishna River
42 Kisaralik River
43 Kuskokwim River
44 South Fork Kuskokwim River
45 Mulchatna River
46 Newhalen River
47 Nushagak River
48 Nuyakuk River
49 Savonoski River
50 Stony River
51 Tlikakila River
52 Togiak River
53 Wood River Lakes System

32 ALAGNAK RIVER AND NONVIANUK RIVER

The Alagnak, known locally as the Branch River, originates in Kukaklek Lake and flows west-southwest 74 miles before entering the Kvichak River and Kvichak Bay, which then empties into Bristol Bay. The Alagnak has several distinctly different sections, both in difficulty and scenery. The first 6 miles out of the lake flows at a moderate speed (3 to 4 miles per hour) through dry upland tundra. The view from the river is open and unobstructed for 2 to 4 miles out over low ridgelines paralleling the river. Hiking in this area is good.

For the next 10 miles, the river flows over shallow Class II boulder gardens and through a riparian spruce forest. The current increases to 7 to 8 miles per hour and the river enters an incised canyon with two sets of Class II to II-plus rapids. This canyon should be scouted, because it has very steep rock walls and portaging is difficult. This area (the upper Alagnak) has been run in 12- to 13-foot rafts at normal water levels with no problem. Below the canyon the next 5 miles are moderately swift, but not difficult. The enclosing bluffs diminish and the floodplain widens.

At Mile 19, the Alagnak reaches its confluence with the Nonvianuk. From here, the Alagnak is Class I. It is braided, with islands, for the next 15 miles, spreading out across flat spruce lowlands, with thick willow brush lining much of the riverbank. Selecting the proper channel and avoiding sweepers can be tricky. The river slows, eventually becoming a broad, single channel moving at 2 miles per hour when it hits the Kvichak.

The Nonvianuk River is an 11-mile tributary of the Alagnak which flows out of Nonvianuk Lake. The mouth of Nonvianuk Lake is a popular fishing spot and many float trips begin here for this reason. The Nonvianuk/Alagnak is the most popular float route in the Bristol Bay region because it is relatively easy and has good fishing for several species of fish. Many fishing guides take their clients on the Nonvianuk and Alagnak, and several lodges are located on private lands within and outside the Wild and Scenic River corridor. Most parties on the river travel in boats without motors.

Nomadic people fished and hunted along the lakes and rivers in the Naknek Lake region, which includes the Alagnak River, more than 4,000 years ago. By 1900 B.C., a new Eskimo group had moved

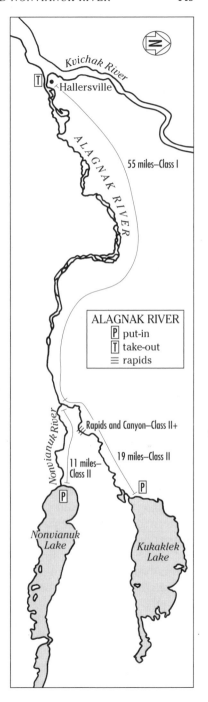

from the Kuskokwim Delta into the Naknek Lake region and displaced the earlier culture. Trade between the lake country dwellers and the seacoast hunters on the Shelikof Strait began, and for 500 years the two groups traveled across the Aleutian Range, through Katmai Pass, to exchange material items and culture. People lived in *barabaras,* or pit houses, dug out to be slightly subterranean, and constructed of mud and wood.

With the first contact between the Eskimos and Russians in 1818, the Russian Orthodox Church and the fur trade made inroads into Native settlement and subsistence patterns. Later, commercial fishing become the major industry in the Bristol Bay region, and it remains so today. Many of the lands along the shore of the lower Alagnak are owned by Natives.

Rating: Class I–II-plus. The upper Alagnak (19 miles) is Class II, with a short Class II-plus canyon. The Nonvianuk is an excellent float for those who don't want to deal with the Class II-plus rapids on the upper Alagnak. Eleven miles of easy Class II on the Nonvianuk followed by 55 miles of Class I on the Alagnak make this a relatively easy float.

Cautions: Sweepers; brown bears. At periods of low water, there may be several Class II rapids on the upper 5 miles of the Nonvianuk. The upper Alagnak has a Class II-plus chute that some have called wicked and others have called a piece of cake. It may be tricky at high water; most paddlers with whitewater experience probably can handle it with no problem. This section is impossible to line and very difficult to portage (requires climbing out of a 100- to 200-foot-deep gorge), so plan on running it.

Trip length: 74 miles from Kukaklek Lake to the Kvichak; allow 7 days; 66 miles from Nonvianuk Lake to the Kvichak; allow 6 days.

Season: May through September. Highest water in May, June, and early July.

Watercraft: Upper Alagnak (first 19 miles)—Raft; whitewater or inflatable kayak. Nonvianuk River, and Alagnak River below its confluence with the Nonvianuk—Raft, kayak, canoe, including folding boats.

Access: In—Scheduled air service from Anchorage to King Salmon. Put in by chartered floatplane from King Salmon to Kukaklek Lake or Nonvianuk Lake. Out—Take out by floatplane from the lower 10 to 30 miles of river to King Salmon. Tidal influence and winds in the last 10 miles makes travel more difficult, but floating out to the Kvichak can be an interesting experience, as you travel through the delta of the Kvichak and pull out at the old Alaska Packers Cannery at the abandoned settlement of Hallersville. There is a wheelplane airstrip for pickup.

Land manager: Katmai National Park and Preserve; private holdings. The Alagnak, including the Nonvianuk, is a National Wild River. (See Land Managers section at back of book for address and phone information.)

Maps: Iliamna A–7, A–8. Dillingham A–1, A–2, A–3.

Fish: Arctic char, arctic grayling, northern pike; king, coho, sockeye, pink, and chum salmon. The Alagnak River system is within the state's Wild Trout Area; check fishing regulations for special fishing restrictions. The lands surrounding Kukaklek Lake, Nonvianuk Lake, and Battle Lake, along with the lands along the Alagnak, are within Katmai National Park and Preserve; check for any special regulations. **Wildlife:** Brown bear (critical habitat during summer and fall), moose, wolf, wolverine, lynx, fox, river otter, golden eagle, bald eagle, rough-legged hawk.

33 AMERICAN CREEK

For the experienced paddler, American Creek offers a brief but exciting whitewater float through an exceptionally pristine wilderness. Nestled in a narrow glacial valley among 3,500- to 4,500-foot peaks at the foot of the Aleutian Range lie jeweled alpine lakes that form the headwaters of American Creek. Small mountain streams cascade into 3-mile-long Murray Lake, and a small stream about 2 miles long empties into 5-mile-long Hammersly Lake. From these crystal-clear lakes flows the equally transparent American Creek.

From its source at about 1,600 feet, the river drops 1,500 feet along its course, traversing distinct ecological zones. The headwater lakes are surrounded by alpine tundra. Hiking and scenic vistas are superb. Of particular interest are two waterfalls on an unnamed tributary 4 miles north of Hammersly Lake. Along the first 10 to 12 miles of river, willow thickets grow adjacent to the river, with the uplands dominated by sedge tussocks interspersed with low shrubs. Below 1,200 feet elevation, cottonwoods and boreal forest appear. In the canyon area, white spruce becomes more dominant. In the last 5 miles of the river, tall willows appear, then give way to broad marshy grasslands in the vicinity of Lake Coville.

Rapids and riffles cover much of the river and the first 20 miles is shallow and rocky, requiring frequent lining. This section can be hard on all but inflatable boats. Below this section, the whitewater is almost continuous.

The river carves two striking canyons where the river constricts and plunges between bedrock and boulders. There are several Class III rapids, consisting of plunge drops over bedrock and boulders. The upper canyon has about 1 mile of major rapids and the lower canyon consists of several 3- to 4-foot drops over the course of 5 miles. The current over the first 30 miles averages 5 to 7 miles per hour. In the last 10 miles, the current slows to 2 to 3 miles per hour and the river becomes braided. Guided parties fly in to fish the lower river.

No early non-Native explorations are known in the American Creek drainage. The only known remnant of historical occupation is a cabin and cache along the river dating from the 1930s, built by trapper Roy Fure.

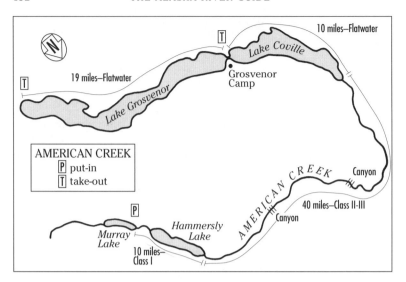

Rating: Class I–III. Boaters get a combination of flatwater paddling on clear lakes and a swift 40-mile whitewater descent, dropping an average of 30 feet per mile (and including a tricky paddle through steep, narrow canyons, where the river drops 60 feet per mile over one 6-mile section). Only experienced paddlers in well-constructed boats should attempt this river.

Cautions: Difficult Class III canyons; continuous whitewater over much of the river; logjams and sweepers in lower river.

Trip length: 50 miles from Murray Lake to Lake Coville; 4 to 10 days. Trip can be extended by paddling down Coville and Grosvenor lakes to Savonoski River. (See this book's entry on Savonoski River.)

Season: June through early September.

Watercraft: Raft; hard-shell or inflatable kayak. Shallow, rocky upper river can be especially hard on boats. Folding boats are *not* recommended. Continuous rocky and occasionally difficult whitewater precludes canoe.

Access: In—Scheduled air service from Anchorage to King Salmon. Put in on Murray or Hammersly lakes by floatplane from King Salmon. Out—Take out on Lake Coville or Lake Grosvenor by floatplane, or continue to outlet of Lake Grosvenor and float Savonoski River.

Land manager: Katmai National Park and Preserve. (See Land Managers section at back of book for address and phone information.)

Maps: Mount Katmai D–4, D–5, D–6.

Fish: Arctic grayling, northern pike, sockeye salmon, Dolly Varden, rainbow trout, lake trout. **Wildlife:** Brown bear, moose, wolf, wolverine, lynx, beaver, bald eagle, rough-legged hawk, osprey.

St. Marys sits on a southfacing shore of the lower Andreafsky River.

34 ANDREAFSKY RIVER AND EAST FORK ANDREAFSKY RIVER

From headwaters on the southern slopes of Iprugalet Mountain, the Andreafsky River and East Fork Andreafsky River traverse alpine tundra and rolling hills, then forests of spruce, as these clearwater streams flow to join as one river about 5 miles above the village of St. Marys. In contrast to the low topographic relief of the Yukon Delta wetlands, the Andreafsky River and the East Fork Andreafsky offer intimate river travel through a broad range of ecosystems. The upper river segments are within designated wilderness in Yukon Delta National Wildlife Refuge and both are National Wild and Scenic rivers.

The most difficult aspect of traveling these rivers is finding a place to land a plane in their upper reaches. The riverbed is small; gravel bars change yearly and may not always be large enough to land on. A Supercub may be the only plane that can get into the upper rivers in some years.

The lower Yukon region, including the Andreafsky River, has historically been inhabited by Yup'ik Eskimos, who lived in small self-sufficient semipermanent villages of 50 to 250 people. Winter villages were composed of partly subterranean houses from which the people traveled seasonally to harvest fish, caribou, waterfowl, and sea mammals. The Yup'ik constructed skin-covered baidarkas and umiaks for their travels. Today, subsistence resources remain an important source of nutrition, and lower Yukon Yup'ik spend time at summer fish camps, gathering the bulk of their annual food supply.

The name Andreafsky is derived from the Andrea family, which settled on the river in the late 1800s. The family built a Russian Orthodox church, establishing the village of Andreafsky in 1899. The town lost its name to St. Marys when the original St. Marys town site (Akulurak) was moved from upriver. St. Marys, with its Catholic mission, was established less than a mile upstream from Andreafsky, the Russian Orthodox village. The two settlements are now one.

Rating: Class I.
Cautions: Grizzly bears.
Trip length: The Andreafsky is 105 miles long; allow 5 to 7 days. The East Fork is 122 miles long; allow 5 to 7 days.
Season: June through September.

Watercraft: Small raft; folding canoe or kayak; inflatable canoe or kayak.

Access: In—Scheduled airline from Anchorage or Bethel to St. Marys. Check with air taxi operator for availability of planes into upper river. Supercub may offer best chance of getting into the headwaters of these rivers, as there are few gravel bars of sufficient length to land a Cessna 185. Out—Take out at St. Marys or continue downriver a couple more miles to the Andreafsky's confluence with the Yukon River and float down less than a mile to Pitkas Point on the Yukon. You can also continue down the Yukon to Mountain Village.

Land manager: Yukon Delta National Wildlife Refuge. The Andreafsky, including the East Fork Andreafsky, is a National Wild River. (See "Land Managers" at back of book for address and phone information.)

Maps: Andreafsky River: Unalakleet A–6; St. Michael A–1; Kwiglik A–2, A–3, B–2, C–1, C–2, D–1. East Fork: Unalakleet A–6; Kwiglik A–2, A–3, B–1, B–2, C–1; Holy Cross C–6, D–6.

Fish: Arctic char, arctic grayling, northern pike, whitefish; king, coho, pink, and chum salmon. **Wildlife:** Grizzly and black bear, moose, wolf, beaver, fox, river otter, muskrat, waterfowl.

35   ANIAKCHAK RIVER

For remote wilderness, solitude, wild weather, and wilder water, a float trip down the Aniakchak is very special. But don't attempt it unless you are an expert paddler and extremely self-reliant in Alaska wilderness camping. Issuing forth from a cerulean lake in the heart of the Aniakchak Caldera, the Aniakchak is truly a wild river. From its beginning, the river quickens and plunges through The Gates, a narrow 1,200-foot-high gap in the crater, dropping an average of 70 feet per mile through frothy, rocky Class II, III, and IV turbulence for about 15 miles. Then it slows to Class I and meanders 17 miles to Aniakchak Bay.

Aniakchak was a 7,000-foot mountain until ancient cataclysmic eruptions blew off its top, leaving a caldera 6 miles across from rim to rim and 36 square miles in area, with enclosing walls 2,000 feet high. In 1931, Aniakchak erupted again, choking the caldera with lava and ash and reducing it to "a valley of death in which not a blade of grass or flower or a bunch of moss broke through the thick covering of deposited ash," reported geologist/priest Father Bernard Hubbard. More than 60 years later many lifeforms have returned, transforming the caldera into a world within a world. Wildflowers bloom, bears roam along the lakeshore, and salmon swim their way up to Surprise Lake.

Aniakchak was unknown to all but native inhabitants of the region until 1922, when a U.S. Geological Survey field party led by R. H. Sargeant and W. R. Smith, and including Father Hubbard, visited the crater. Sargeant and Smith are credited with naming the crater. Father Hubbard was overwhelmed by the abundant life inside the crater—bear, wolf, fox, salmon, birds. He reported the crater was "a world complete in itself . . . a world inside a mountain." After the 1931 eruption, he returned to the caldera as soon as he could, finding "an abomination of desolation . . . the prelude to hell. Black walls, black floor, black water, deep black holes and black vents. . . . Beautiful Surprise Lake . . . was choked and muddy and black. . . . We stood awestricken on the edge, looking, like Dante, into a real inferno."

A hike to the caldera today is an opportunity to observe the rate of revegetation in an area completely wiped out little more than 60 years ago.

Rating: Class I–III/IV. Numerous closely spaced boulders and swift shallow water make maneuvering very difficult.

Cautions: Weather is often miserable, with rain, cold, and high winds, especially through The Gates. Winds have been known to reach 100 miles per hour. Aniakchak Bay is often too rough for landing floatplanes; expect weather delays for flying in or pickup. Brown bears.

Trip length: 32 miles. Float takes 3 days from Surprise Lake to Aniakchak Bay. Recommend a minimum of 7 days to explore this unique area.

Season: May to September. The weather usually worsens as the summer wears on.

Watercraft: Medium-size raft or inflatable kayak.

Access: In—Scheduled airline to King Salmon, then charter floatplane to put-in on Surprise Lake. Out—By wheeled plane (from King Salmon or Port Heiden) on beach at Aniakchak Bay or by floatplane (from King Salmon) on the bay itself.

Land manager: Aniakchak National Monument and Preserve. The Aniakchak is a National Wild River. (See Land Managers section at back of book for address and phone information.)

Maps: Chignik D–1; Sutwik Island D–5, D–6.

Fish: Dolly Varden, sockeye salmon. **Wildlife:** Caribou, brown bear, wolf, wolverine, fox, porcupine, bald eagle.

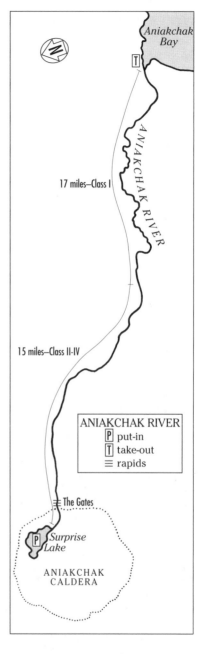

36 CHILIKADROTNA RIVER

Originating in the azure waters of Twin Lakes, surrounded by peaks in Lake Clark National Park and Preserve, the Chilikadrotna races west 60 miles through forested hills in western Alaska to its confluence with the Mulchatna River. At the outlet of Lower Twin Lake lie scattered boulders and some whitewater. The first 8 miles of the river are Class I–II, followed by 31 miles of continuous Class II with one Class III rapid. The riverbed is narrow and winding, and races through a forested valley where sweepers, boulders, rocky rapids, and shallows are a constant threat. On one stretch the river drops 50 feet in less than a mile. About halfway through this section, a Class III rapid appears (about 5 miles below the Little Mulchatna River). Below here, the rapids subside and the river glides through lowland forest. The last 21 miles are Class I to the Mulchatna River, which is also Class I.

For an excellent wilderness hiking/float trip, spend a few days exploring the mountains, glaciers, and alpine meadows around Twin Lakes before descending the clear, swift waters of the Chilikadrotna.

The Chilikadrotna offers good sport fishing as well as fine whitewater.

Spectacular jagged peaks in the Alaska Range cradle Twin Lakes. Along the river, spruce-covered hills and ridges slope gracefully up from the river to tundra-covered peaks. The Chilikadrotna offers continuous swift water and long stretches of exciting yet readily navigable rapids for the intermediate boater.

The Lake Clark region, including the Chilikadrotna, was once occupied by Eskimos and Aleuts. At some point after contact with Russians, Dena'ina Athapaskans settled in the region, pushing the Aleuts more toward the Aleutians and the Eskimos more to the east side of the Alaska Peninsula. Dena'ina villages were scattered throughout the Mulchatna-Chilikadrotna region. Reliable salmon runs and the availability of large land mammals made it possible to live in semipermanent villages. These villages were basically abandoned in the early 20th century as residents settled in Nondalton or Lime Village, where there were opportunities to fish commercially.

The first documented travel to the Lake Clark region by Americans was in 1881 by C. L. McKay of the U.S. Signal Service. Ten years later the lake was named for John Clark, the agent in charge of the Alaska Commercial Company's post at Nushagak. In 1898, gold prospectors began settling on Portage Creek, the Mulchatna River, and on Bonanza Creek.

Rating: Class II, with one Class III rapid. Long stretches of swift water along a narrow riverbed make for an exciting run. This river is suitable for intermediate boaters.

Cautions: Sweepers; logjams; swift current; narrow, twisting watercourse; Class III rapid about 5 miles below Little Mulchatna River; standing waves up to 4 feet high; sharp turns.

Trip length: 72 miles (60 miles on Chilikadrotna and another 12 miles down Mulchatna to a straight stretch on the river for pickup); allow 4 to 5 days.

Season: June through September.

Watercraft: 10- to 13-foot raft; inflatable, folding or hard-shell kayak. Canoes for experienced boaters only.

Access: In—Put in by floatplane on Twin Lakes from Anchorage or Port Alsworth. Out—Take out by floatplane on Mulchatna River 12 miles below confluence with the Chilikadrotna, or continue down Mulchatna River. (See this book's entry on the Mulchatna River.)

Land manager: Lake Clark National Park and Preserve. The upper Chilikadrotna is a National Wild River. (See Land Managers section at back of book for address and phone information.)

Maps: Lake Clark C–3, C–4, C–5, C–6, C–7.

Fish: Arctic grayling, king and chum salmon, Dolly Varden, rainbow trout; northern pike and lake trout in Twin Lakes. **Wildlife:** Brown and black bear, moose, wolf, river otter, beaver, bald eagle, migratory waterfowl.

37   COPPER RIVER (ILIAMNA LAKE)

From its headwaters above Meadow Lake, the Copper River begins as a series of lakes (Meadow Lake, Upper Copper Lake, Lower Copper Lake) and flows westerly for 32 miles into Intricate Bay on Iliamna Lake. (This Copper River is not to be confused with the glacier-fed Copper River, described elsewhere in this guide, which flows into the Gulf of Alaska.) Traversing spruce and cottonwood forests, the run from Upper Copper Lake begins with 2 miles of Class III–IV whitewater. Then you paddle across Lower Copper Lake to the outlet, where there are 3 miles of Class III whitewater.

The water now moves swiftly over a boulder-strewn bottom to two waterfalls. The first waterfall drops 15 feet, the second drops 32 feet. Approaching the falls, watch for a tall cutbank on the right, half a mile above the first falls. Just upriver from the falls is a tall cutbank on the left. Take out on the left side of the river *before* reaching this cutbank and follow a portage trail half a mile to a point below the two falls. From this point, there are 6 miles of Class II and occasional Class III followed by 6 miles of Class I to Intricate Bay. Approach sharp bends in the river with caution; there often is whitewater in these spots.

To avoid the area of difficult whitewater and the waterfalls, you can opt for a short float (11 miles) beginning at Upper Pike Lake and ending at Intricate Bay. From Upper Pike Lake, the first 5 miles of the river are Class II, followed by 6 miles of Class I, with a few Class III rapids spiking the route. The Class III portions occur mostly where the river bends sharply to the right, and it is possible to portage these.

Rating: Class I–IV.
Cautions: Class III–IV rapids; impassable waterfalls about 3 miles below Lower Copper Lake (12 miles before Intricate Bay).
Trip length: 31 miles from east end of Meadow Lake to Intricate Bay; allow up to 4 days. Or 11 miles from Upper Pike Lake to Intricate Bay; allow 1 day.
Season: Late June to September.
Watercraft: Raft or whitewater kayak.
Access: In—Fly to town of Iliamna on scheduled airline. Put in by floatplane at Meadow Lake or Upper Pike Lake. Out—Take out by

floatplane or hired boat on Intricate Bay or Lower Pike Lake.

Land manager: State; private. (See Land Managers section at back of book for address and phone information.)

Maps: Iliamna C–3, C–4, C–5.

Fish: Northern pike, sockeye salmon, Dolly Varden, rainbow trout. Fly fishing only below Lower Copper Lake. **Wildlife:** Brown bear, moose, porcupine, waterfowl.

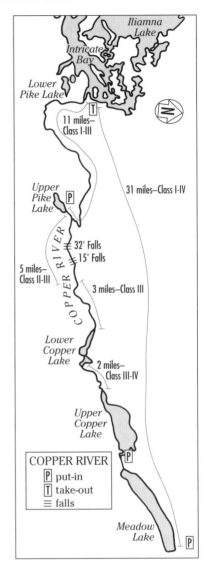

38   GOODNEWS RIVER

The Goodnews is an easy river with beautiful scenery and wonderful fishing. Beginning at a small lake in the Togiak National Wildlife Refuge, the Goodnews River flows about 15 miles to Goodnews Lake, nestled within the Ahklun Mountains, then flows southwesterly over 60 miles before emptying into Goodnews Bay. For more than half its length, it flows through designated wilderness in the Togiak Refuge. While western Alaska and the Bristol Bay region is generally characterized as flats and wetlands, the Goodnews stays in the emerald-green, tundra-covered mountains for much of its length. The lower river has a very slow or nonexistent current due to the tidal influence of Goodnews Bay. Upriver winds can also make downriver travel more difficult.

During summer salmon runs, fish are sometimes so thick in the Goodnews that you can hardly paddle. The Goodnews is popular with sport fishermen, and Natives frequent the river to harvest fish for subsistence use. You may see fish camps along the river, or sod shelters used for camping. The lower 15 miles of the river are surrounded by lands of the Bureau of Land Management and of Kuitsarak Inc. (the Goodnews village corporation).

The Goodnews River was one of several travel and trade routes used by Native people going between the Kuskokwim River and the Nushagak River. The report by Warburton Pike, a non-Native writer, of his journey in 1896 up the Goodnews makes today's downriver jaunts in high-tech boats seem like sweet desserts:

> For two days we pushed up this river, poling, towing and wading . . . through a dry rolling country with mountains of some elevation, till it became merely a deep little ditch, in some places too narrow for the canoe. When we could follow it no longer we began to abuse Moses (Pike's Native guide) for bringing us the wrong way, but he was quite equal to the occasion, and taking his kayak on his shoulders stalked off towards a grassy ridge that lay right ahead, making signs for us to do the same. About a mile away we found a little lake. . . . We made altogether five portages in passing through a chain of lakes, and finally dropped on to another little ditch draining toward the southwest.

The journey Pike took was actually part of one of the best routes from the Yukon to the Nushagak River. Many other people later followed this same route, using poling boats and kayaks to transport supplies up to mining camps.

Rating: Class I.
Cautions: Sweepers.
Trip length: 60 miles from Goodnews Lake to Goodnews Bay; allow 5 days.
Season: June through September.
Watercraft: All.
Access: In—Scheduled airline from Anchorage to Dillingham or Bethel. Charter floatplane to Goodnews Lake. Out—Take out at village of Goodnews Bay on Goodnews Bay. Take scheduled airline to Bethel or Dillingham, and on to Anchorage.
Land manager: Togiak National Wildlife Refuge; Bureau of Land Management; Kuitsarak Inc. (See Land Managers section at back of book for address and phone information.)
Maps: Goodnews Bay A–6, A–7, B–5.
Fish: Arctic char, arctic grayling, Dolly Varden; king, coho, sockeye, chum, and pink salmon. Lake trout in Goodnews Lake. **Wildlife:** Brown bear, beaver, wolverine, otter, mink, red fox, waterfowl, shorebirds.

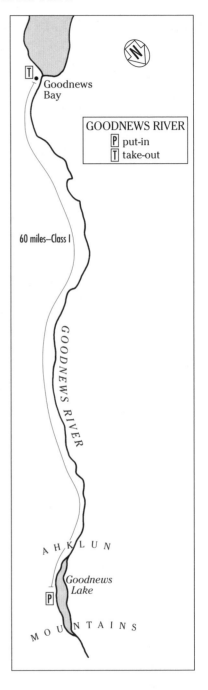

39   HOLITNA RIVER

The Holitna, a meandering Interior river flowing through an isolated region, is recommended for paddlers with good wilderness skills. Beginning at the confluence of the Kogrukluk River and Shotgun Creek, the Holitna flows northerly for about 200 miles to its confluence with the Kuskokwim River near the village of Sleetmute. With a watershed of 4,180 square miles, the Holitna is the largest in the lower Kuskokwim basin. The river meanders across a broad, low valley, with gentle slopes rising to thousand-foot hills. In the southwestern part of the Holitna basin, northeast and southwest of the Chukowan River and lower Oksotalik Creek, are high, smoothly rounded hills. The most conspicuous feature is Kazik Hill, an isolated sharp pinnacle about 8 miles northwest of Kashegelok Village.

The Holitna's gentle current makes it an easy float, except for sweepers and occasional logjams created when riverbanks erode into the boreal forest, knocking whole trees into the river. The surrounding country is covered with forests of spruce, birch, and cottonwood. For paddlers who want to spend time traveling in a remote forested region on a totally nontechnical river, with an opportunity to visit a small Native village on the Kuskokwim, this is a good choice.

The Holitna River, long used by Natives as part of a travel and trade route between Bristol Bay and the Interior, was the Russians' first route to the Interior. Sometime in the early 1790s, a Russian by the name of Ivanof, employed by the Lebedev-Lastochkin Company at its Lake Iliamna trading post, led a small party of men on skis from Lake Iliamna to the headwaters of the Nushagak River, then crossed a low divide to the Holitna River, followed it to the Kuskokwim River, portaged over to the Yukon River, and descended the Yukon to explore the coast.

Another Russian, Baron Ferdinand P. von Wrangel, sent a trading expedition to the Kuskokwim during the winter of 1832-1833. Fedor Komakov and a small party built a small cabin at the mouth of the Holitna River to serve as a trading post. Then they marched upriver on foot, establishing contacts with the Natives, and returned with 1,150 beaver pelts. From 1833 to 1861, an average of 1,500 pelts was taken annually from the Kuskokwim watershed.

Sleetmute, a village at the mouth of the Holitna River, is a

Native name meaning "whet-stone people," and was named for slate deposits found in the area.

Rating: Flatwater Class I.
Cautions: Sweepers; logjams.
Trip length: 200 miles; allow 8 to 10 days.
Season: June through September.
Watercraft: Folding or inflatable kayak or canoe. Raft not recommended due to slow current. Hard-shell boats difficult to transport.
Access: In—Fly to Bethel on scheduled airline. Put in by float-plane on upper river, at confluence of Shotgun Creek and Kogrukluk River. Out—Take out at Sleetmute. Take scheduled airline or charter flight to Bethel and on to Anchorage.
Land manager: Yukon Delta National Wildlife Refuge; Kuskokwim Corporation. (See Land Managers section at back of book for address and phone information.)
Maps: Taylor Mts. D–5; Sleetmute A–4, A–5, B–3, C–3.
Fish: Northern pike, sheefish; king, coho, pink, sockeye, and chum salmon. **Wildlife:** Moose, black bear, fox, beaver, muskrat, waterfowl.

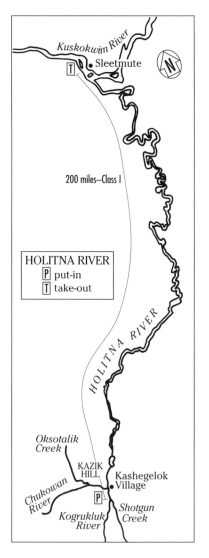

40   KANEKTOK RIVER

From its source at Kagati Lake (an Eskimo word meaning "the source") in the Ahklun Mountains in Togiak National Wildlife Refuge, the Kanektok River flows westerly for 85 miles to Kuskokwim Bay near the village of Quinhagak. Draining an area of 752 square miles, the river has an average width of 200 feet and a gradient of 15 feet per mile. The upper river flows through a valley lined with mountains; the lower river meanders in a braided fashion across a broad floodplain of flat tundra. There are several fishing guide camps in the area. Motorboats are allowed, so if you are looking for a pristine wilderness experience, don't float the river between mid-July and mid-August, the height of sportfishing season.

The upper 5 to 10 miles are shallow and may require lining or dragging boats. Below, the current moves swiftly through a braided channel where sweepers are a constant hazard. Avoiding

A floatplane is often the only reliable transport into remote rivers.

the numerous trees is difficult, as is choosing the correct channel, so this is not a trip for beginners. According to Noel B. Granzow, who floated the river for the Bureau of Outdoor Recreation in the 1970s: "The topographic maps are out of date as they do not show the new channels. . . . The river can be run but it should not be attempted by one canoe as there are literally hundreds of sweepers waiting to clutch a canoe and hold it fast. . . . The prospective traveler should be prepared to line and even portage often."

Josiah Spurr led a U.S. Geological Survey party in 1898 that ascended the Kanektok River in 18-foot cedar canoes. Spurr ascended the Yentna River to the headwaters of the South Fork Kuskokwim, then descended the Kuskokwim to Bethel. Then the party split up, half ascending the Kuskokwin to Kalstag and then crossing a portage to the Yukon, while the other half, including Spurr, went by boat to Quinhagak and ascended the Kanektok River, hoping to find a route to either the Togiak River or the Nushagak River. The Eskimos he hired to guide him tried to dissuade him, saying the river was too swift. They found many Native camps along the river. From Kagati Lake, they followed up a narrow unnamed creek for 8 or

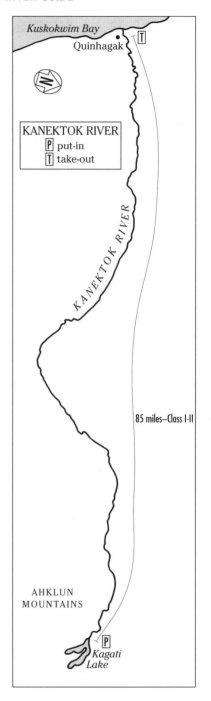

9 miles, then portaged over several lakes to a steep pass to reach a small creek that emptied into Togiak Lake. They then descended Togiak River to Togiak.

Rating: Class I–II. The first 25 miles are Class I; the next 30 miles are Class I–II, and the last 30 miles are flatwater. The upper 55 miles constitute a swift winding watercourse, requiring quick maneuvering. In high water, difficulty increases to Class II–III, with increased danger of sweepers and submerged trees.

Cautions: Swift current, twisting course, sweepers, logjams.

Trip length: 85 miles; allow 5 to 7 days.

Season: June through September.

Watercraft: All.

Access: In—Scheduled airline from Anchorage to Dillingham or Bethel. Charter floatplane to Kagati Lake. Out—Take out at Quinhagak on Kuskokwim Bay. Scheduled airline from Quinhagak to Bethel, and on to Anchorage.

Land manager: Togiak National Wildlife Refuge; Qanirtuuq Inc. (See Land Managers section at back of book for address and phone information.)

Maps: Goodnews Bay C–5, C–6, D–3, D–4, D–5, D–6, D–7, D–8.

Fish: Arctic char, arctic grayling, rainbow trout; king, coho, sockeye, chum, and pink salmon. The Kanektok is one of the premier sportfishing rivers in North America because of the variety of species and trophy size of fish. **Wildlife:** Brown bear, moose, fox, beaver, river otter, mink, waterfowl.

41 KANTISHNA RIVER

The Kantishna, a good family wilderness float on a nontechnical, meandering Interior river, begins in the foothills of Mount McKinley and heads northerly for over 200 miles to its confluence with the Tanana River. From the outlet of Lake Minchumina, Muddy River flows 25 miles to Birch Creek, which quickly joins the McKinley River and becomes the Kantishna River near Chilchukabena Lake. The Kantishna flows through forests of spruce and hardwood, leaving the foothills behind. More advanced paddlers may want to float Moose Creek, which is spiked with Class II rapids on its journey from Kantishna outside of Denali National Park to its confluence with the Kantishna River. Few travelers penetrate this region.

The Kantishna River was an ancient travel and trade route between the Tanana and Kuskokwim regions. Later, prospectors, trappers, traders, and government parties traveled up and down the river, along the foothills of Mount McKinley. There once was a Dena'ina village at Lake Minchumina. A flu epidemic in the early 20th century killed many of the residents. The Minchumina airstrip was built in 1941, and trappers and homesteaders moved into the area.

Rating: Class I.
Cautions: Sweepers.
Trip length: 220 miles; allow 10 days to confluence with Tanana River.
Season: June through early September.
Watercraft: Canoe; folding canoe or kayak; inflatable canoe or kayak.
Access: In—Charter flight from Anchorage or Fairbanks or scheduled airline from Fairbanks to Lake Minchumina village. Put in on lake and follow Muddy River down to confluence with Kantishna River. Out—Take out on gravel bar near the Kantishna's confluence with the Tanana River, or continue down the Tanana to Manley Hot Springs (accessible via the Elliott Highway).
Land manager: Denali National Park and Preserve; state. (See Land Managers section at back of book for address and phone information.)
Maps: Mount McKinley A–3, B–3, B–4, C–4, D–3, D–4; Kantishna River

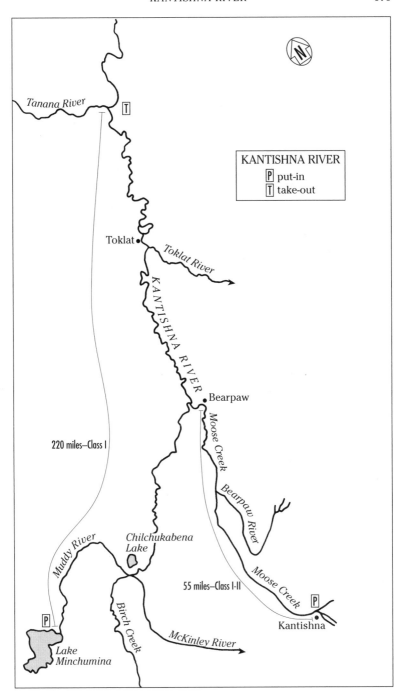

KANTISHNA RIVER
P put-in
T take-out

Tanana River

Toklat

Toklat River

KANTISHNA RIVER

Bearpaw

Moose Creek

220 miles—Class I

Bearpaw River

Chilchukabena Lake

Muddy River

Moose Creek

55 miles—Class I-II

Kantishna

Birch Creek

McKinley River

Lake Minchumina

The appearance of a sow and cubs along a river is a thrilling experience.

A–2, A–3, B–1, B–2, C–1; Fairbanks C–6, D–6.
Fish: Arctic grayling, chum salmon; northern pike in Lake Minchumina. **Wildlife:** Caribou, grizzly bear, moose, fox, beaver, marten, migratory waterfowl.

42   KISARALIK RIVER

The Kisaralik is an exciting whitewater trip for experienced intermediate paddlers. The Kisaralik offers diverse scenic contrasts—blue-green waters and rugged mountains of sandstone and shale; smooth tundra-covered hills and beautiful forests; challenging whitewater cutting through rocky bluffs; deep pools and huge smooth boulders; narrow, twisting valleys that carry tributary streams into the river.

Beginning at Kisaralik Lake, bordered by the snowcapped Kuskokwim Mountains, the Kisaralik flows northwest 111 miles to the Kuskokwim River, 20 miles northeast of Bethel. A deep, clearwater river, the Kisaralik flows swiftly along a rocky streambed spiked with rapids for most of its course, with an overall river gradient of 14 feet per mile. The Kisaralik River drainage covers about 1,100 square miles.

From its headwaters, the river flows through a tundra-covered basin for the first 20 miles. The river then cuts a valley, up to a mile wide, for 40 miles through the Kilbuck Mountains, which rise dramatically 2,000 to 3,000 feet. The hiking and backpacking are excellent around Kisaralik Lake (elevation 1,577 feet) and in the Kilbuck Mountains. Once out of the mountains, the river flows through forests of birch, aspen, spruce, alder, and cottonwood, descending in elevation and becoming a gentle meandering river.

The Kisaralik traverses four major ecosystems: alpine tundra, moist tundra, wet tundra, and upland spruce/hardwood forest. At its confluence with the Kuskokwim, the river flows at an altitude of less than 250 feet. The lower Kisaralik is traveled by residents of Bethel, Akiachak, Akiak, and Tuluksak in motorboats for sportfishing, hunting, gathering, and camping, and there are many Native allotments along the river.

Human occupation of the area goes back 11,000 years to nomadic hunters of Pleistocene animals. Early Eskimos moved into the area about 3,000 years ago. The region is now populated by Yup'ik Eskimos, who continue to practice a subsistence lifeway.

Rating: Class I–IV. Several short Class III–IV rapids can all be portaged. The first occurs 24 miles below Kisaralik Lake and consists of 20-yard-long Upper Falls (Class IV). Quicksilver Creek and the ridge on the left-hand side through which the river cuts are recognizable landmarks about 1.5 miles above Upper Falls. The falls can be scouted and portaged on the left side of the river. Upper Falls is followed by about 12 miles of Class II before Lower Falls, a narrow Class IV canyon which can be portaged. You'll know you're almost to Lower Falls when the river begins to make a long left turn. Several miles of Class I–II follow. The last difficult rapid, Golden Gate, is Class III. Run or portage on either side. Below Golden Gate are 40 miles of Class I. Watch for sweepers. The last 25 miles are meandering flatwater to the confluence with the Kuskokwim.

Cautions: Upper Falls, Lower Falls, Golden Gate Rapids; sweepers in middle section of river; high water can make canyons unrunnable.

Trip length: 111 miles from Kisaralik Lake to confluence of Kisaralik and Kuskokwin rivers; allow 6 to 8 days.

Season: May to early September.

Watercraft: Medium-size raft; whitewater kayak or inflatable kayak. No folding kayaks.

Access: In—Scheduled airline to Bethel. Put in by floatplane from

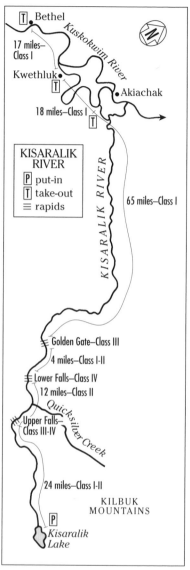

Bethel to Kisaralik Lake. Out—Take out at Kwethluk on the Kuskokwim River, or arrange to be picked up by motorboat. The mouth of the Kisaralik is two to four hours from Bethel by motorboat.

Land manager: State of Alaska (upper 18 miles); Yukon Delta National Wildlife Refuge (middle and lower river); Native allotments and private land selections along middle and lower river. (See Land Managers section at back of book for address and phone information.)

Maps: Bethel B–1, B–2, B–3, B–4, C–4, C–5, C–6, C–7, C–8.

Fish: King, coho, sockeye, chum, and pink salmon; Dolly Varden and rainbow trout; lake trout in Kisaralik Lake. **Wildlife:** Brown and black bear, moose, wolf, wolverine, fox, river otter, peregrine falcon, large variety of waterfowl.

Mosquitoes are sometimes so thick that recreationists wear head nets.

43 KUSKOKWIM RIVER

Second in size to the Yukon River, and nearly paralleling it southwesterly to the Bering Sea, the Kuskokwim is one of Alaska's greatest rivers, draining 50,000 square miles. Several large tributaries drain into this mighty river which flows 540 miles to the sea. The North Fork Kuskokwim River begins in the rolling hills of the Kuskokwim Mountains and flows 260 miles to meet the South Fork just above the village of Medfra. The East, Middle, and South Forks drain extensive silty flats. The South Fork flows 152 miles to its confluence with the North Fork. These forks are sluggish, meandering bodies of water, characterized by many oxbows.

The main Kuskokwim River officially begins at the junction of the North and South forks above Medfra. From here the river is wide and meandering, flowing through forests of spruce, birch, and willow and across swampy wetlands.

Kolchan and Dena'ina Athapaskans lived in the upper Kuskokwim area and traveled the rivers and through passes in the Alaska Range to trade in Cook Inlet. Widespread and well-traveled trade routes connected the Kuskokwim drainage with the Yukon drainage via a portage near Lake Minchumina. These Natives lived in small bands and utilized territory along one or more clearwater tributaries of the main Kuskokwim. They traveled in frail but quickly constructed birchbark canoes or canoes made of moose hide, often decked over in kayak fashion. To ascend rivers, they used poles to push the canoes, or went overland and built canoes along the way for the journey downriver. Not more than a few hundred Natives have lived in the upper Kuskokwim during the last 140 years. Present-day Kolchan reside primarily at Nikolai on the South Fork of the Kuskokwim and at Telida on the Swift Fork.

The Kuskokwim was "discovered" by non-Natives before the Yukon. In 1829, Ivan Filipovich Vasilev of the Russian American Company ascended the Nushagak River, portaged to the Holitna River headwaters, and floated the Holitna to the Kuskokwim and thence back to the coast. The first steamers ascended the river in 1910.

The Kuskokwim has had commercial traffic continuously since the early part of the century. The upper Kuskokwim continues to be heavily traveled by the local population. The largest settlements along the Kuskokwim are McGrath, Sleetmute, Aniak, Chualthbaluk, and Bethel.

Rating: Class I flatwater from Medfra to the coast.
Cautions: Sweepers.
Trip length: 500 miles or less; allow 1 week to 5 weeks, depending on length.
Season: June through late September.
Watercraft: All.
Access: In—Scheduled airline from Fairbanks or Anchorage to Aniak, Bethel, or McGrath. Charter wheelplane to upper river, or begin trip from Medfra (scheduled air service). Out— Take out by air charter or scheduled air from Sleetmute, or continue downriver to any of the villages, which are served by scheduled or charter air services out of Aniak and Bethel.
Land manager: Yukon Delta National Wildlife Refuge (lower river); private; Calista Corporation; Kuskokwim Corporation. (See Land Managers section at back of book for address and phone information.)
Maps: Kantishna River A–5, B–5,

B–6; Mount McKinley D–6; Medfra A–3, A–4, A–5, B–2, B–3, C–1, C–2, D–1; McGrath B–6, C–6 D–5, D–6; Iditarod A–1, B–1; Sleetmute C–3, C–4, C–6, C–7, C–8, D–1, D–2, D–4, D–5, D–6; Russian Mission A–5, A–6, B–4, B–5, C–1, C–2, C–3, C–4, C–5; Bethel C–8, D–6, D–7, D–8; Baird Inlet A–2, B–1, B–2.
Fish: Arctic char, arctic grayling, northern pike; king, coho, pink, and chum salmon. **Wildlife:** Grizzly and black bear, moose, wolf, fox, beaver, marten, bald eagle, migratory waterfowl.

44   SOUTH FORK KUSKOKWIM RIVER

Beginning as glacial meltwater on the northeast slope of Snowcap Mountain in the Alaska Range, the South Fork Kuskokwim flows north-northwest for 152 miles to its confluence with the North Fork, just above Medfra, to form the main Kuskokwim River. Draining an area of 3,070 miles, the South Fork begins as a raging torrent, swift and turbid. The gradient in the upper 50 miles is more than 30 feet per mile. Below here, the river gradually becomes a sluggish, meandering stream with a gradient of less than 3 feet per mile.

With its many oxbows and gravel bars, the South Fork drains extensive silty flats and flows through forests of spruce, birch, and willow and through wetlands. The South Fork spreads out into shallow braids, particularly where tributaries empty into it. The middle section of the South Fork is referred to as "Snag Flats" because, often, one or more of the channels are choked with dead trees. The lower river is more consolidated within its banks and much easier to travel. Also known as Echeatnu, Istna, or Nando River, the South Fork now has just one village, Nikolai, along its entire length. Nikolai is situated on the north side of the river in its lower reaches.

The South Fork was used by Indians and Eskimos as a travel route from hunting grounds in the Alaska Range to villages on the many tributaries of the Kuskokwim. When Josiah Spurr explored the South Fork in 1898 for the U.S. Geological Survey, he kept the first written account of a descent of this river (published as part of the Survey's 1898–1899 annual report). Spurr and his party traveled in 18-foot canoes, mapping huge expanses of previously unmapped territory in the Yukon and Kuskokwim drainages.

When the Spurr expedition fell short of supplies, they decided to run the rapids of the upper South Fork. As he described that section:

> The fall of the river was very great, and rapids were almost continuous; but as the state of our provisions did not admit of much delay nearly all of those rapids were run through in the canoes, and in this downstream traveling our progress was as rapid as it had before been slow.

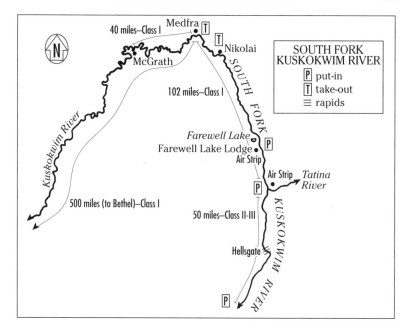

Rating: Class I–III. Upper 40 to 50 miles is very swift, constricted, and hazardous Class II–III whitewater. Below here, Class I.

Cautions: Upper river has very steep gradient with many sweepers and logjams; sweepers along entire river.

Trip length: 152 miles from headwaters to confluence with North Fork (forming the main Kuskokwim). Recommend floating just lower 100 miles of South Fork; allow 4 to 5 days; allow another half-day to Medfra or another 3 days to McGrath.

Season: June through late September.

Watercraft: All.

Access: In—Scheduled airline from Fairbanks or Anchorage to Aniak, Bethel, or McGrath. Then air charter to upper river. There is a landing area at confluence with the Tatina River. It is also possible to fly by charter floatplane or wheelplane to Farewell Lake or the airstrip near Farewell Lake Lodge. Out—Take out by scheduled air from Nikolai, Medfra, or McGrath, or continue downriver to any of the villages, which are served by scheduled and charter air services out of Aniak and Bethel.

Land manager: State; private; Kuskokwim Corporation. (See Land Managers section at back of book for address and phone information.)

Maps: Lime Hills D–4, D–5; McGrath B–4, B–5, C–4, C–5, D–4.
Fish: Arctic char, arctic grayling, northern pike; king, coho, pink, and chum salmon. **Wildlife:** Grizzly and black bear, moose, wolf, fox, beaver, marten, bald eagle, migratory waterfowl.

45 MULCHATNA RIVER

A wild river beginning in the jeweled alpine lake region of Lake Clark National Park and Preserve, the Mulchatna offers paddling experiences from swift Class III rapids to a gentle float through pristine forested lowlands. From Turquoise Lake in the Neacola and Chigmit mountains, the Mulchatna flows roughly southwest for 220 miles to its confluence with the Nushagak River, 65 miles northeast of Dillingham.

Leaving the glacier-clad Chigmit Mountains to the east, the first 22 miles of the river are shallow, rocky, and swift Class II–III whitewater. Sometimes this section of the river is too shallow to run. Around the headwaters, high, well-drained slopes and ridges are covered with alpine tundra, offering excellent hiking. As the river descends, it leaves the open tundra country and cuts through forested foothills of spruce and birch. The low, tundra-covered Bonanza Hills rise above the forested valley and offer good hiking. A deep, extremely narrow gorge, the Bonanza Hills Canyon, constricts the river in this area. A 2-mile section of rocky, tight Class II–III whitewater courses through the canyon, which begins near the confluence with Summit Creek. Portaging this section can be arduous.

About 24 miles below Bonanza Hills Canyon, boulders and ledge drops begin as Class I as the river bends right, then left, in a long oxbow, cutting into a small gorge with a Class III 3-foot drop and several other ledge drops stretching across most of the river. On the west side is one large chute partially obstructed by a boulder. Huge haystacks and holes characterize this Class III section.

Below Bonanza Creek the Mulchatna mellows and meanders, becoming an easy Class I float for about 180 more miles. The land becomes somewhat marshy and brushy, and hiking is not easy. Below its confluence with the Chilikadrotna River, the Mulchatna widens, the current increases, and the river braids across a forested floodplain to the Nushagak River. Watch for sweepers and logjams.

Rating: Class I–III. The first 22 miles from Turquoise Lake to the Bonanza Hills are Class II–III shallow, rocky rapids; Class II–III ledge-drop rapids 4 miles below Half Cabin Lake. The rest of the river is Class I.
Cautions: Sweepers; logjams; 3-foot ledge drop (T8N, R33W, Sec. 13

on Lake Clark D–6 topo map).

Trip length: 230 miles between Turquoise Lake and New Stuyahok on the Nushagak River; allow 10 to 13 days. For shorter trip, put in or take out by floatplane on small lakes west of Bonanza Hills (180 miles from Bonanza Hills lakes to New Stuyahok; allow 9 to 11 days). Can also put in or take out by floatplane at Dummy Creek (140 miles from Dummy Creek to New Stuyahok; allow 7-10 days) or at confluence with Koktuli River (6 to 9 days from Koktuli River to New Stuyahok).

Season: June through September.

Watercraft: Raft; hard-shell, folding, or inflatable kayak; canoe suitable below Bonanza Hills or in the hands of experienced paddlers.

Access: In—Floatplane from Anchorage, Iliamna, or Port Alsworth to Turquoise Lake. For family Class I river voyage of 180 miles, put in by floatplane at any of the small lakes west of Bonanza Hills or on the river itself near Big Bonanza Creek. Out—Take out by charter wheelplane on gravel bars on lower Mulchatna, or by floatplane on the straight stretch of river 12 miles below the confluence of the Mulchatna and the Chilikadrotna. Or take out at New Stuyahok, or float another 95 miles down the Nushagak to Bristol Bay.

Land manager: Lake Clark

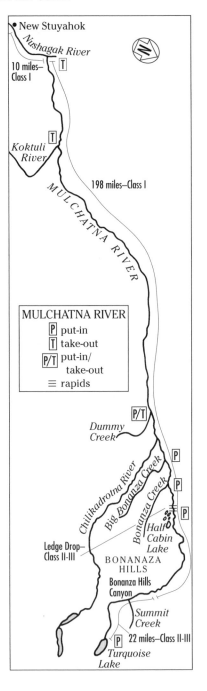

Paddlers running ledge drops and whitewater on the Mulchatna River.

National Park and Preserve; private; state. The upper 24 miles of the Mulchatna is a National Wild River. (See Land Managers section at back of book for address and phone information.)

Maps: Lake Clark B–7, B–8, C–4, C–6, C–7, D–3, D–4, D–5, D–6; Taylor Mountains A–1, A–2, B–1; Dillingham B–4, C–3, C–4; D–2, D–3.

Fish: Arctic grayling, Dolly Varden, rainbow trout; king, sockeye, and chum salmon. **Wildlife:** Caribou, brown and black bear, Dall sheep, moose, wolf, beaver, rough-legged hawk, osprey, bald eagle, Harlan's hawk, great horned owl.

46 NEWHALEN RIVER

Beginning at Sixmile Lake, the Newhalen flows southerly for 22 miles to empty into Iliamna Lake at the village of Newhalen. A large, swift, and unusually turquoise-blue river, the Newhalen is rarely run in its entirety due to waterfalls and difficult Class IV whitewater below the falls. The upper 11 miles, to Upper Landing at the end of the Iliamna Road, are a pleasant Class I paddle.

If you decide to continue down the river past Upper Landing, pull out on the left side of the river at the sharp right-hand bend at Mile 17 in order to avoid a nearly river-wide Class V ledge. Then portage on a trail for more than a mile to skirt the ledge.

If you miss the take-out at this point, you have one more chance to take out, but it is not recommended. Run a series of narrower ledges on a long straight stretch. Run these through the middle of the river. Then you will come to a left-hand bend. Below is an island that separates the river into two chutes. The left chute has a rock pillar in the center; the right chute has dangerous falls. Pull out on the left just as the river starts bending to the left. This is difficult, as you have to work to get from the center of the river through the ledges and over to the left side in time to catch an eddy. Otherwise you are committed to running the chute. The left chute is narrow, with severe boils and turbulence created by the rock pillar. Descend on the left side of the pillar.

Once through this part, seven sections of Class IV whitewater are still to come. If you portaged your boat, you are probably beat by now. The rest of the river should be scouted before running. In some places, the banks are too steep to climb.

Rating: Class I–V. Upper 8 miles are Class I; next 5 miles are Class I–II; last 5 miles begin with dangerous Class V ledges, which may be portaged, then Class IV whitewater (seven sets of rapids). Rafters and kayakers who attempt this river should be experienced boaters; kayakers must be proficient in Eskimo roll.

Cautions: Don't paddle past the point where portage of Class V whitewater is possible.

Trip length: 22 miles; long one-day paddle from Sixmile Lake to Newhalen; allow 2 days if traveling by raft. Or 11 miles; short one-day paddle from Sixmile Lake to Upper Landing.

Season: June through September, with September being the least reliable weather.

Watercraft: Minimum 13-foot raft with rowing frame, or hardshell whitewater kayak.

Access: In—Scheduled airline from Anchorage to Nondalton. Put in at Sixmile Lake. For Class IV–V section only, drive to end of road from Iliamna and put in at Upper Landing. Out—For a flatwater float of the upper Newhalen (8 miles), take out at Upper Landing, then drive to Iliamna. For Class IV–V run, take out at village of Newhalen and take a taxi to the Iliamna airport. (It's also possible to pull out 1.5 miles earlier at a road that leads to the Iliamna airport.) Fly on scheduled airline back to Anchorage.

Land manager: Alaska Peninsula Corporation; Iliamna Natives Ltd.; Bureau of Land Management, Anchorage. (See Land Managers section at back of book for address and phone information.)

Maps: Iliamna C–6, D–5, D–6.

Fish: Arctic char, arctic grayling, rainbow trout, lake trout; king, sockeye, coho, pink, and chum salmon. **Wildlife:** Brown and black bear, moose, porcupine, snowshoe hare, migratory waterfowl.

Map labels:

Iliamna Lake

safest portage route

falls

possible portage route Class V

Newhalen — T

5 miles—Class IV

ILIAMNA ROAD

Iliamna

T — portage—see inset

ILIAMNA ROAD

NEWHALEN RIVER

9 miles—Class I-II

Upper Landing P/T

8 miles—Class I

NEWHALEN RIVER

P put-in
T take-out
P/T put-in/take-out
≡ rapids
— road
--- portage

Fish Village

P

Nondalton

Sixmile Lake

47 NUSHAGAK RIVER

The Nushagak provides a good family float for paddlers with wilderness camping experience, and is especially interesting for people who would like to visit Yup'ik villages in Southwest Alaska. With headwaters rising in the Nushagak Hills, the Nushagak flows southwest 275 miles to Nushagak Bay, picking up major tributaries along the way (the Nuyakuk and Mulchatna rivers). Scattered forests of spruce and hardwood line the river, with open tundra just beyond. While the upper river is remote, there are Native villages below the Nuyakuk River, so you are likely to meet others traveling on the Nushagak. The river flows past the villages of Koliganek, New Stuyahok, and Ekwok. Much of the land surrounding these villages is owned by Native corporations or is privately owned.

Historically, the Eskimo groups in this area eventually separated into two groups: the Aglegmiut, who lived along the Nushagak Bay coast, and the Nushagagmiut, who lived inland along the Nushagak River. The Nushagak became the first river in the Bristol Bay region to be explored by non-Natives when the Russians arrived in the 1800s. Because the Nushagak had long been a travel and trade route for Natives going between Bristol Bay and the Interior, it was only natural that the Russians would eventually go up the river in search of furs.

A fort was established at Nushagak (named Alexandrovski Redoubt), and the Russians made peace between the formerly antagonistic Aglegmiut and the Nushagagmiut. In 1829 Ivan Vasilev took Native guides and followed the Nushagak up to the Nuyakuk River and on to the Tikchik Lakes. He later made the trip again and went over to the Kuskokwim. The Nushagak remained an important travel route for years.

With the U.S. purchase of Alaska, the Russian American Company was replaced by the Alaska Commercial Company. Fishing became the dominant industry and two canneries opened at Nushagak in 1899. By the 1930s the canneries closed because of declining salmon runs and because the channel of the Nushagak River changed its course so that the deepest portion was no longer on the Nushagak side of the Bay.

Rating: Class I.

Cautions: Sweepers; logjams.

Trip length: 275 miles, or less, depending on where you take out; allow 10 to 14 days.

Season: May through September.

Watercraft: All.

Access: In—Fly to Dillingham on scheduled airline. Take charter flight to put in on gravel bar in upper river. Out—Take out at Koliganek, New Stuyahok, or Ekwok, or continue downriver to Dillingham.

Land manager: State; private; Stuyahok Ltd.; Choggiung Ltd.; Ekwok Natives Ltd. (See "Land Managers" at back of book for address and phone information.)

Maps: Dillingham D–4, D–5, D–6; Taylor Mountains A–4, B–2, B–3, B–4, C–20.

Fish: Arctic char, arctic grayling, northern pike, rainbow trout; king, coho, sockeye, chum, and pink salmon. **Wildlife:** Caribou, brown and black bear, moose, migratory waterfowl.

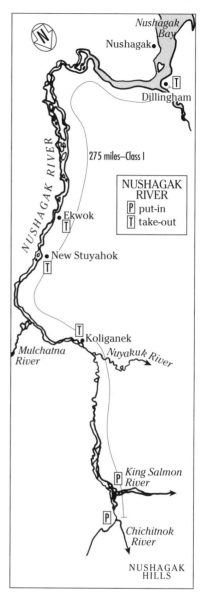

48 NUYAKUK RIVER

This an excellent river for families or novices, with experience in portaging, who want a taste of western Alaska—especially those who enjoy fishing. The Nuyakak River is a 43-mile tributary of the Nushagak River. The Nuyakak begins at Tikchik Lake, the lowest of six large interconnected lakes. It flows east, then slightly southeast, to its confluence with the Nushagak about 65 miles from Dillingham.

Deep and clear, with a moderate (3 to 4 miles per hour) current, the Nuyakuk has a gradient in the first 6 miles that averages 17 feet per mile. Three sets of rapids come within these 6 miles, the last being a large Class IV–V cataract a half mile long that requires portaging. Once past the rapids the river flattens, with a gradient averaging 1 to 2 feet per mile to the river's mouth.

The upper river is flanked by a forest of black spruce and by wet bottomlands where tamarack grows. Paper birch and white spruce grow on better-drained sites. The vegetation is rather brushy along the river, with adjacent uplands being more open. Campsites are good on the first three-fourths of the river but are difficult to find on the lower river.

Rating: Class I–V. The river is Class I except for two sections of Class II in the first 4 miles below the outlet of Tikchik Lake and the Class IV–V falls 6 miles below the outlet. These sections can be portaged (see Cautions below). Boaters who want to avoid white-water completely can arrange with their floatplane pilot to land on the river below the first 7 miles.

Cautions: Rapids. The first two rapids (Class II) can be portaged or lined on the left side of the river. The falls (Class IV–V; actually a series of ledges) 6 miles from the outlet (topographic map reference T3S, R51W, Sec. 18-19) can be easily portaged on a visible, well-used trail on the right side of the river.

Trip length: 55 miles from Tikchik Lake to Koliganek; allow 4 days.

Season: Late May to early September.

Watercraft: All.

Access: In—Scheduled air service to Dillingham, then charter float-plane to Tikchik Lake. Out—Take out at Koliganek or farther down-river on the Nushagak at New Stuyahok. Floatplanes can land on most of the Nuyakuk and Nushagak rivers.

Land manager: Wood-Tikchik State Park (upper 12 miles); Nushagak and Mulchatna Rivers Recreation Management Area (state); private; Koliganek Natives Ltd. (See Land Managers section at back of book for address and phone information.)

Maps: Dillingham D–4, D–5, D–6.

Fish: Arctic grayling, northern pike, rainbow trout; king, coho, sockeye, chum, and pink salmon. **Wildlife:** Caribou, brown and black bear, moose, lynx, beaver, mink, migratory waterfowl.

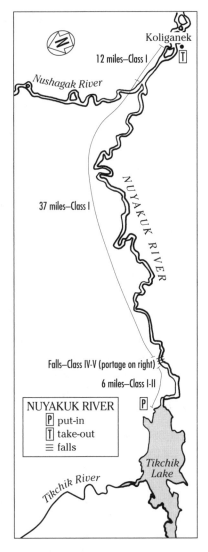

49   SAVONOSKI RIVER

As the glaciers receded after the last ice age, they left behind deep depressions many miles long in Southwest Alaska. These depressions filled with water and now form a vast lake system. Paddling the Savonoski River Loop, you have an opportunity to sample this rich lake and river system while exploring several interconnected waterways within Katmai National Park and Preserve. This trip should only be attempted by persons with intermediate skills who are experienced wilderness travelers and know how to travel in dense brown-bear territory.

At Brooks Camp, you'll want to hike to Brooks Falls, a prime bear gathering place, where there is a platform for viewing the bears fishing at the falls. From Brooks Camp, paddle about 24 miles on Naknek Lake to the lake's Bay of Islands. Paddle close to shore, crossing at the closest two points of land on Naknek Lake when the weather is calm. Camp well away from any streams because these are frequented by brown bears once the salmon return from the sea. The Bay of Islands, one of the most sheltered areas in all of Naknek Lake, is filled with small islands ranging from rocky outcrops to several acres in size. The islands are great for camping, as they are generally safe from bears.

Portage to Lake Grosvenor by crossing a narrow neck of land between Naknek and Grosvenor lakes. To find the 1.2-mile trail, look for a small promontory (145 feet high) sticking out from the north shore. The historic cabin of Roy Fure is at the head of a small cove just east of the promontory, and the trail is nearby. Follow the trail northwest. About halfway across, you'll encounter a small pond. Paddle across and continue on the trail, which is often knee-deep in mud, to Lake Grosvenor.

The paddle route along the shore of Lake Grosvenor to Grosvenor River is about 16 miles, followed by a 3-mile float on the river to its confluence with the Savonoski River. The meeting of these two rivers is visually fascinating, as the clear blue Grosvenor meets the pumice- and silt-filled Savonoski. Listen for the sound of floating pumice rocks grinding their way down the river.

The Savonoski is braided, with a moderate current (3–5 miles per hour) and a gradient of 6 feet per mile. Nesting tundra swans are often seen along the upper Savonoski; the river is also prime brown-bear habitat. It's probably best to float the entire 15 miles from Lake Grosvenor to the mouth of the Savonoski River (at Iliuk Arm on Naknek Lake) all in one day, camping north of the mouth. You could also paddle another 2 to 3 miles to good camping spots on the south shore of Iliuk Arm. The south shore generally offers the most protection from wind.

The return to Brooks Camp to complete the Savonoski loop requires a 20-mile paddle from the mouth of the Savonoski. Margot Creek, a tempting campsite along the way, is frequented by bears; it's best to camp away from the creek mouth or on an island. Bears travel the shorelines of all streams and lakes in Katmai National Park. The highest preventive measures are required to avoid conflicts with the animals. When you finish the loop by paddling around the moraine 2.5 miles from Brooks Camp, be sure the weather is calm, as this finger of land places you in an exposed position.

A Native village existed near the mouth of the Savonoski River until the Novarupta Volcano eruption in 1912, when people abandoned the area. American Pete, the chief of Savonoski village, and a small party of Eskimos were the only human beings anywhere near the volcanic eruption when it occurred. The village of Savonoski was only 20 miles from Novarupta. With the eruption, the villagers fled in terror to the safer village of Naknek. American Pete described

Grosvenor Lake, Katmai National Park and Preserve.

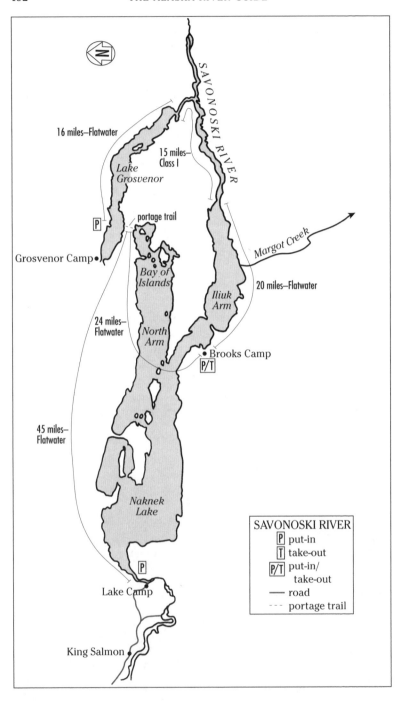

16 miles—Flatwater

15 miles—Class I

Lake Grosvenor

SAVONOSKI RIVER

portage trail

Margot Creek

Grosvenor Camp

Bay of Islands

20 miles—Flatwater

Iliuk Arm

24 miles—Flatwater

North Arm

Brooks Camp

P/T

45 miles—Flatwater

Naknek Lake

P

Lake Camp

King Salmon

SAVONOSKI RIVER

P   put-in

T   take-out

P/T put-in/ take-out

—— road

---- portage trail

it (as reported by Robert F. Griggs in *The Valley of Ten Thousand Smokes;* 1922):

> The Katmai Mountain [Novarupta] blew up with lots of fire, and fire came down trail from Katmai with lots of smoke. We go fast Savonoski. Everybody get in baidarka. Hellava job. We come Naknek one day, dark, no could see. Hot ash fall. Work like hell. Now I go back every year one month maybe after fish all dry and kill bear. Too bad. Never can go back to Savonoski to live again. Everything ash. Good place too, you bet. Fine trees, lots moose, bear and deer. Lots of fish in front of barabara. No many mosquitoes. Fine church, fine house.

Rating: Class I–II. Savonoski River is generally fast Class I, with the likelihood of Class II standing waves in the lower river as it nears Iliuk Arm.

Cautions: Brown bears; sandbars and sweepers on Savonoski River. Strong winds appearing without warning can create williwaws that turn the lakes into whitecapped, wave-covered maelstroms. Stick close to shore and paddle only when conditions are safe.

Trip length: 75 to 95 miles around the loop from Brooks Camp back to Brooks Camp; allow 7 to 10 days.

Season: June through September. Bears frequent the Savonoski River and the shores of Iliuk Arm in greater numbers after late July; strongly recommend that you not camp on the river in July or August.

Watercraft: Canoe or kayak (rigid, folding, or inflatable).

Access: In—Scheduled airline to King Salmon. Then scheduled or charter flight to Brooks Camp or Grosvenor Camp in Katmai National Park and Preserve. It is also possible to put in on Naknek Lake via road from King Salmon. Take the road from the airport to Lake Camp. From here, it is about a 45-mile paddle to the portage from Bay of Islands to Lake Grosvenor. Out—Brooks Camp on Naknek Lake.

Land manager: Katmai National Park and Preserve. (See Land Managers section at back of book for address and phone information.)

Maps: Mount Katmai C–5, C–6.

Fish: Arctic char, northern pike, sockeye salmon, rainbow trout, lake trout. **Wildlife:** Brown bear, moose, wolf, lynx, beaver, river otter, bald eagle.

50   STONY RIVER

Beginning as glacier melt at Stony Glacier near the foot of Sled Pass, the Stony River flows north for 190 miles, braiding its way to a wide valley at the southern end of the Revelation Mountains. The Necons River empties into the Stony, and the Telaquana River joins the river 20 miles downstream. Below the Telaquana, in a 10-mile stretch, the river meanders sluggishly across a 200-yard-wide channel, moving at about 2 miles per hour. Then it cuts a series of scenic canyons in a 100-yard-wide channel over the course of 19 miles. The current speeds up to 5 to 7 miles per hour as the river drops over a couple miles of short Class II rapids (located in T12N, R30W, Lime Hills topo map).

At high water, there may be up to 8-foot standing waves. The canyons end about 22 miles above Lime Village as the river braids through islands and gravel bars of the Kuskokwim lowlands at a moderate speed (about 5 miles per hour) for another 90 miles. Here the only relief on the landscape are groups of small isolated hills. The river flows past Lime Village. Then several creeks and tributaries feed in as the river braids and eventually empties into the Kuskokwim River about a mile from Stony River village.

Like most of the tributaries in the Kuskokwim watershed, the Stony was occupied by Natives hunting and gathering at different times of the year. Eskimos and Athapaskans used the Stony as a route to the foothills of the Kuskokwim Mountains and the Alaska Range to hunt caribou, moose, and bear. Then they built boats to go back downriver.

The Stony River region was never really settled by trappers and prospectors because an expedition to the area was considered to be a two-year undertaking—the first year for poling supplies and equipment upriver to the head of navigable waters and then waiting for freezeup to transport everything by dogsled; the winter for building shelter and trapping; and the following summer for the start of prospecting. Interest didn't really increase until the advent of bush airplane travel. In the late 1920s, people flew into the headwaters of the Stony in floatplanes, and the country was no longer inaccessible.

Rating: Class I–II. The Stony is suitable for moderately experienced boaters with good wilderness skills, and for families with good boating and wilderness experience.

Cautions: Rocky rapids through canyons.

Trip length: 119 miles from confluence of Stony and Telaquana rivers to Stony River village; allow 5 to 6 days.

Season: June through September.

Watercraft: Kayak, canoe, small to medium-size raft. Inflatable canoes and kayaks suitable; folding boats could be used, but in the hands of inexperienced paddlers may sustain damage from rocky riverbed.

Access: In—Scheduled airline to McGrath or Aniak, then by charter wheelplane to gravel bars at confluence of Stony and Telaquana rivers or by floatplane. Out—Take out at Stony River village on right bank at mouth of the Stony. Then via scheduled airline to Aniak or McGrath and on to Anchorage or Fairbanks.

Land manager: Bureau of Land Management, Anchorage; Lake Clark National Park and Preserve; Kuskokwim Corporation; state; private. (See Land Managers section at back of book for address and phone information.)

Maps: Lime Hills A–4, A–5, A–6, B–5, B–6, B–7, B–8; Sleetmute B–1, C–1, C–2, D–2.

Fish: Arctic char, arctic grayling, northern pike; king, coho, chum, and pink salmon.

Wildlife: Grizzly and black bear, moose, wolf, fox, beaver, marten, bald eagle, migratory waterfowl.

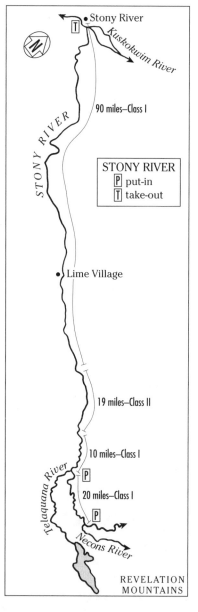

Stony River

Kuskokwim River

90 miles–Class I

STONY RIVER
P put-in
T take-out

STONY RIVER

Lime Village

19 miles–Class II

10 miles–Class I

20 miles–Class I

Telaquana River

Necons River

REVELATION MOUNTAINS

51   TLIKAKILA RIVER

The Tlikakila offers a beautiful, but all-too-short, wilderness float for intermediate boaters with good wilderness skills in a splendid mountain setting. Closely flanked by glaciers, 10,000-foot-high mountains, and perpendicular cliffs, the Tlikakila exits from Summit Lake and pours through a deep, narrow valley in the Alaska Range. Known locally as Big River, the Tlikakila is the largest tributary into Lake Clark. The Tlikakila is a small but fast-moving glacial river fed by meltwater and runoff from the Lake Clark Pass area. Its braided course races through forests of spruce, poplar, willow, and alder, with rugged mountains rising steeply above the valley. The scenery is superb. On busy summer weekends, recreational planes flying through Lake Clark Pass and above the Tlikakila River break the silence.

Rating: Class I–II, with short sections of Class III whitewater.
Cautions: Class III rapids just below confluence with the North Fork (can be portaged on the left side of the river) and 10 more miles of

The Tlikakila braids through a spectacular peak-rimmed valley.

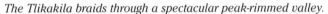

Class II below. Areas of quicksand in the lower river. Bears.

Trip length: 51 miles; allow 3 days.

Season: June through September.

Watercraft: Raft, whitewater kayak, inflatable kayak.

Access: In—Scheduled air to Port Alsworth or Iliamna, then by charter floatplane to Summit Lake in Lake Clark National Park and Preserve. Or charter floatplane from Anchorage to Summit Lake. Out—Take out on Lake Clark by floatplane or charter boat to Port Alsworth.

Land manager: Lake Clark National Park and Preserve; private. The Tlikakila is a National Wild River. (See "Land Managers" at back of book for address and phone information.)

Maps: Lake Clark B–2, B–3; C–1, C–2; Kenai C–8, D–8.

Fish: Arctic char, arctic grayling, sockeye salmon, lake trout.

Wildlife: Brown and black bear, Dall sheep, moose, wolf, fox, marten, mink, bald eagle.

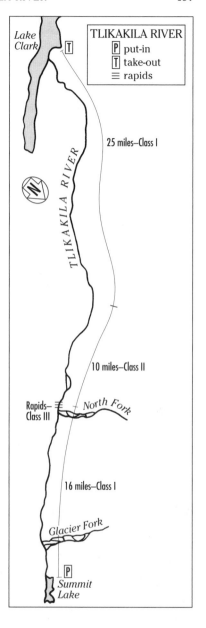

Lake Clark

TLIKAKILA RIVER
P put-in
T take-out
≡ rapids

25 miles–Class I

TLIKAKILA RIVER

10 miles–Class II

Rapids–Class III   North Fork

16 miles–Class I

Glacier Fork

P
Summit Lake

52 TOGIAK RIVER

This is an easy trip on an outstanding river in western Alaska, with exceptional wilderness scenery in its upper reaches. From headwaters at Upper Togiak Lake, the river flows from the southern foothills of the Kilbuck Mountains to Togiak Bay, draining about 2,000 square miles. Exceptionally clear, the river flows 40 to 80 feet wide in its upper reaches and 150 to 250 feet wide near its mouth over a distance of 60 miles from Togiak Lake. The distance from Upper Togiak Lake to the outlet of Togiak Lake is 22 miles, making for a 60-mile paddle and float.

The upper Togiak valley is clothed in tundra, which reaches up the surrounding mountains. A rare geological phenomenon is found in this valley: a *tuya*—a flat-topped, steep-sided volcano formed when lava erupted under a glacier. The 2-mile-long tuya is not within the immediate river corridor and requires a long hike to see. In its lower reaches, the Togiak slows, with large meanders and oxbows. The lower river corridor is flat, with distant hills and mountains visible inland. From the mouth of the river and from the village of Togiak, the offshore islands of Walrus Islands State Game Sanctuary are visible.

Archaeological evidence reveals that the Bristol Bay area has been inhabited by Native people for at least 2,000, and as many as 5,000, years. Yup'ik Eskimos still live here. Togiak and Twin Hills, along and near the Togiak River, are two of six Yup'ik villages in the Bristol Bay region.

Rating: Class I and occasional Class II.
Cautions: Sweepers; logjams; river section between Upper and Lower Togiak lakes is very shallow. Winds at the mouth of the river, entering Togiak Bay, often make it difficult to cross the bay to the village of Togiak. Depending on the wind, paddling to Togiak Fisheries, on the south side of Togiak Bay, may be easier.
Trip length: 82 miles from Upper Togiak Lake to river's mouth, and another mile or so to Togiak or Togiak Fisheries; allow 5 to 6 days.
Season: June to late September.
Watercraft: All.
Access: In—Scheduled airline to Dillingham. Fly by charter float-plane to Upper Togiak Lake. Out—Take out at village of Togiak or at

Togiak Fisheries. Both are served by scheduled airline to Dillingham.

Land manager: Togiak National Wildlife Refuge; Togiak Natives Ltd. Corporation; Twin Hills Native Corporation. (See "Land Managers" at back of book for address and phone information.)

Maps: Goodnews A–4, B–3, B–4, C–2, C–3, D–2.

Fish: King, coho, sockeye, chum, and pink salmon; northern pike, Dolly Varden, rainbow trout, burbot, lake trout in the lakes. **Wildlife:** Brown bear, fox, beaver, river otter, mink, waterfowl.

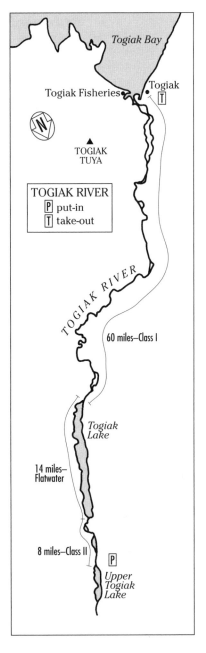

Togiak Bay

Togiak Fisheries

Togiak T

N

▲ TOGIAK TUYA

TOGIAK RIVER
P put-in
T take-out

TOGIAK RIVER

60 miles–Class I

Togiak Lake

14 miles– Flatwater

8 miles–Class II

P

Upper Togiak Lake

53 WOOD RIVER LAKES SYSTEM

This is an excellent trip for intermediate boaters or for families who want to sample a mountain and water environment in western Alaska—especially those who enjoy fishing. Bordered by the Nushagak lowlands on the east and the Wood River Mountains to the west and north, the interconnecting lake system consists of five large lakes and a few small lakes that are connected by short, swift, boulder-strewn streams. The system slowly moves south through the various lakes and their outlet creeks to the mouth of Lake Aleknagik, where the Wood River begins its southerly course to meet the Nushagak River above Dillingham.

The Wood River Lakes System is part of the 1.7-million-acre Wood-Tikchik State Park, largest state park in the nation, which was created in 1978. The park's guiding philosophy is to protect its wilderness character. Although powerboats are allowed and there are several commercial fishing lodges within the lake system, the area is essentially primitive, with rustic state park facilities and ranger stations.

The lake system encompasses several terrain and vegetative zones. Jagged peaks, high alpine valleys, and deep V-shaped inlets give the lake's western arms a fjordlike appearance. The east side of the lakes looks toward islands, gravel beaches, and the Nushagak lowlands. White spruce, birch, willow, and alder cover the hills and mountains up to the 900-foot elevation. Above are tundra meadows, along with rugged rock. In the lowlands, muskeg and wet tundra is found. Hiking is difficult because alder and willow grow thickly around the lakeshores. Persistence and patience, however, reward you with incredible views from the Wood River Mountains.

From Lake Kulik, paddle down the Class II Wind River to Mikchalk Lake, down the Peace River to Lake Beverley, then down Agulukpak River to Lake Nerka, then down 5-mile-long Agulowak River to Lake Aleknagik, and finally down the Wood River to Dillingham.

The Yup'ik people in this area were nearly wiped out by a flu epidemic in 1918–1919. The surviving people basically cleared out and did not resettle at the mouth of Lake Aleknagik until 1928, when they slowly rebuilt the village, including a school, church, and sawmill.

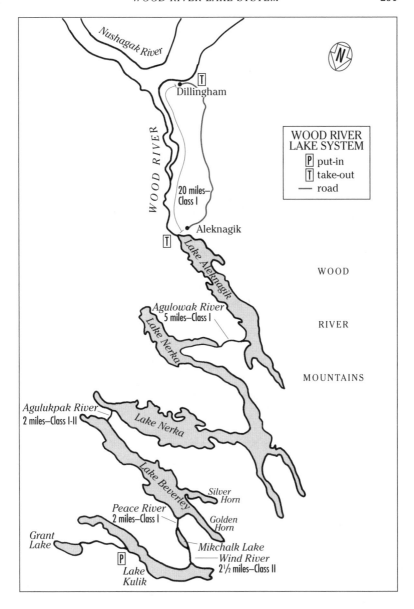

Rating: Class I–II. Lakes are flatwater, except when very windy. Wind River is Class II, with boulder–strewn rapids. The Peace River is flatwater Class I. Agulukpak River is Class I or II, depending on water level, with a swift, shallow, boulder-filled watercourse. Agulowak River is Class I. Wood River to Nushagak River and on to Dillingham

is Class I. Portage of any of the short connecting streams is possible.
Cautions: Wind can create whitecaps capable of capsizing boats; paddle close to shore and don't venture out when it's windy. Insects can be fierce; porcupines like to chew on folding boats; suitable campsites are few.

Trip length: 120 to 140 miles from Lake Kulik to Dillingham; allow 7 to 10 days.

Season: Late May through September.

Watercraft: Canoe or kayak. Folding varieties are suitable.

Access: In—Scheduled air service to Dillingham, then charter floatplane to Lake Kulik or any of the lakes farther south. Out—Take out at Dillingham on the Nushagak River, or arrange to be picked up by charter floatplane on any of the lakes, or take out at Aleknagik village, connected by 25-mile road to Dillingham.

Land manager: Wood-Tikchik State Park (upper 12 miles); Nushagak and Mulchatna Rivers Recreation Management Area (state); Aleknagik Natives Ltd. (See Land Managers section at back of book for address and phone information.)

Maps: Dillingham B–1, B–2, C–1, C–2, D–1, D–2; Goodnews Bay B–1, C–1.

Fish: Arctic grayling, northern pike, Dolly Varden, rainbow trout, lake trout; king, coho, sockeye, chum, and pink salmon. **Wildlife:** Brown bear, moose, lynx, beaver, river otter, mink, muskrat, golden eagle, migratory waterfowl.

SOUTHCENTRAL ALASKA

The Copper and Susitna rivers form the heart of the Southcentral region, while subregions of Kodiak Island and the Gulf of Alaska form the limbs. The Copper drains 24,400 square miles in Alaska and Canada, and the Susitna drains 20,000 square miles. Rugged mountainous terrain characterizes much of the region, and most of the rivers originate in glaciers.

Dominating the watershed are Alaska's greatest mountain ranges: the Alaska Range, with Mount McKinley, tallest mountain in North America; the Wrangell Mountains; and the Aleutian Range, with the great volcanic peaks of the Alaska Peninsula. Most of the rivers coursing to Cook Inlet and the Gulf of Alaska are swift, silty, braided glacial streams flowing from the mountains. The exceptions to this terrain are the lower Susitna Valley, the lowlands bordering Cook Inlet, the Copper River plateau, and intermittent areas along the coast, where clear rivers spring forth and meander across wetlands. In the Kodiak-Shelikof coast subregion, rivers and streams are short and steep, with fairly small drainages.

Breakup in the Southcentral region usually occurs in late April, with peak flow in late April and early May. Freezeup begins in mid-October. The climate in much of the region is maritime, with continental influences in the inland mountain areas. The Japanese Current and the mountains both create many local climatic variations. Annual precipitation ranges from about 15 inches to more than 79 inches, with about half of this occurring as rain during the ice-free season.

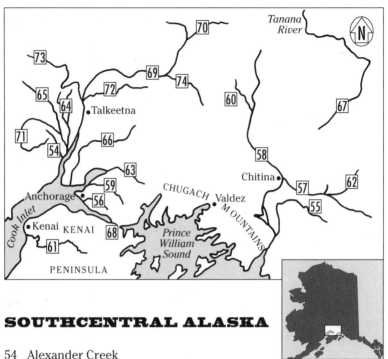

SOUTHCENTRAL ALASKA

54 Alexander Creek
55 Bremner River
56 Campbell Creek
57 Chitina River
58 Copper River
59 Eagle River
60 Gulkana River
61 Kenai River
62 Kennicott River
    and Nizina River
63 Knik River
64 Kroto Creek, Moose Creek,
    and Deshka River

65 Lake Creek
66 Little Susitna River
67 Nabesna River
68 Portage Creek
69 Susitna River (Upper)
70 Susitna River (Lower)
71 Talachulitna Creek and
    Talachulitna River
72 Talkeetna River
73 Tokositna River
74 Tyone River

54   ALEXANDER CREEK

Alexander Creek is one of the most popular fishing and hunting rivers in Southcentral Alaska. From its source at Alexander Lake, Alexander Creek flows southeast about 40 miles to meet the Susitna River. The terrain around the lake is flat, and views of the Alaska Range, including Mount McKinley (Denali), are excellent. Alexander Lake Lodge lies on the south end of the lake, and a half-dozen cabins are scattered around the lakeshore. A platform at the southeast end of the lake provides a dry area for inflating rafts. Otherwise, there is little dry ground on public land near the lake's outlet. Three sites are used informally by campers on private lands around the lake.

The creek is 1 to 5 feet deep and from 50 to 200 feet wide, with an average gradient of 3.5 feet per mile. It meanders through spruce, birch, and cottonwood forest, often between high banks or through willow thickets and tall grasses, so scenic vistas below the lake are generally poor. Motorboats are not allowed from Creek Miles 23 to 38.3 (almost to Alexander Lake) from May 15 to August 20. The state keeps this section in an essentially unmodified natural state in order to provide a primitive setting. Once you have descended the first few miles below the lake, the creek has no structures along it until Sucker Creek. Below this point are increasing numbers of cabins and frequent powerboat use.

Motorboats are allowed on the lower 23 miles of Alexander Creek. A sign at its confluence with Pierce Creek at Mile 7.4 cautions large boats against going farther upstream, where the creek is narrow, shallow, and winding. Most motorized traffic is found near the mouth. Alexander Creek is extremely popular for sportfishing, particularly during king and coho salmon runs in June. Campsites are scarce in the last 11 miles. Along the last 2 miles, there are quite a few cabins and commercial establishments. A large, well-established Dena'ina Athapaskan village once existed at the mouth of Alexander Creek.

Rating: Class I; slow-moving (1-2 miles per hour).
Cautions: Sweepers; bears. Prevailing winds from the south, particularly below Sucker Creek, and the sluggish current of the lower river often make paddling a slow, monotonous chore. Some rafters carry a small outboard motor.

Trip length: 41 miles; 4 to 5 days.
Season: May through September.
Watercraft: All.
Access: In—Put in at Alexander Lake by charter floatplane. Motorboats can travel from Anchorage or Deshka Landing to access the lower creek. Out—Take out at mouth of Alexander Creek by charter floatplane.
Land manager: Alexander Creek State Recreation River; private.
Maps: Tyonek B–2; C–2, C–3.
Fish: Arctic grayling, northern pike, burbot, rainbow trout; king, coho, sockeye, chum, and pink salmon. **Wildlife:** Brown and black bear, moose, beaver, nesting trumpeter swans.

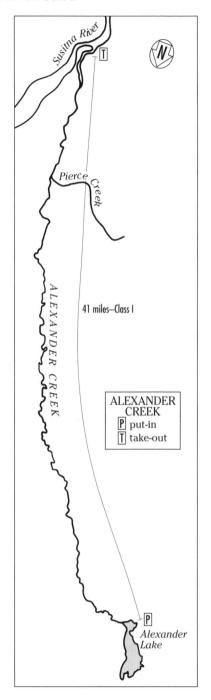

55   BREMNER RIVER

Rising in glaciers of the Chugach Mountains, the Bremner River flows westerly for 64 miles through a coastal trough that separates the Canadian border ranges and the Pacific mountain system (the Chugach and Wrangell mountains). The Bremner traverses a vast, rugged wilderness of glaciated peaks and swift, turbid rivers. These barriers are formidable to the would-be explorer. The area is primitive, revealing little of its past human history, and few have penetrated it. Vegetation is influenced by both the Interior and the coast, so there is a mixture of alpine tundra, coastal forests of Sitka spruce and hemlock, and dense alder thickets. The hiking can be very difficult below the alpine zone, unless you have an affinity for alder.

The river is made up of three forks. The North Fork begins at 1,600 feet and provides most of the river's volume. The average gradient from its headwaters is 26 feet per mile. The Middle Fork begins at 2,300 feet at the foot of a glacier and descends steeply. In one section it drops 1,200 feet in 8.5 miles, an average fall of more than 140 feet per mile. The South Fork, smallest of the three, begins as meltwater of the Fan and other glaciers at about 1,600 feet and drops an average of about 89 feet per mile, meeting the main Bremner River some 14 miles downriver. The Bremner is generally considered unrunnable above the confluence of the Middle and North forks. The Middle Fork has been floated at least twice, however: by a National Park Service party and by a Bureau of Outdoor Recreation party conducting a study of wild and scenic rivers in the 1970s.

The North and Middle forks are large-volume, braided rivers carrying heavy loads of silt. A capsize can be serious, as clothing quickly fills with sediment and the water is extremely cold. There are narrow canyons to descend, passing through steep bluffs. In the upper canyon of the North Fork (Twelvemile Canyon) are several miles of continuous whitewater, with plunge pools and waterfalls. High glaciated mountains border the river valley, and the valley floor is heavily forested. Just below Twelvemile Canyon, the Middle and North forks meet to become the main stem. About 13 miles below the confluence, the river flows through another constricted whitewater gorge, Threemile Canyon. Then the South Fork enters, and the river courses about 29 miles before joining the mighty

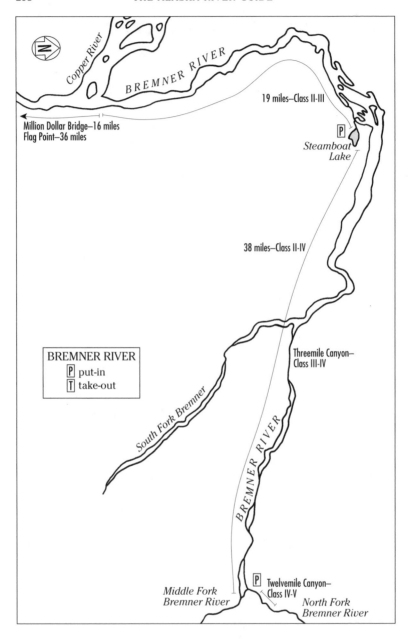

Copper River. There are extensive sand dunes at the mouth of the Bremner.

The name that the Ahtna, an Athapaskan group occupying the

Copper River region, gave to the Bremner is Tetahina, which means "flowing river." The Ahtna avoided the river valley, choosing instead to inhabit the middle and upper Copper River regions.

Lieutenant Henry Allen named the Bremner in 1885 for John Bremner, a local prospector who accompanied him up the Copper River and all the way to the Koyukuk River. Bremner has the distinction of being the only person to have more than one Alaskan river named after him (the John River also took his name). Gold was discovered in the area on Golconda Creek at the turn of the century, and miners worked the valley until 1909.

Rating: Class II–IV, due to remoteness. This river is suitable only for seasoned Alaska wilderness travelers with advanced to expert boating skills.

Cautions: A cold, swift, silty glacial river traversing an isolated wilderness area; narrow canyons; brown bears.

Trip length: 50 miles or less on the Bremner River plus about 36 miles on the Copper River to Flag Point; allow 4 to 7 days. (See this book's entry on the Copper River in Southcentral Alaska.)

Season: July through September.

Watercraft: Raft; hard-shell kayak.

Access: In—From Cordova, Tolsona Lake, or Gulkana, fly by charter floatplane to Steamboat Lake, 20 river miles above the mouth of the Bremner River. This is the easiest, most feasible access. You could also land a Supercub on gravel bars in upper river. Out—Take out at Flag Point on the Copper River for pickup by vehicle. (Take-out is also possible 20 miles earlier at the Million Dollar bridge, but beware of possible entrapping mud on side sloughs when pulling boats out.)

Land manager: Wrangell-St. Elias National Park and Preserve; state. (See Land Managers section at back of book for address and phone information.)

Maps: Gulkana D–7, D–8; Cordova B–3, C–2, C–3, D–1, D–2.

Fish: Arctic grayling, Dolly Varden; king, coho, and sockeye salmon.

Wildlife: Grizzly and black bear, Dall sheep, wolf, wolverine, mountain goat, waterfowl (including trumpeter swans).

56   CAMPBELL CREEK

A free-flowing stream in the heart of Alaska's largest city, Campbell Creek is a resource to treasure and protect. Many Anchorage paddlers use the creek for early season paddling practice; others enjoy the quiet paddling amidst a protected greenbelt in the city.

Campbell Creek begins in the wetlands of Campbell Tract, the last large undeveloped tract of land within the Municipality of Anchorage. A small stream with a width of 7 to 12 feet, Campbell Creek is normally only 7 to 12 inches deep. Early in the season, swollen with snowmelt, the creek may be up to 3 feet deep, exceeding its banks and making sweepers even more hazardous than later in the summer. The creek meanders through a residential, office, and industrial area of South Anchorage. Campbell Lake also is a great place to canoe or kayak and is a safe location to practice paddling techniques before you head out for a wilderness adventure.

The Dena'ina living in Southcentral Alaska called Campbell Creek "crying ridge creek." Campbell Lake and Campbell Creek

Canoeing through sweepers and overhanging branches on Campbell Creek.

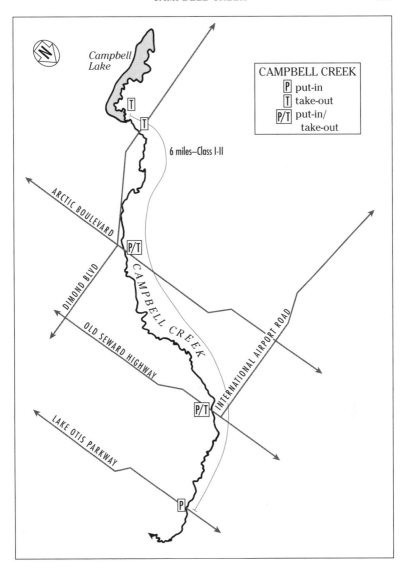

today are contaminated with oil, grease, heavy metals, and fecal matter. A lawsuit filed by four environmental groups in 1992 spurred the state into greater action to clean up the creek, and we can do our part to see that the creek and other waterways are not contaminated by our own activities. "Clean Creeks Day," an annual mid-May event in Anchorage and Wasilla, offers an opportunity to help clean debris from creeks.

Rating: Class I, with short, rocky Class II sections and narrow, tight 90-degree turns overhung with sweepers. Rocky sections can be lined.

Cautions: Narrow channel; sweepers; beaver dams. Strainers (submerged trees and branches that trap boats while allowing water to strain through) and overhanging branches are numerous; some trees completely block the channel and boats must be carried around. Bring a folding camp saw to clear out some of the more persistent sweepers.

Trip length: 6 miles, but length will depend on choice of put-in and take-out locations; float an hour or all day. Allow 1.5 to 2 hours from Lake Otis Parkway to intersection of Old Seward and International Airport Drive and an additional 1.5 to 3 hours to continue to the intersection of Dimond and Arctic boulevards. Some paddlers enjoy creekside dining at the Peanut Farm restaurant, during or after their trip.

Season: Late April to October.

Watercraft: Canoe or kayak.

Access: Some suggested put-ins and take-outs (there are many in Anchorage) are: Folker Street off Tudor Road; Campbell Creek Park on Lake Otis Parkway; Shelikof/Rakof streets near New Seward Highway and Tudor Road; Old Seward Highway near International Airport Road (near the Peanut Farm); Keyhole Drive off East Potter Drive; Dimond Boulevard and C Street; along the Campbell Creek Greenbelt all the way to Campbell Lake. The river narrows along the greenbelt and there are many more sweepers and overhanging branches.

Land manager: Municipality of Anchorage; private.

Maps: Anchorage A–8.

Fish: Dolly Varden, rainbow trout; king, coho, sockeye, silver, and pink salmon. The state stocks the creek each spring with thousands of silver fry. **Wildlife:** Moose, beaver, muskrat, waterfowl.

57   CHITINA RIVER

Boaters with good intermediate paddling skills and wilderness survival skills will find the Chitina to be an excellent wilderness trip in the heart of the nation's largest national park—Wrangell-St. Elias National Park and Preserve, encompassing more than 13 million acres. Born in the St. Elias Mountains where four glaciers meet at the Canadian border, 100 miles northwest of Yakutat, these glaciers flow about 30 miles to become the terminus of the Chitina Glacier. The Chitina River begins at 2,000 feet and flows 112 miles in a profusely braided manner past spectacular mountain scenery, carving its way through a glacial valley with peaks rising over 16,000 feet, before emptying into the Copper River.

The Chitina Valley is a rift separating the Wrangell Mountains from the St. Elias Mountains. One of the scenic highlights is floating past MacColl Ridge, where waterfalls cascade from steep cliffs of multicolored rock, carving deep ravines through bedrock to expose rich strata of geologic history. Hiking is excellent in the upper river, especially in the desertlike terrain surrounding the Chitina Glacier, where the river first emerges.

As the river descends, each new tributary adds force and volume. The clearwater tributaries are very tempting as camping spots, but grizzlies also find these spots attractive, particularly when the salmon are running. Respect wildlife and your own safety, and camp away from these spots. The river is big and cold, with silt so dense you can hear it singing on the bottom of your boat. The Chitina, a fast-moving complex of shallow channels with numerous gravel bars, requires good skills in reading turbid water. Though only moderately technical, the river runs through a region that is wild and remote.

Small bands of Athapaskans moved into the region of the Wrangell Mountains and the Chitina Valley about 2,000 years ago. These Ahtna called the river Chitina, which means "copper river." The Ahtna utilized copper long before non-Natives ever appeared in the valley. Beginning in 1819, traders made several attempts to ascend the Chitina River, but all failed, in part because of the hostility of the Ahtna. In 1885, Lieutenant Henry Allen became the first American to ascend the Chitina. He found the Ahtna friendly, but the environment harsh. He and his men nearly starved to death.

Prospectors followed in the footsteps of Allen's expedition and many mines were established in the late 1800s. The big discovery, a large vein of copper named Bonanza, was not found until 1900, beginning the boom days of the Chitina Valley. By 1911, with construction of the Copper River and Northwestern Railway, Chitina had a population of 2,000 people.

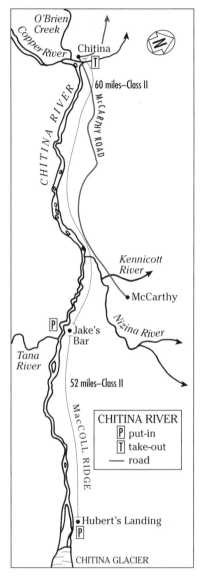

Rating: Class II. May involve 2.5-mile portage (5 hours or more) to get to the main river channel.

Cautions: Grizzlies often frequent the mouths of clearwater tributaries (Chalkina, Gilahina, Lakina, and Tebay). Cold, silty glacial water; harsh weather.

Trip length: 112 miles between Hubert's Landing and Chitina, at the confluence of the Chitina and Copper rivers; allow 7 days. 60 miles from Jakes's Bar to Chitina; allow 4 days.

Season: Late May through mid-September. River flow fluctuates tremendously depending on time of day (glacier melt during sunny weather) and precipitation. The Chitina generally hits peak flow in late July and early August.

Watercraft: Rafts of all sizes, inflatable or hard-shell kayaks, decked canoes.

Access: In—Put in by air from Chitina, McCarthy, or Gulkana to Hubert's Landing area, a bumpy tundra strip just below the terminus of the Chitina Glacier. Then portage 2.5 miles to the main river channel. To avoid this grueling portage, put in by wheelplane at Jake's Bar, Mile 52 on the Chitina. Out—Take out on right side of the

Flood waters on McCarthy Creek, after three days of heavy rainfall.

river at the Copper River bridge at Chitina. To do this, stay on the far right side of the Chitina for at least a mile above its confluence with the Copper. When you begin to see steep bluffs on the right, get ready to pull in on the right immediately at the end of the bluff. Then drag or carry your boat between a quarter-mile and a half-mile upstream. Or, take out at O'Brien Creek, the first obvious creek entering the Copper River, 3.5 miles downstream from Chitina. If you take out at that point, be sure to get way over on the right-hand side as soon as you enter the Copper River. If you miss O'Brien Creek, you'll have to run 100 more miles on the Copper to the next take-out point.

Land manager: Wrangell-St. Elias National Park and Preserve; state; Ahtna Inc. (See Land Managers section at back of book for address and phone information.)

Maps: McCarthy A–2, A–3, A–4, A–5, A–6, B–6, B–7, B–8; Valdez B–1, C–1, C–2.

Fish: Sockeye, coho, chum, and pink salmon spawn in clearwater tributaries of the Chitina. **Wildlife:** Brown and grizzly bear, Dall sheep, moose, wolf, coyote, bald eagle, migratory waterfowl. The Chitina bison herd may be seen in the vicinity of the Chitina's confluence with the Tana River.

58 COPPER RIVER (WRANGELL MOUNTAINS)

The Copper River originates on the north side of the Wrangell Mountains and flows south 287 miles to the Gulf of Alaska, draining an area of more than 24,000 square miles. Thirteen major tributaries contribute to the flow. The drop in elevation between Copper River headwaters and the ocean is 3,600 feet, or an average of about 12 feet per mile, giving the river a swift current, averaging 7 miles per hour. Though accessible by road from many locations, the Copper offers a wilderness whitewater experience on a high-volume glacial river through varied magnificent scenery.

The snowclad peaks of the Wrangell Mountains dominate the upper river, while Wood and Baird canyons offer geological diversity and a bit of hydrological challenge in the lower river. Four glaciers enter the Copper River Valley at a point where the valley is about 2.5 miles wide, less than 40 miles inland from where the Copper River meets the Gulf of Alaska. Allen Glacier intrudes into the valley from the west. Just below this point is Abercrombie Rapids. Grinnell Glacier hangs on the west side below the rapids. Miles Glacier enters from the east and extends across the valley to force the river against mountain walls on the west. A 3.5-mile ice face confronts the river, and peripherally touches the river for a 12-mile stretch.

Where glaciers actually meet the river they act as a dam, causing rapids opposite the snout of the glacier and large lake-like areas in the river upstream. Where Childs Glacier enters from the west, there is a vertical wall of ice towering to 300 feet and extending for more than 2.5 miles along the river. Great icebergs are constantly discharged from the terminus of the glacier. As they drop into the river, which is only 10 to 20 feet deep in front of the glacier, the water creates "tidal" waves as high as 200 feet. The resulting swells sometimes wash across the river to the east bank, which rises 25 feet above the river, and have been known to flood 100 to 200 feet into the alder thickets. Boats caught on the river or on shore in front of the glacier have been thrown as far as 150 feet up on shore. Below the glacier constrictions, the river valley widens to a maximum of 13 miles.

The lower Copper River was historically inhabited by Eyaks, a Native group distantly related to Athapaskan groups of the Interior but with much of their culture similar to that of the Yakutat Tlingit and the Chugach Eskimos. The middle and upper Copper River was, and continues to be, inhabited by the Ahtna Athapaskans. The lower river Ahtna discovered copper and learned to work it, and later traded with other groups. The Russians discovered the Copper River in 1781 and tried unsuccessfully several times over the course of six decades to ascend the river. The U.S. government sent Lieutenant William Abercrombie to look at the Copper River delta in 1884. The next year, Lieutenant Henry Allen led the first non-Native expedition up the Copper River.

Prospectors found copper in the Chitina Valley in 1899, and a year later two prospectors discovered the Bonanza Mine of what later became the great Kennecott mine complex (near present-day McCarthy). The Copper River and Northwestern Railway, completed in 1911, wound 195 miles to the Kennecott Mines. In the Cordova-to-Chitina section alone, 129 bridges were used and 95 miles of track were laid on bridges or trestles. By the 1920s the price of copper and gold decreased and the mine was no longer profitable. The Kennecott Mine closed in 1932. The Alaska Road Commission began converting the railway into a road, and by 1964, conversion was completed from Cordova to Mile 59. The 1964 earthquake destroyed bridges and road grades, thus reverting the route to wilderness once more.

Rating: Class II–III. Class III 12 miles below Copper Lake; Class III at confluence with Sanford River.

Cautions: Large hydraulics between Gakona and Tazlina rivers; Haley Creek headwall and whirlpool on right below Wood Canyon; Abercrombie Rapids above Miles Glacier (can be scouted on right); high winds and unstable calving ice and icebergs at Childs Glacier. Recommend not camping directly across from glaciers due to tidal waves from calving ice.

Trip length: 220 miles from Slana River bridge to Cordova Road at Flag Point; allow 8 to 10 days. For shorter trip, 100 miles from Chitina to Flag Point, allow 4 to 5 days. Other trip lengths are possible depending on your put-in and take-out locations.

Season: May to late September.

Watercraft: Raft or kayak. Experienced paddlers can run section between Slana River and Chitina. Experienced paddlers have also run the river in sea kayaks all the way out to the Copper River Delta and the Gulf of Alaska. This involves good navigation skills and likely will involve dragging boats through shallow channels, as the Copper splits into a myriad of braids on the delta.

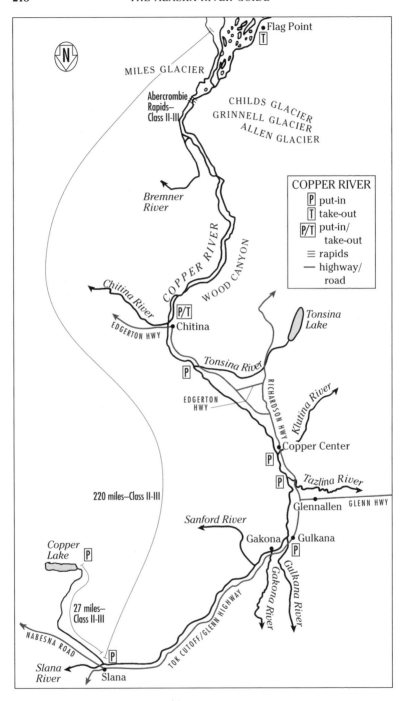

N

Flag Point
T

MILES GLACIER

Abercrombie
Rapids—
Class II-III

CHILDS GLACIER
GRINNELL GLACIER
ALLEN GLACIER

*Bremner
River*

COPPER RIVER

WOOD CANYON

COPPER RIVER

P	put-in
T	take-out
P/T	put-in/ take-out
≡	rapids
—	highway/ road

Chitina River

P/T
Chitina

EDGERTON HWY

Tonsina River

*Tonsina
Lake*

P

EDGERTON
HWY

RICHARDSON HWY

Klutina River

P
Copper Center

P

P

Tazlina River

Glennallen   GLENN HWY

220 miles—Class II-III

Sanford River

Gakona   Gulkana
P

*Copper
Lake* P

27 miles—
Class II-III

Gakona River

Gulkana River

NABESNA ROAD

TOK CUTOFF/GLENN HIGHWAY

P

*Slana
River*   Slana

The Copper splits into a myriad of braids as it nears the Gulf of Alaska.

Access: In—Drive Glenn Highway to Nabesna Road. Put in at Slana River bridge at Mile 1.5 on the Nabesna Road. It is also possible to charter a floatplane out of Tolsona Lake at Mile 170.5 on the Glenn Highway to put in on Copper Lake, adding about 15 miles to the trip. There are many road-accessible put-in and take-out points along the Glenn Highway (such as bridges across the Chistochina, Gakona, and Gulkana rivers). On the Richardson Highway, it is possible to put in or take out at bridges across the Tazlina, Klutina, and Tonsina rivers. On the Edgerton Highway, it is possible to put in or take out on the lower Tonsina bridge and at Chitina. Out—Most convenient take-out near the end of the river is near Cordova at Mile 26.4 on the Copper River Highway at Flag Point. Make prior arrangements for transport into town. (Take-out is also possible 20 miles earlier at the Million Dollar bridge, but beware of possible entrapping mud on side sloughs when pulling boats out.)

Land manager: Bureau of Land Management, Glennallen; Wrangell-St. Elias National Park and Preserve; Ahtna Inc.; state. (See Land Managers section at back of book for address and phone information.)

Maps: Copper Lake to Chitina: Nabesna B–6, C–6; Gulkana A–3, B–2, B–3, C–1, C–2; Valdez C–2, C–3, D–3, D–4. Chitina to Cordova: Valdez A–3, B–2, B–3, C–2; Cordova B–3, C–2, C–3, D–2, D–3.

Fish: Arctic grayling, whitefish, burbot; king, sockeye, and coho salmon; steelhead, Dolly Varden, rainbow, and lake trout. **Wildlife:** Caribou from two herds (Mentasta and Nelchina), brown and black bear, Dall sheep, moose, wolf, lynx, coyote, Dusky Canada geese, trumpeter swan.

59   EAGLE RIVER

Beginning in the Chugach Mountains of Chugach State Park, Eagle River emerges from Eagle Glacier as a cold, turbid, swift glacial stream. In its upper reaches, it is most known to those who traverse from Eagle River Valley over Crow Pass to Girdwood. This icy, knee- to waist-high crossing is forbidding to some, but is only a minor inconvenience to the people who run the 28-mile Crow Pass Marathon. This section of the river is not generally accessible to boaters.

To launch from the Eagle River Visitor Center, portage boats about a mile to the river by trail and then paddle through the sloughlike tributary that leads to the main river from the canoe landing. This area is often shallow and rocky and the portage is arduous, so most people choose to begin floating farther downriver at the North Fork Access. You'll float through a forested valley, with sweepers, and minimal maneuvering is required.

The best take-out for beginners and families is at the Eagle River Briggs bridge off Hiland Road or Eagle River Loop Road, on the left side of the river just a few miles above Eagle River Campground. If you choose to paddle another mile farther to the gauging station, which is 1 mile above the campground, scout the take-out before you run this section. There is a mile of Class II rapids just upriver of the take-out and Class III rapids just downstream of the take-out.

In early explorations, Captain Edwin F. Glenn's Army expedition in Southcentral Alaska in 1898 successfully crossed from Prince William Sound, near present-day Whittier, to Portage and Turnagain Arm. Later, Luther Kelly, a guide for Glenn, took a party up the Twentymile River and climbed over Crow Pass, then down Crow and Raven creeks and the Eagle River. They found scattered Indian camps, large numbers of Dall sheep, and innumerable mosquitoes, and described the valley as a "miniature Yosemite." This route was surveyed by the U.S. Army's Alaska Road Commission in 1910 and became part of the Iditarod Trail from Seward to Nome.

Rating: Class I–III, between Eagle River Visitor Center and the Glenn Highway bridge (just below Eagle River Campground). Starting at the visitor center, upper 13 miles is Class I; then 1 mile of Class II rapids just above gauging station take-out; then 2 miles of Class II–III before Glenn Highway bridge. Recommend taking out at the gauging station above Class III rapids. (Below the Glenn Highway bridge are Class II–IV rapids.)

Cautions: Class III rapids (Campground Rapids) just below the gauging station. Scout before running.

Trip length: 14 miles from Eagle River Visitor Center to gauging station above Eagle River Campground; allow 6 to 8 hours. Or about 8 miles from North Fork Access to gauging station; allow 2 to 4 hours.

Season: First of May through September.

Watercraft: All.

Access: In—Drive to Eagle River and take Eagle River Road 12 miles to the Eagle River Visitor Center (Chugach State Park). Portage boats about a mile to the river by trail. An alternative put-in (and the easiest, particularly for families) is about 5 miles downriver at North Fork Access point off Eagle River Road (parking lot and rest rooms). **Out**—First take-out is at the Eagle River Briggs bridge off Hiland Road or Eagle River Road, a few miles above the campground. The main take-out is at the gauging station 1 mile above the campground. To find this take-out, pass under the Eagle River Briggs bridge to Eagle River Road and look for the cable running overhead to

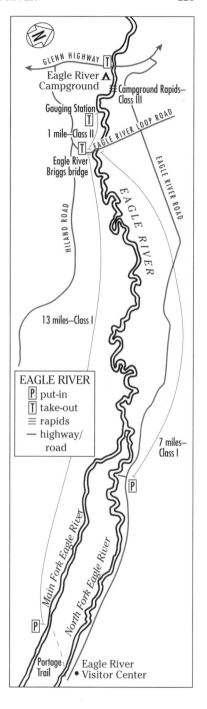

the gauging station. Some people use this location as a put-in for running Campground Rapids. Below Campground Rapids, take out on the left side at the campground. Paddlers who wish to continue downriver below the campground to run Lower Eagle River must obtain permission from Fort Richardson Army Reservation.

Land manager: Alaska Division of Parks (Chugach State Park); private. (Below Glenn Highway: Fort Richardson Army Reservation.) (See Land Managers section at back of book for address and phone information.)

Maps: Anchorage A–7, B–6, B–7.

Fish: King and coho salmon. Alaska Department of Fish and Game stocks Eagle River with king salmon fry. **Wildlife:** Moose, beaver, bald eagle.

60   GULKANA RIVER

The Gulkana is one of the most popular whitewater rivers in Alaska because of its road accessibility. From its headwaters in the lake and plateau country at the foot of the Alaska Range, the Gulkana flows through forested rolling hills for 80 miles before meeting the Copper River. The first 3 miles out of Paxson Lake are shallow, rocky Class II rapids. Here the river drops about 25 feet per mile; continuous fast water and rapids require alertness. Several old cabins with sagging sod roofs can be seen on the riverbanks.

From the river's confluence with its Middle Fork are 15 miles of Class I paddling. Here the river becomes deep and quiet as it meanders lazily through spruce forests. At River Mile 18, a canyon begins and a sign marks a quarter-mile portage on the left side of the river, around Canyon Rapids. Experienced paddlers may wish to run the Class III–IV canyon after scouting. As the current quickens, the river drops 50 feet per mile for the next 8 miles, and many a canoe has been crushed here.

From River Mile 18.5 to Mile 26 are rocky Class II rapids, with lots of maneuvering around rocks and logs. At the first bend below the portage, there is a trail that leads 1 mile to Canyon Lake—a nice hike. The river then flattens in gradient and the float to Sourdough Campground is generally Class I.

From Sourdough, the river flows 35 miles to Richardson Highway bridge (Highway Mile 127). This section is Class I, with some Class II water in the last 8 miles, with an average gradient of 15 to 25 feet per mile. Because the river closely parallels the highway, it is popular with less experienced boaters who want the challenge of trying a Class II river. At high water, there may be a 50-yard Class III rapid 2 to 3 miles below Poplar Grove Campground. On the lower end of the river you may encounter powerboats, likely en route to campsites along the river to fish for salmon. Summer weekend use of the lower Gulkana is heavy.

Ahtna Athapaskans occupied the Gulkana River Valley at least 1,000 years ago. In the 1890s, there were many villages and sod houses at Paxson Lake, a strategic spot for caribou hunting where the animals were driven into the lake and speared from skin boats. The Ahtna traveled between Tangle Lakes, Paxson Lake, and the tributaries of the Gulkana River, using the rivers and overland trails to take advantage of hunting, fishing, and gathering opportunities throughout the spring, summer, and fall, and returning to winter villages before the first snows.

Mining gained prominence after 1903. Prospectors, trappers, and opportunists moved into the Gulkana Valley. Roadhouses and lodges were built along the Gulkana and its tributaries as these became travel routes for the miners. Sourdough Lodge (Mile 147.5 on the Richardson Highway) was established in 1903 and housed travelers until December 1992, when it burned to the ground.

Rating: Class I–IV. River is Class I, with Class II rapids from Paxson Lake to the Middle Fork, Class III–IV at Canyon Rapids (can be portaged), and Class II for 8 miles below Canyon Rapids. The upper river, from Paxson Lake to Sourdough Campground, should only be run by experienced paddlers who are prepared to portage boats and gear around quarter-mile-long Canyon Rapids.

Cautions: Canyon Rapids (Class III–IV); sweepers; logjams. The upper 45 miles are far from the road; water is fast and cold.

Trip length: 80 miles from Paxson Lake to Richardson Highway bridge; allow 4 to 7 days. 45 miles from Paxson Lake to Sourdough Campground; allow 3 to 5

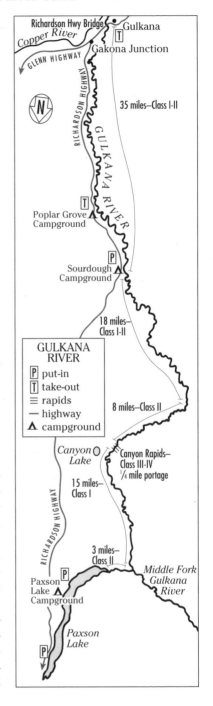

Richardson Hwy Bridge • Gulkana
Copper River   T
Gakona Junction
GLENN HIGHWAY

N

35 miles–Class I-II

GULKANA RIVER

RICHARDSON HIGHWAY

T
Poplar Grove ▲
Campground

P
Sourdough ▲
Campground

18 miles–
Class I-II

GULKANA RIVER
P put-in
T take-out
≡ rapids
— highway
▲ campground

8 miles–Class II

Canyon ○
Lake

Canyon Rapids–
Class III-IV
¼ mile portage

15 miles–
Class I

3 miles–
Class II

Middle Fork Gulkana River

RICHARDSON HIGHWAY

P
Paxson
Lake ▲
Campground

Paxson Lake

P

days. 35 miles from Sourdough Campground to Richardson Highway bridge; allow 2 days.

Season: Mid-June to mid-September.

Watercraft: Raft; inflatable kayak; hard-shell kayak or canoe for experienced paddlers.

Access: In—Put in at Paxson Lake off the Richardson Highway, either at Mile 179.5 (Paxson Lake Wayside) or Mile 175 (Paxson Lake Campground). Launching at Paxson Lake Wayside requires a 5-mile paddle down Paxson Lake to its outlet. For a shorter trip, and to avoid Canyon Rapids, put in at Sourdough Campground (35 miles above Richardson Highway bridge) or at Mile 147.4 Richardson Highway (20 miles above the bridge). Out—Take out at Mile 127 at the Richardson Highway bridge. (For a one-day Class I family trip of about 13 miles, put in at Sourdough and take out at Poplar Grove.)

Land manager: Bureau of Land Management, Anchorage; Ahtna Inc. The upper Gulkana River is a National Wild and Scenic River. (See Land Managers section at back of book for address and phone information.)

Maps: Gulkana B–3, B–4, C–4, D–4.

Fish: Arctic grayling, whitefish, burbot, king and sockeye salmon, rainbow trout. **Wildlife:** Caribou, grizzly and black bear, moose, wolf, fox, beaver, river otter, bald eagle.

61   KENAI RIVER

Beginning at Kenai Lake, the Kenai River flows west 75 miles to Cook Inlet at Kenai. Most of the river lies within Kenai National Wildlife Refuge. Ranging from Class I to III, with excellent fishing, the Kenai is one of the most popular rivers in Southcentral Alaska. Although the river is glacial in origin, the lake allows the silt to settle before the river begins its journey to the sea. Incredibly aquamarine in color, the Kenai is a beautiful river. It's no wonder so many people love it. Here are three possible trips:

Upper Kenai: Kenai Lake to Jean Creek; 13 miles; allow one day. Fishermen's Bend is a Class II stretch along the Sterling Highway. The next whitewater stretch is at Schooner Bend. Stay close to the right bank through this Class III section, which is about a mile or two above the Russian River confluence. Both of these stretches can be lined or portaged. Below the Russian River, the Kenai is Class I to Jean Creek. Pull out on the right side of the river to Jean Creek Campground. When the sockeye are running, it may be difficult to float past the Russian River through the barrier of fishing lines and lures in the hands of sportfishers on the banks and in the river.

A large raft with an oar frame is ideal for a family trip on the Kenai River.

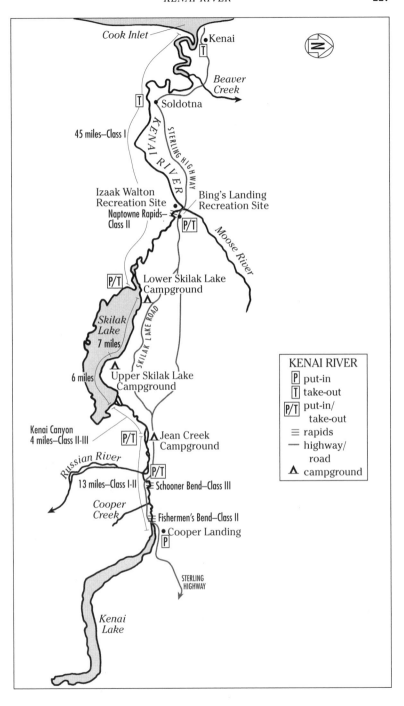

Cook Inlet

•Kenai

T

Beaver Creek

T •Soldotna

45 miles—Class I

KENAI RIVER

STERLING HIGHWAY

Izaak Walton
Recreation Site
Naptowne Rapids—
Class II

Bing's Landing
Recreation Site

P/T

Moose River

P/T Lower Skilak Lake
Campground

▲

Skilak Lake
7 miles

6 miles

SKILAK LAKE ROAD

▲
Upper Skilak Lake
Campground

Kenai Canyon
4 miles—Class II-III

P/T ▲Jean Creek
Campground

Russian River

P/T

13 miles—Class I-II ≡Schooner Bend—Class III

Cooper Creek

≡Fishermen's Bend—Class II
•Cooper Landing
P

STERLING
HIGHWAY

Kenai Lake

KENAI RIVER
P put-in
T take-out
P/T put-in/
     take-out
≡ rapids
— highway/
   road
▲ campground

Kenai Canyon: Jean Creek to lower Skilak Lake; 17 miles; allow one day to Lower Skilak Lake Campground (but if the wind comes up, you may end up waiting out the weather and spending two days). The 4 miles of the canyon (above Skilak Lake) are for experienced paddlers only: Class III, with vertical river walls that make lining or portaging impossible. Below the canyon, the river braids, and logjams and sweepers may be a hazard. From Skilak Lake, views of the Kenai Mountains are outstanding. The lake is a long haul, especially in a raft. There are 6 miles of rock bluffs to paddle or row past to the Upper Skilak Lake Campground. Watch for winds and don't attempt the lake unless the weather is calm. From the campground it's another 7 miles to Lower Skilak Lake Campground. From here, take out for access to Skilak Lake Road.

Lower Kenai: Skilak Lake to Kenai; 45 miles; allow two to three days. The lower river, basically flatwater, is one of the most heavily used rivers in Alaska. World-class king salmon and other species of salmon are produced in the river, so it may be crowded with other boats and people. Class II Naptowne Rapids is encountered about 10 miles below the outlet of Skilak Lake, just below the boat landing at Bing's Landing State Recreation Site. Below the rapids, the river passes its confluence with Moose River and Izaak Walton State Recreation Site. There are spots all along the way from Soldotna to Kenai to take out if you wish.

The Kenai Peninsula was originally inhabited by Dena'ina Athapaskans, known as Kenaitze. With the arrival of the Russians, the Kenaitze became pawns of the traders, first wooed and then forced to serve the best interests of the Russians. The hunt for sea otters was taken up with fervor; in 1785, a total of 3,000 pelts were taken from Cook Inlet, and just 15 years later the otters were nearly extinct. Many of the old villages were abandoned as the Natives were forced by necessity to move close to the trading posts. Smallpox ravaged the peninsula in the mid-1830s. The population of 3,000 in 1805 had dropped to fewer than 800 by the time the epidemic ended in 1840.

The first documented trip by a non-Native up the Kenai River was in 1850 by prospector Peter Doroshin, who found gold. Ivan Petroff followed in Doroshin's footsteps in 1875 to find gold and to pursue "business with some of the beaver trappers in the mountains." He made the journey with two companions in a three-hole, 15-foot-long baidarka made of tanned seal skin attached to a light willow frame. They made it as far as Skilak Lake.

Rating: Class I–III, depending on which section of the river is floated.
Cautions: Sweepers; logjams; collisions with people who are sport-fishing and with their lines. All whitewater sections can be scouted prior to running. Schooner Bend Rapids can be seen from Russian River Campground road at Mile 52.7 Sterling Highway. Kenai Canyon can be scouted by turning off at Mile 58 Sterling Highway to the Skilak River Road. Drive seven-tenths of a mile and then walk down a trail two-tenths of a mile to the river. Then follow the trail uphill and parallel to the river until you can see the canyon rapids. You can also get to this trail from Mile 2.3 Skilak River Road. Naptowne Rapids may be seen by taking the Sterling Highway at Mile 80.3 to Bing's Landing State Recreation Site and walking down to the end of the campground.
Trip length: See above, in description of each river section.
Season: May through October.
Watercraft: All.
Access: Trip 1. Upper Kenai—Drive the Seward Highway to Sterling Highway. Put in along Sterling Highway at any of several locations: outlet of Kenai Lake; Fishermen's Bend; Cooper Creek Campground; Sterling Highway at the Kenai River bridge; Russian River Campground access road; gravel pull-offs along Sterling Highway. Take out at Jean Creek Campground.
Trip 2. Kenai Canyon—Put in at Jean Creek Campground on Skilak Lake Road. Take out at Lower Skilak Lake Campground on Skilak Lake Road.
Trip 3. Lower Kenai—Put in at Lower Skilak Lake Campground. Take out at Kenai public dock and Ames bridge, off Beaver Loop Road and Kalifornsky Beach Road in Kenai. (Other take-out locations along the route include the Moose River bridge on the Sterling Highway; Kenai River bridge in Soldotna; Beaver Creek on the Kenai Spur Road.)
Land manager: Chugach National Forest; Kenai National Wildlife Refuge; Alaska Division of Parks; private; Native. (See Land Managers section at back of book for address and phone information.)
Maps: Seward B–8; Kenai B–1, B–2, B–3, C–2, C–3, C–4.
Fish: Whitefish, Dolly Varden, rainbow trout; king, coho, sockeye, and pink salmon. Consult Alaska Department of Fish and Game for latest sportfishing regulations. **Wildlife:** Brown and black bear, moose, wolverine, beaver, river otter, marten, waterfowl.

62 KENNICOTT RIVER AND NIZINA RIVER

These tributaries of the Copper River are alternative floats for getting onto the Chitina River. The Nizina gushes forth as silty meltwater from the Nizina Glacier. Big water and waves are encountered immediately. The scenery along the Nizina is outstanding and there is good hiking in the upper river area. Folded gray limestone cliffs rise from the water, topped by lava and igneous rocks, with jagged peaks towering above. Sourdough Peak stands out for its unique rock glaciers—slides of rock mixed with ice that flow slowly down the mountain, creating the visual effect of a glacier.

The Kennicott issues from the Kennicott and Root glaciers in the Wrangell Mountains and enters the Nizina just above Nizina Canyon. The canyon, narrow and sheer-walled, is comparable in size to the canyons in Yosemite and Zion national parks. Take care as you enter the canyon, as the turns are tight, continuous, and

Nizina River, Wrangell-St. Elias National Park and Preserve.

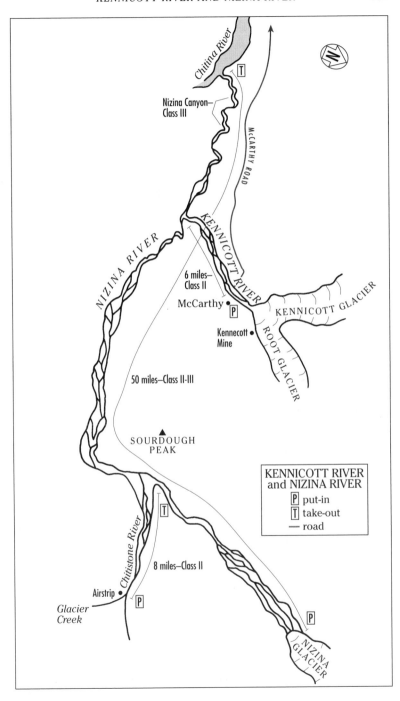

strenuous. There are big holes, eddies, and whirlpools in the Class III rapids. Below the canyon, the Nizina churns along swiftly, Class II all the way to its confluence with the Chitina River.

Rating: Class II–III.

Cautions: The Kennicott is shallow, fast, and braided and during low water levels requires lining or portaging. The upper Nizina has a 20-mile section with fast water and difficult rapids. Difficult Class III rapids in Nizina Canyon.

Trip length: 14 miles on the Kennicott River from end of McCarthy Road to the Kennicott's confluence with the Nizina; allow 1 day. 45 to 50 miles on the Nizina River from the Nizina Glacier to the river's confluence with the Chitina River; allow 5 to 8 days.

Season: Late May/early June through September.

Watercraft: 10- to 15-foot raft; inflatable or hard-shell whitewater kayak.

Access to the Kennicott River: In—Launch boats at end (Mile 61) of the McCarthy Road. To visit historic town of McCarthy, cross the Kennicott River on two handpulled trams for several hundred feet, then follow the road a quarter mile to a fork. McCarthy is 1 mile to the right; the Kennecott copper mine is 5 miles to the left. Out— Take out at confluence of Nizina and Chitina rivers by charter wheelplane out of McCarthy or Chitina, or continue down the Chitina River. (See the Chitina River trip description in this book.)

Access to the Nizina River: In—Fly to Nizina Glacier via Supercub out of McCarthy or Chitina, landing on short gravel strip on rock terrace above the Nizina. Portage for half a mile to a mile down multi-level terraces to the riverbank. Alternative put-in by charter wheelplane to Glacier Creek airstrip. Float Glacier Creek to Chitistone River, then down Chitistone to the Nizina. Out—Take out at confluence of Nizina and Chitina rivers by wheelplane out of McCarthy or Chitina, or continue down the Chitina River.

Land manager: Wrangell-St. Elias National Park and Preserve; state; private. (See Land Managers section at back of book for address and phone information.)

Maps: McCarthy A–6, B–6, B–7, B–8; Valdez B–1, C–1, C–2.

Fish: Arctic grayling; coho, sockeye, chum, and pink salmon spawn in clearwater tributaries of the Chitina. **Wildlife:** Brown/grizzly bear, moose, wolf, coyote, migratory waterfowl.

63   KNIK RIVER

The Knik River offers a short float on a glacial river. Flowing swift, cold, and silty out of the Knik Glacier, the river courses about 26 miles through the lower Matanuska Valley, in the shadow of Pioneer Peak, to Knik Arm. The upper river is accessible from Knik River Road for paddlers who wish to try its more challenging braided waters. The lower river is easily accessible from the Old Glenn Highway bridge at Mile 9. Launch boats from the north side of the bridge and enjoy a leisurely 9-mile float to the New Glenn Highway bridge at Mile 30.

Some paddlers continue floating down into Knik Arm all the way to Anchorage, but silty waters, weird currents, wind, and extreme tides all combine to make this a risky venture. Don't try it without local knowledge and experience. Even powerboaters approach this body of water with great caution.

Dena'ina Athapaskans living near the mouth of the Knik River in the 19th century traveled up to Jim Creek and Swan Lake to hunt in the mountains and catch salmon in the fall. They dried the salmon

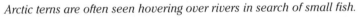

Arctic terns are often seen hovering over rivers in search of small fish.

there and before freezeup would return to the winter village in skin boats.

Rating: Class I–II.

Cautions: Cold, silty glacial water; sweepers, clumps of cutbanks, and partially submerged tree roots.

Trip length: 15 miles from end of Knik River Road to Old Glenn Highway bridge (Class II); 4 hours. 9 miles from Old Glenn Highway bridge to the New Glenn Highway bridge (Class I); 4 hours.

Season: Late April through September.

Watercraft: All.

Access: In—Take Glenn Highway 29.6 miles north of Anchorage and turn onto Old Glenn Highway. Put in at Old Glenn Highway bridge, Mile 9, on the north side. To float upper river, follow Knik River Road 11.4 miles to where it dead ends, and put in on the river. Out—Take out at New Glenn Highway bridge, Mile 30, on the north side.

Land manager: Private; state; Matanuska-Susitna Borough.

Maps: Anchorage B–5, B–6, B–7, C–6.

Wildlife: Waterfowl and birds, particularly early in the spring, just after breakup.

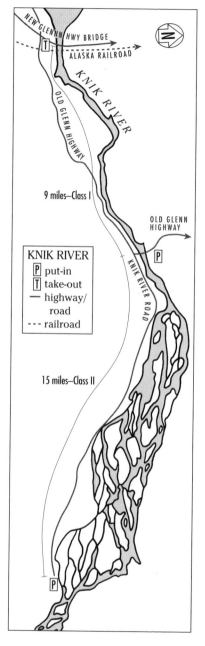

KNIK RIVER
P put-in
T take-out
— highway/road
--- railroad

64   KROTO CREEK, MOOSE CREEK, AND DESHKA RIVER

Beginning at Kroto Lake, Kroto Creek flows south through forested hills, flats, and wetlands to meet Moose Creek, forming the Deshka River. Kroto Creek meanders and twists freely across the Susitna Valley, roughly paralleling the Susitna River, providing paddlers an opportunity to explore a stream free of powerboats. Moose Creek begins at a small unnamed lake several miles east of Kroto Creek and flows roughly parallel to that creek for about 40 miles before the two join to become the Deshka. In the upper reaches of Kroto and Moose creeks, there are rolling hills and forested flatlands.

The Deshka meanders southward with many shallow riffles and midchannel gravel bars over the course of nearly 30 miles before entering the Susitna River about 8 miles southwest of Willow. For most of its course, it traverses rich wetlands. In open areas on the river, there are spectacular views of the Alaska Range and the Talkeetna Mountains. The river is darkish in color from the tannins draining off wetlands. There are many camps, buildings, and docks below Neil Lake. (Upstream, however, Kroto and Moose creeks are relatively pristine.)

The mouth of the Deshka is very congested from late May to mid-June when the salmon are running. Powerboats anchor in midchannel, and floatplanes land and take off. The Deshka offers excellent fishing in an accessible, moderately developed river corridor. If you want to avoid the congested lower river, take out at Neil Lake. If you don't mind crowds, float all the way to the mouth.

The rich fish and wildlife habitat of the Deshka River attracted the Dena'ina to its riverbanks, where they built winter houses on the bluffs and fish camps along the river for summer and fall. At the mouth of the Deshka River at Kroto is the site of a former Dena'ina village first reported by Robert Muldrow of the U.S. Geological Survey in 1900.

Rating: Class I. Upper Kroto Creek has some sharp bends that require vigilant maneuvering.
Cautions: Sweepers; logjams; powerboats on the Deshka River.
Trip length: Option 1—About 25 miles down Kroto Creek from Amber Lake to Neil Lake, just below confluence of the two creeks;

allow 2 days. **Option 2**—About 35 miles down Moose Creek from Oilwell Road to Neil Lake; allow 2 to 3 days. **Option 3**—About 25 miles from Neil Lake to Deshka mouth; allow 2 to 3 days.

Season: June through August. Low water in September may hinder progress.

Watercraft: Canoe, kayak, or small raft. Larger rafts are suitable on Deshka River.

Access: Option 1—Amber Lake is accessible by floatplane from Talkeetna, Kashwitna Lake, Willow, or Anchorage. Float down Amber Creek about a mile to reach Kroto Creek. Take out by floatplane at Neil Lake. A slough below Neil Lake and a couple portage trails provide access to Neil Lake from the Deshka River. **Option 2**—Take Petersville Road (Mile 243.2 on the George Parks Highway) for about 6 miles; then turn left on Oilwell Road and follow it for about 5.5 miles to Moose Creek. Take out by floatplane at Neil Lake. **Option 3**—Continue down Deshka River to its confluence with the Susitna River for pickup by floatplane. Boat taxi may also be arranged from mouth of Deshka. It is also possible to continue downriver on the Susitna (see Lower Susitna River description).

Land manager: Kroto Creek/Moose Creek State Recreation River; Matanuska-Susitna Borough; private. (See Land Managers section at back of book

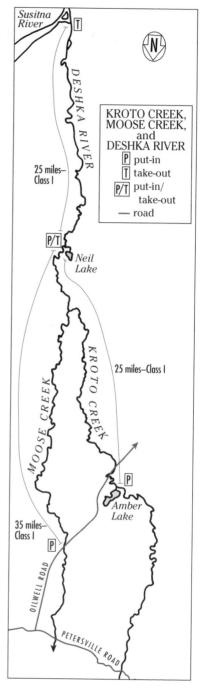

Moose are a common sight along many of Alaska's rivers and streams.

for address and phone information.)

Maps: Talkeetna A–1, A–2, B–2; Tyonek C–1, D–1, D–2.

Fish: Rainbow trout; king, coho, sockeye, chum, and pink salmon. Kroto and Moose creeks are closed to king salmon fishing above their confluence; catch-and-release only for rainbow trout. **Wildlife:** Grizzly and black bear, beaver, moose, muskrat, bald eagle, trumpeter swan, merganser.

65   LAKE CREEK

From Chelatna Lake in the foothills of the Alaska Range, Lake Creek flows southeast 54 miles to its confluence with the Yentna River. Seven-mile-long Chelatna Lake is the largest lake in the Matanuska-Susitna Valley. Lake Creek varies in width from 150 to 250 feet and falls an average of 25 feet in elevation per mile. A popular fishing stream, Lake Creek offers outstanding views of Mount McKinley, Mount Foraker, and the Alaska Range.

After the first couple miles of placid water, Lake Creek becomes swift, rocky, and wild. The first 36 miles are Class I–III, with continuous stretches of exposed rocks and whitewater. A canyon beginning about 3 miles below Shovel Lake reaches its climax just below Quiet Lake with a challenging set of Class III–IV rapids. The last 8 miles are Class I and in this section you are likely to encounter motorboats. A 43-mile section between Mile 2.8 and Mile 45.9 is off limits to motorboats from May 15 to August 20.

There are numerous mining claims, cabins, lodges, and private lands in the area, particularly around Chelatna Lake and along the lower 6 miles of the stream. Good camping sites are available along Lake Creek except at its mouth, which can be congested and noisy with floatplanes and powerboats during peak fishing season (mid-June through early August).

Prospectors and trappers moved up into the Lake Creek country around the turn of the century, traveling overland rather than trying to pole upriver. By 1910, there were many gold mines in the Yentna and Lake Creek areas.

Rating: Class I–IV. Continuous stretches of Class III whitewater; a serious Class IV canyon exists about halfway down the river. This river should be attempted only by expert paddlers.
Cautions: Class IV canyon beginning about 3 miles below Shovel Lake; you can scout and then portage or line boats along the right side of the river on a portage trail. The portage is 150 to 200 yards. Class IV rapids about 5 miles above Yenlo Creek.
Trip length: 54 miles from Chelatna Lake to Lake Creek's confluence with the Yentna River; allow 4 to 5 days.
Season: Late May through end of September. Check with local pilots to see if Chelatna Lake is ice-free.

Watercraft: Kayak or raft.

Access: In—Put in on Chelatna Lake by floatplane from Kashwitna Lake, Willow, or Anchorage, or at the public airstrip at the south end of Lake Creek by wheelplane from Talkeetna or Anchorage. Out—Take out by floatplane on the Yentna River, or continue down Yentna River to the Susitna River, a distance of about 32 miles.

Land manager: Lake Creek State Recreation River; Matanuska-Susitna Borough; private. (See Land Managers section at back of book for address and phone information.)

Maps: Talkeetna A–2, A–3, B–3; Tyonek D–3.

Fish: Rainbow trout, grayling, Dolly Varden; king, chum, silver, and pink salmon. **Wildlife:** Moose, brown/grizzly and black bear, bald eagle.

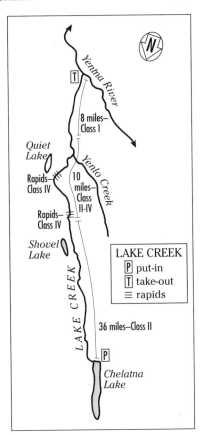

66 LITTLE SUSITNA RIVER

Because of easy road access and closeness to Anchorage and Palmer-Wasilla, the Little Susitna (Susitna means "sandy river" in Dena'ina) is one of Southcentral Alaska's most popular fishing streams. The lower river is a perfect paddle for novices who enjoy getting out into the wilds and doing some fishing.

Beginning as meltwater from the Mint Glacier in the Talkeetna Mountains, the Little Susitna, or Little Su, begins as a clear, rushing mountain stream flowing through a constricted canyon over huge rocks and boulders, dropping at a rate of 20 feet per mile. It eventually slows to just 2 to 4 miles per hour, meandering muddily across marshy lowlands, and reaches Cook Inlet after 110 miles. The terrain changes from steep mountain and hillsides to flat and rolling lowlands covered with forests of spruce and hardwood. The middle section of the river, particularly in the Nancy Lake Creek area, is characterized by wetlands.

Above the George Parks Highway, the river is closed to salmon fishing. Below the highway, powerboats are used widely on the river, so you may want to plan your trip to take advantage of non-motorized weekends. On the first and third weekends of each month, a 27-mile section of the river from just above the Little Susitna Access Road to 1 mile below Nancy Lake Creek is designated a nonmotorized area. On the second and fourth weekends, this section is designated for powerboats only. On the fifth weekend of the month and on weekdays, there are no restrictions. The Little Su is most heavily used when salmon fishing is at its peak, from late May to late June.

The Iditarod National Historic Trail, the winter mail and supply route from Seward to Nome, crosses the lower Little Susitna River near Yohn Lake. The Iditarod Trail Sled Dog Race travels this same section.

Rating: Class I (14.5 miles) from Schrock Road to George Parks Highway; below George Parks Highway to the river mouth are an additonal 69.5 miles of Class I.

Cautions: From Schrock Road to George Parks Highway—Sweepers; two permanent logjams (easy to portage or line). Below George Parks Highway—Sweepers, jetboats, airboats.

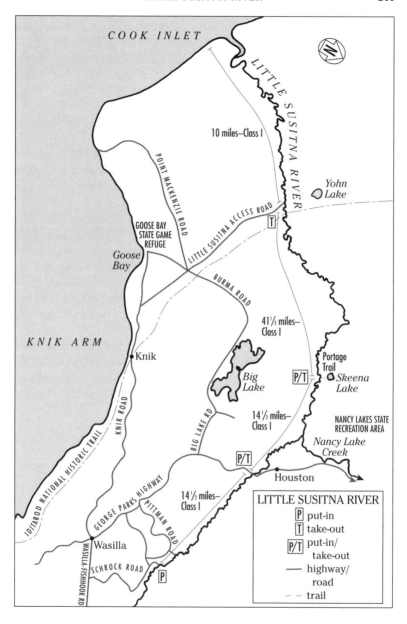

Trip length: 84 miles from Schrock Road bridge to river mouth; allow 4 to 5 days. Floats of various lengths, from a half-day to 3 days, are possible, with put-ins and take-outs accessible by road. Most popular float, from the George Parks Highway to Little Susitna

Access Road off the Burma Road, is about 56 miles; allow 3 to 4 days. Another popular trip is to paddle 14.5 miles downriver from the George Parks Highway to Skeena Lake trail, portage three-quarters of a mile to Skeena Lake, and then paddle on the Nancy Lakes State Recreation Area canoe trail system; allow 3 days.

Season: Late May through September.

Watercraft: All craft are suitable for floats beginning below Schrock Road bridge.

Access: In—Put in from Schrock Road by turning right off the George Parks Highway (at Mile 48.5) onto Pittman Road, a few miles west of Wasilla. Follow Pittman to Schrock Road and look for unimproved road leading to the river. You can also put in where the Little Susitna crosses under the George Parks Highway, at Mile 57.1. Out—Take out (or put in) at the Nancy Lakes State Recreation Area or at the Little Susitna Access Road, which is also called Burma Road. This road begins two-tenths of a mile west of the Lake Marion turnoff on Big Lake Road. Burma Road can also be reached from Knik Road. Take Knik Road from Wasilla and drive past Knik to the Point Mackenzie Road. This road intersects with Burma Road and leads to the Little Susitna Access at Burma Landing.

Land manager: Hatcher Pass Public Use Area, Little Susitna State Recreation River; Susitna Flats State Game Refuge; Matanuska-Susitna Borough; private. (See Land Managers section at back of book for address and phone information.)

Maps: Anchorage C–7, C–8; Tyonek B–1, C–1.

Fish: Whitefish, burbot, Dolly Varden, rainbow trout, whitefish; king, coho, sockeye, chum, and pink salmon. **Wildlife:** Grizzly and black bear, moose, beaver, muskrat, bald eagle, merganser.

67   NABESNA RIVER

Flowing from the terminus of the Nabesna Glacier on the north side of the Wrangell Mountains within Wrangell-St. Elias National Park and Preserve, the Nabesna River flows northerly for about 80 miles to its confluence with the Chisana River, where the two streams become the Tanana River. The Nabesna cuts through a deep canyonlike valley before entering a broad outwash plain. The river is steep and swift in its upper reaches, gradually lessening as it enters Tetlin National Wildlife Refuge.

Once in the flats, the Nabesna flows across an undulating plain broken by hills, forests of spruce and birch, lakes, and extensive marshes. The upper 20 miles of the river are Class I–II, with a gradient of 20 feet per mile. Fast choppy water and gravel bars require maneuvering skills. The next 20-mile section continues to have a swift current, with an average gradient of 12 feet per mile, and also requires maneuvering skill through the many braided channels, shallows, bends, and back eddies. The lower 40 miles has a slow current and an average gradient of 5 feet per mile.

Tetlin Athapaskans historically lived a nomadic hunting life in the upper Tanana region. At the time of first non-Native contact, the Tetlin had seven communities on the Nabesna. When Lieutenant Henry Allen made his trip up the Copper River and down the Tanana River in 1885, the Tetlin Athapaskans referred to the Tanana River as the Nabesna. When Allen returned 13 years later, he found that the name Nabesna was no longer being used. Allen liked "this euphonious Indian name," and so applied the name to the chief tributary of the upper Tanana. Northway, near the confluence of the Nabesna and Chisana rivers, is a traditional Tetlin Native village which continues the rich tradition of hunting, trapping, fishing, dancing, and crafts.

Rating: Swift Class I–II. Recommended for intermediate or better paddlers.
Cautions: Cold, swift, silty water; braided channels. Glacially fed rivers pulse with the weather, with water level rising significantly by afternoon on warm, sunny days or on warm, rainy days. Keep this in mind when planning your paddling day.
Trip length: 80 miles or less; allow 3 days.

Season: June through September.
Watercraft: Raft, hard-shell kayak, or decked canoe.
Access: In—Fly by charter wheel-plane from Northway to Orange Hill airstrip near terminus of Nabesna Glacier. Or, drive the Glenn Highway to Tok cutoff at Gakona Junction and follow for 60 miles to the Nabesna Road. Follow the Nabesna Road, a 4-wheel-drive, poorly maintained route, to Mile 41. Ford several creeks along the way. Follow a 5-mile-long trail from Mile 41 to the river (including lining boat down Cabin Creek). Out—Take out at Northway or at the Alaska Highway at the confluence of the Nabesna and Chisana rivers, where they become the Tanana River.
Land manager: Wrangell-St. Elias National Park and Preserve; Tetlin National Wildlife Refuge; Northway Natives Inc. (See Land Managers section at back of book for address and phone information.)
Maps: Tanacross A–2; Nabesna B–4, C–3, C–4, D–2, D–3.
Fish: Arctic grayling, chum salmon. **Wildlife:** Grizzly and black bear, Dall sheep, moose, wolf, lynx, red fox, trumpeter swans, osprey.

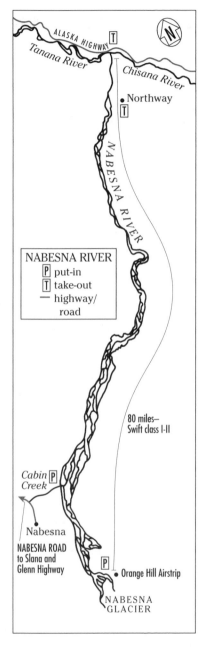

NABESNA RIVER
P put-in
T take-out
— highway/ road

80 miles–
Swift class I-II

Cabin P
Creek

Nabesna
NABESNA ROAD
to Slana and
Glenn Highway

P Orange Hill Airstrip

NABESNA
GLACIER

68   PORTAGE CREEK

Portage Creek offers a short, swift paddle from Portage Lake to the Seward Highway, through forest and past steep mountains with hanging glaciers—a very pleasant day trip from Anchorage when the weather is good. The stream braids and twists its way over gravel bars and around cutbanks as it flows through a deeply etched glacial valley, with the Chugach Mountains on one side and the Kenai Mountains on the other, offering dramatic looks at Explorer and Middle glaciers. On a sunny day, the views are breathtaking. But beware: often you can depart Anchorage on a beautiful sunny day, then drive around Turnagain Arm only to find windy, rainy, whiteout conditions in Portage Valley. The clouds and storms from Prince William Sound spill over Portage Pass into the valley.

Portage and Burns glaciers were well-traveled portage routes in the past as Dena'ina Indians and Chugach Eskimos traveled between Cook Inlet and Prince William Sound. Russian fur traders learned of the route and traversed the region. During the winter of 1902–1903, James Ward and a local prospector helped two other prospectors drag a 24-foot boat over Portage Glacier to Portage Creek; in the

Northway is a logical take-out for a trip on the Nabesna. (See page 243.)

spring they floated down to Hope. At that time, there was no Portage Lake, because the terminus of Portage Glacier reached nearly to the site of the present-day Begich- Boggs Visitor Center. By 1914 the glacier had retreated, forming the lake. Now the face of the glacier is nearly 4 miles away, across 660-foot-deep Portage Lake.

Rating: Class I, unless swollen by snowmelt or rain, when the upper 2 miles can become Class II.

Cautions: Brush, submerged logs, shallow water; high winds during storms.

Trip length: 6 miles; allow 2 to 3 hours.

Season: May through September.

Watercraft: All.

Access: In—Drive the Seward Highway to Mile 78.9 and take Portage Glacier turnoff; follow the Portage Glacier Road 5 miles to the parking lot at the outlet of Portage Lake. Put in at the outlet. Out—Take out at the Portage Creek bridge at Mile 79 on the Seward Highway.

Land manager: Chugach National Forest. (See Land Managers section at back of book for address and phone information.)

Maps: Seward D–5, D–6.

Fish: Dolly Varden; king, coho, sockeye, chum, and pink salmon. **Wildlife:** Moose, beaver, river otter, weasel, bald eagle, waterfowl.

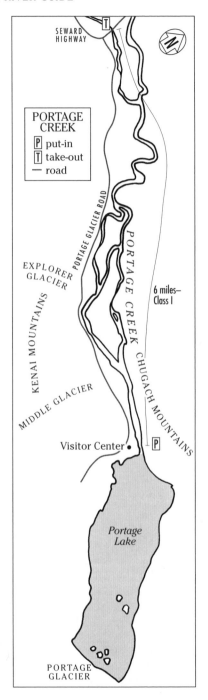

69 UPPER SUSITNA RIVER

Originating in three glacial tributaries on the southern flanks of the Alaska Range, the Susitna flows southward through a network of braided channels for about 60 miles, then curves southwest and winds its way in a single deep channel for 140 miles through forested country to Gold Creek on the Alaska Railroad, and then braids again for another 90 miles to Cook Inlet.

A cold, silty, powerful river, the Susitna offers different paddling experiences in different sections. Devils Canyon on the upper Susitna is one of the most formidable and challenging stretches of big whitewater in North America. The 15-mile canyon is rated up to Class VI, a rating that, to many expert paddlers, means the river section is nearly impossible to run. But several boaters have actually run the canyon, which begins at the river's junction with Devil Creek and encloses Gorge Rapids (or The Pearly Gates, as kayakers refer to it) as it squeezes the frothing whitewater through narrow, confining walls.

The headwaters of the Susitna offer spectacular views of rugged glaciated mountains in the Alaska Range. With the exception of the Denali Highway bridge crossing the upper river and the development in that area, the Susitna basin remains undeveloped.

In 1958, a U.S. Army group attempted to run the upper Susitna in a 50-foot boat with a decked bow, equipped with two engines. Two days after the group departed, legendary bush pilot Don Sheldon spotted the wreckage of the boat floating downriver and the eight men huddled on a narrow ledge at the base of the canyon wall. In his small floatplane, he rescued all of them, making numerous daring runs into the high canyon and landing in the river rapids to retrieve the men.

Russians may have been the first non-Natives to penetrate the Susitna. In 1844, Malakov, an employee of the Russian American Company, went a short way upstream to look for good fur-bearer country. In 1881, Hieromonk Nikita and another churchman took two three-holed baidarkas into Knik Arm and up the Susitna on missionary work. Before the century was over, American adventurers and prospectors were dragging boats and sledges upriver as far as Devils Canyon. Gold was discovered at Valdez Creek in 1903 and great efforts were made to transport supplies in and gold out.

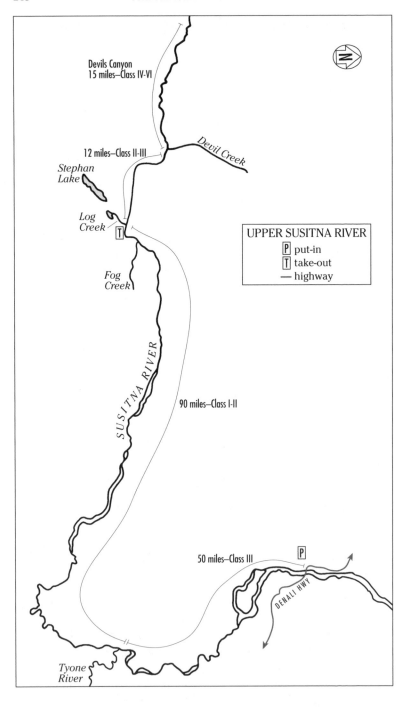

Devils Canyon
15 miles—Class IV-VI

12 miles—Class II-III

Devil Creek

*Stephan
Lake*

*Log
Creek*

T

*Fog
Creek*

UPPER SUSITNA RIVER
P put-in
T take-out
— highway

SUSITNA RIVER

90 miles—Class I-II

50 miles—Class III

P

DENALI HWY

*Tyone
River*

Rating: Class I–III (before Devils Canyon).

Cautions: Cold, swift, silty water; difficult to read channels. Don't miss the turnoff into Log Creek or you will enter Class VI Devils Canyon.

Trip length: About 140 miles from Mile 79.5 Denali Highway to Log Creek (before Devils Canyon); allow 7 to 10 days.

Season: June through September.

Watercraft: Raft, hard-shell kayak, or inflatable kayak.

Access: In—Put in at Mile 79.5 Denali Highway at Susitna River bridge. Take out at Log Creek on left side of river, third creek downstream after a sharp right bend in the river (in T31N, R3E, Sec. 23, Talkeetna Mts. D–4 topo map). Paddle up Log Creek to small lake at head of creek or portage to Stephan Lake. Out—Fly out from small lake or from Stephan Lake by floatplane to Kashwitna Lake, Willow, or Anchorage. Or you can arrange for pickup by wheelplane on a gravel bar upriver of the sharp bend. Check with pilots, as gravel bars change every year.

Land manager: State; private. (See Land Managers section at back of book for address and phone information.)

Maps: Healy A–2; Talkeetna Mountains C–1, C–2, C–4, D–1, D–2, D–3, D–4.

Fish: Arctic grayling, northern pike, whitefish, burbot, rainbow trout, lake trout; king, coho, pink, sockeye, and chum salmon.

Wildlife: Caribou, grizzly and black bear, moose, wolf, beaver, bald eagle, migratory waterfowl.

70 LOWER SUSITNA RIVER

With Denali (Mount McKinley) and the Alaska Range dominating the view, a float down this section of the swift, powerful Susitna is a pleasure. Ten miles into the trip that begins at Gold Creek, Curry Ridge rises on the west side of the river between the Parks Highway and the Alaska Range. Be sure to take the far left channel above Talkeetna if you want to go ashore at Talkeetna. The Susitna is highly braided, with many shallow riffles and sweepers. A cold, glacial river, it cannot be taken lightly. Paddle carefully, and enjoy the scenery.

Rating: Fast Class I; in high water can become Class II; standing waves may be encountered which can swamp canoes.
Cautions: Cold, swift, silty water; difficult to read channels and see rocks; logjams.
Trip length: About 35 to 40 miles from Gold Creek to Talkeetna; allow 2 days. About 90 miles from Talkeetna to the mouth of

The Susitna River courses through a mosaic of forest and wetlands.

Alexander Creek; allow 4 to 5 days. Other trip lengths can be planned, depending on take-out location. An additional 12 miles down Skwentna River to Skwentna.

Season: June through September.

Watercraft: All.

Access: In—Take the Alaska Railroad from Talkeetna to Gold Creek. Put in on Gold Creek at its confluence with the Susitna River. Out—Take out at Talkeetna. Or you can take out at the George Parks Highway bridge at Mile 104 above Willow, 12 miles downstream from Talkeetna. You can also continue paddling down to Willow Creek Parkway, Mile 70.8 on the George Parks Highway. You may also decide to go on to Susitna, the mouth of Alexander Creek, or Cook Inlet; make arrangements for boat, wheelplane, or floatplane pickup if you decide to continue.

Land manager: State; private.

Maps: Talkeetna A–1, B–1, C–1; Talkeetna Mountains C–6, D–6; Tyonek D–1.

Fish: Arctic grayling, Dolly Varden; king, coho, sockeye, pink, and chum salmon. **Wildlife:** Caribou, grizzly and black bear, moose, wolf, beaver, bald eagle, migratory waterfowl.

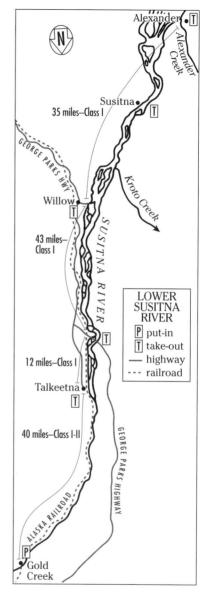

35 miles–Class I

43 miles–Class I

12 miles–Class I

40 miles–Class I-II

LOWER
SUSITNA
RIVER
P put-in
T take-out
— highway
--- railroad

71 TALACHULITNA CREEK AND TALACHULITNA RIVER

From headwaters flowing off Beluga Mountain, the Talachulitna River courses south then northerly for 64 miles to join the Skwentna River. Talachulitna Creek, a major tributary, begins northwest of Judd Lake and flows easterly through Talachulitna and Judd Lakes to empty into the Talachulitna River. A small clearwater river with excellent fishing, the Tal is one of Southcentral Alaska's most popular fly-in fishing float trips.

Tal Creek is shallow, meandering, and narrow. Beaver dams occasionally go across the main channel. Tal Creek is a designated nonmotorized area between June 15 and August 20, and is rarely used at all by motorboaters. For this reason, most paddlers begin their Talachulitna trips on the creek. Undeveloped and relatively remote, the creek offers a quality wilderness-type float. The first couple miles are shallow and rocky; lining or dragging boats is usually necessary. Normally slow Class I, at higher water there may be some Class II sections.

Below The Forks (confluence of Tal Creek and Tal River), powerboats will likely be encountered. In this section the river widens to 100 feet. Lodges and fishing guides operate fishing trips on this section. The river also is closed to motorized use from June 15 to August 20 from Hell's Gate to the river's confluence with Thursday Creek.

Hell's Gate, about 14 miles below the confluence of Tal Creek and Tal River, is unrunnable at all water levels due to large boulders, but this 100-yard-long section can be lined. Hell's Gate is the beginning of narrow, steep Talachulitna Canyon (T19N, R12W, Sec. 34 on Tyonek topo map), where over the course of about 15 miles, the river plummets into four major gorges, with rapids up to Class IV, separated by swift Class II water. Below Hell's Gate, the current quickens and there are more rocky rapids in quick succession. About 5 miles downriver is another canyon with Class II–III rapids. Below are two more canyons with Class II–III whitewater as the river pushes through narrow slots and over boulders. The canyons end about 3 miles above the mouth of the river, and it becomes Class I–II, approximately 500 feet wide, to its mouth at the Skwentna River.

Rating: Class I–IV. Upper 18 miles (Tal Creek) is Class I, suitable for

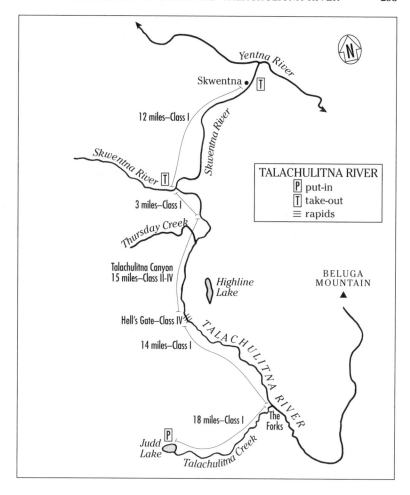

relatively inexperienced floaters. Lower river requires technical skill for Class III–IV canyons; suitable for experienced whitewater paddlers.

Cautions: Rocks; logjams; sweepers; whitewater through canyons. Some of the rapids can be lined.

Trip length: 18 miles on Talachulitna Creek from Judd Lake to confluence with Talachulitna River; allow 3 days. An additional 32 miles down Talachulitna River to confluence with Skwentna River; allow 5 to 7 days for entire 50-mile trip.

Season: Late May to October.

Watercraft: Small to medium-size raft; whitewater kayak; canoe might be suitable for expert canoeists.

When a squall hits or winds are high, why fight it? Take a break and relax.

Access: In—Fly by charter floatplane from Anchorage, Willow, or Skwentna to Judd Lake. Out—Several possibilities: Take out at settlement of Skwentna on the Skwentna River; or take out by charter wheelplane from beach on left side of the Skwentna 1 mile below the mouth of the Talachulitna, across from the USGS gauging station; or take out by floatplane from the mouth of the Tal (a couple miles down the Skwentna) or at midpoint on the Tal at Mile 18 (above the rapids). You may also be able to catch the mail plane from Skwentna to Anchorage.

Land manager: Talachulitna State Recreation River; Matanuska-Susitna Borough; private. (See Land Managers section at back of book for address and phone information.)

Maps: Tyonek C–4, C–5, D–4.

Fish: Arctic grayling, rainbow trout; king, coho, sockeye, chum, and pink salmon. Catch-and-release only for rainbow trout. **Wildlife:** Grizzly and black bear, moose, wolf, beaver, bald eagle, trumpeter swan.

72 TALKEETNA RIVER

Originating at the terminus of Talkeetna Glacier in the Talkeetna Mountains, this swift, silt-laden river flows northwest, then southwest, for more than 90 miles to its confluence with the Susitna River. Draining an area of 1,790 miles, the Talkeetna River is fed by several small clear tributaries. The river traverses forests of spruce and birch and offers an exciting and scenic float, with a dramatic canyon on the upper river. The upper Talkeetna is considered by some to be the premier wilderness whitewater trip in Alaska.

Talkeetna Canyon, which begins about 45 miles from the river's headwaters and a couple miles below Prairie Creek, is a steep-walled 12.5-mile slot that constricts the river into a surging froth of whitewater. This section presents 14 miles of continuous Class III–IV rapids. The river drops an average of 30 feet per mile through the canyon, with a maximum drop of 40 feet per mile. There are a few trails for scouting the rapids in the canyon, and their location is fairly obvious from the topography of the land. At the entrance to the canyon lies a serious Class IV rapid, known as Toilet Bowl, which has been known to flip rafts. The rapids continue down to Iron Creek.

Campsites in this section are poor because of the steep terrain and because there are few eddies to safely land a boat. Below the canyon, the river is Class I, and campsites are numerous but generally best at creek junctions. Below Iron Creek, you may encounter powerboats. From mid-June to mid-July, the peak king salmon fishing period, the Talkeetna is used by many powerboaters and fishers.

Dena'ina Athapaskans historically used the Talkeetna throughout the year, traveling with sleds in the winter and in birchbark boats during the summer. The name Talkeetna is a Dena'ina name meaning "river of plenty."

Rating: Class I–IV, with one of the longest stretches of continuous whitewater in North America (14 miles). The upper Talkeetna is a remote wilderness whitewater trip, suitable for only for experienced kayakers and rafters. Lower half is swift Class I and suitable for intermediate boaters.

Cautions: Class IV rapids in deep, inaccessible canyon; sweepers and powerboats in lower river.

Trip length: About 69 miles from Yellowjacket Creek airstrip to Talkeetna; allow 3 to 5 days. About 30 miles from Iron Creek to Talkeetna; allow 2 days.

Season: June through September.

Watercraft: Raft or whitewater kayak.

Access: In—To run the upper river, fly by charter wheelplane to Yellowjacket Creek airstrip along the Talkeetna River. To float lower river, put in at confluence of Talkeetna River and Iron Creek by jetboat. Out— Take out at public boat launch a mile above the mouth of the Talkeetna.

Land manager: Talkeetna State Recreation River; private. (See Land Managers section at back of book for address and phone information.)

Maps: Talkeetna B–1; Talkeetna Mountains B–4, B–5, B–6, C–4, C–5.

Fish: Arctic grayling, burbot, rainbow trout, Dolly Varden; king, coho, sockeye, pink, and chum salmon. **Wildlife:** Grizzly and black bear, moose, bald eagle.

73   TOKOSITNA RIVER

The Tokositna provides a fine one-day paddle for intermediate boaters. Beginning as meltwater at the snouts of Tokositna and Kanikula glaciers, the Tokositna River meanders southeast, then northeast, for about 30 miles to its confluence with the Chulitna River.

The upper portion, northwest of Home Lake, is extremely swift and braided. East of Home Lake, the river is still moderately swift, but is not difficult to float. The scenery is spectacular, with glaciers and mountains towering above the river valley to the north. The lower river becomes a single channel and the current slows dramatically toward its confluence with the Chulitna.

Early climbers seeking access to Mount McKinley ascended the Chulitna and lower Tokositna rivers in boats, going as far as 2 miles up the Tokositna, then hiking overland to the Ruth Glacier. Frederick A. Cook was the first; in 1906, he ascended the river to Alder Creek in a narrow, 40-foot-long launch with a 25-horsepower motor. He commented on the "boiling rapids" running over huge boulders.

Alaskan painter Sydney Laurence was also drawn to Mount McKinley via the Chulitna and Tokositna rivers. In 1913, he hauled his art supplies by dogsled to the glaciers at the headwaters of the Tokositna and spent the summer painting. He later descended the river with his wife, Jeanne, and a group of 10 miners, 11 dogs, and a mountain of gear.

Rating: Swift Class II.
Cautions: Swift current, icy water.
Trip length: 25 miles; allow 1 to 2 days.
Season: June through September.
Watercraft: Hard-shell kayak; inflatable kayak; canoe; small to medium-size raft.
Access: In—Fly by charter plane from Talkeetna to gravel bars in vicinity of Home Lake, or by floatplane to Home Lake and portage to the river. Out—Take out below confluence of Tokositna and Chulitna rivers on George Parks Highway at Mile 132.8.
Land manager: Denali State Park. (See Land Managers section at back of book for address and phone information.)

Maps: Healy A–5, A–6; Talkeetna B–1, C–1; Talkeetna Mountains D–6.
Fish: All five species of salmon inhabit the river, but with the swift current and silty water, it's unlikely you'll see any of them. **Wildlife:** Grizzly bear, wolf, moose, waterfowl.

74   TYONE RIVER

The Tyone River makes a nice trip for families or novice paddlers who are experienced wilderness travelers. Rising in the vast lake-studded region southeast of the Susitna River, the Tyone River connects a series of lakes—Louise, Susitna, and Tyone—for about 20 miles, then flows as a 28-mile tributary of the Susitna. Susitna Lake has one large island, scattered small islands, and a long irregularly shaped peninsula. Paddling on the lakes can be dangerous if the wind picks up; paddle close to shore and watch for wind-generated waves. There are sport lodges and recreational cabins on the lakes.

The river meanders slowly northwest across the flats, with many bends in the lower river before it meets the Susitna. Powerboats are used on the river. If you are not a very experienced boater, be sure to take out on the Tyone and not continue down the Susitna, which is a swift, cold, silty river with Class II–III whitewater.

Rating: Class I.
Cautions: Wind on the lakes.

Waterfowl and shorebirds like the lesser yellowlegs are a common sight.

Trip length: 48 miles; allow 5 days.

Season: June through October.

Watercraft: All.

Access: In—Take Glenn Highway to Tazlina Lodge at Mile 156. Smokey Lake across from the lodge has a floatplane anchorage. You can fly into Lake Louise by charter floatplane, or fly in to the landing strip on the southwest end of Lake Louise from the airport north of Tazlina Lodge. The cheapest alternative is to take the Lake Louise Road from Mile 159.8. Turn left onto this gravel road and drive 19.3 miles to the south end of Lake Louise and put in at boat launch. Out—Take out by charter wheelplane on gravel bar around the mouth of the Susitna. Experienced boaters can continue down Susitna River to Log Creek (see Upper Susitna River entry in this book for more information).

Land manager: State; Cook Inlet Regional Corporation; private. (See Land Managers section at back of book for address and phone information.)

Maps: Talkeetna Mountains C–1; Gulkana A–5, A–6, B–6, C–6.

Fish: Arctic grayling, burbot, lake trout; king, coho, and chum salmon. **Wildlife:** Grizzly and black bear, lynx, beaver, river otter, marten, waterfowl.

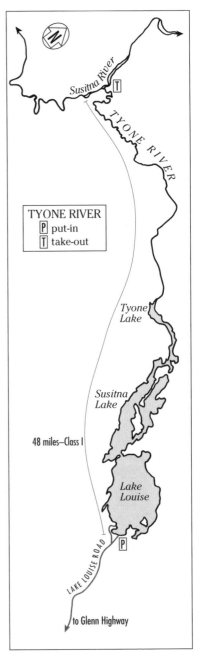

Susitna River

T

TYONE RIVER

TYONE RIVER
P put-in
T take-out

Tyone Lake

Susitna Lake

48 miles—Class I

Lake Louise

P

LAKE LOUISE ROAD

to Glenn Highway

SOUTHEAST ALASKA

The Southeast region is dominated by three major river systems originating in Canada: the Taku, draining 6,700 square miles; the Alsek, draining 9,500 square miles; and the Stikine, draining 19,700 square miles. These systems are new in terms of geologic time. Only in the last thousand years or so have many of the rivers in this region emerged from beneath great sheets of ice from the Wisconsin Ice Age. Large ice fields and glaciers still dominate the mountainous mainland, while the islands of Southeast Alaska are now ice-free.

The coast typically is rugged, with little flat land except where broad glaciers spreading out from the base of the mountains (known as piedmont glaciers) have receded, leaving huge outwash moraines that have since produced forests, such as on the Yakutat Forelands or at Gustavus at the mouth of Glacier Bay. From the coast moving inland, elevations increase dramatically to the summits of some of the highest mountains in North America. No permafrost exists in this region; instead, extensive glaciers clothe the peaks and valleys.

Just four mainland rivers have carved their way through the coastal mountains to the sea—the Stikine, Unuk, Tatshenshini-Alsek, and Taku. These river valleys have proven to be vital transportation routes for flora, wildlife, fish, and humans. The rivers are rich with anadromous fish populations.

Lying along the Gulf of Alaska, this region has a maritime climate, with many storms. The weather is typically cloudy, with moderate temperatures and rain. Average annual precipitation is more than 100 inches, and in some places it is over 200 inches; much of that falls as rain. Rivers generally remain ice-free all year, with heaviest flow in the summer. These cool, moist conditions produce lush, junglelike vegetation. Coastal rainforests of Sitka spruce and western hemlock, interspersed with muskeg, dominate the land below timberline.

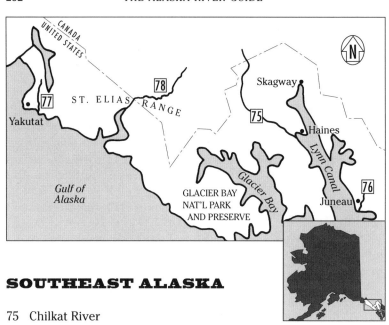

SOUTHEAST ALASKA

75   CHILKAT RIVER

The Chilkat River offers a delightful, swift float through the Chilkat Valley. Glacial in origin, the Chilkat runs silty for much of the year except January through April, when its clear waters sparkle with the movement of Dolly Varden trout. The Chilkat river system drains an area of 958 miles, with tributary rivers coming off glaciers and mountain lakes in British Columbia. The Chilkat itself flows 52 miles to Chilkat Inlet.

The Tsirku River, a major tributary, begins in the Takhinsha Mountains and courses 25 miles to meet the Chilkat at the village of Klukwan. Tsirku is the Tlingit name for "big salmon." Six-mile-long Chilkat Lake feeds into the Tsirku. The Klehini River, beginning as meltwater on Mineral Mountain in British Columbia, flows 42 miles to meet the Chilkat.

The Chilkat River is the centerpiece and lifeblood of the Alaska Chilkat Bald Eagle Preserve near Haines. Each autumn, more than 3,000 eagles gather along a 5-mile stretch of the river to feed on spawned-out salmon. A small year-round population of resident

Bald eagles gather in trees along the Chilkat River in the fall.

eagles, including some which nest, are drawn to the river for its plentiful salmon and trout, and by the fact that warm springs prevent parts of the river from completely freezing over during winter. The Haines Highway parallels the Chilkat River system for 15 miles. When driving, you enter the Bald Eagle Preserve at Mile 9.2 on the Haines Highway. The eagle-viewing area begins at Mile 17; 2 miles north, the highway crosses the Chilkat River. From this point, the highway follows the Klehini River. At Mile 26.3, the highway crosses the Klehini. At Mile 30.9, you leave the preserve.

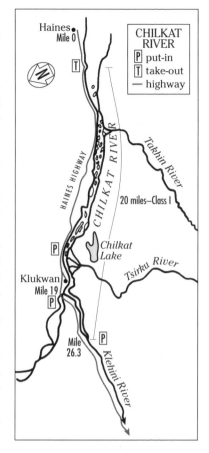

During midwinter, most of the eagles fly to warmer climes. During the summer, the population grows steadily and by October or November, the river provides habitat for the largest eagle council grounds in the world. The bald eagle preserve encompasses 48,000 acres and surrounds the Chilkat River. Please do not float the river through the preserve in late May when the bald eagles are beginning to nest or in the fall (late September through November), to avoid spooking the eagles.

The Chilkat Tlingit have lived along the Chilkat and its tributaries for hundreds of years. Klukwan is the only surviving village of four original villages in the Chilkat Valley. As the only inland village in Southeast Alaska, Klukwan has always been strategically located. When the first non-Natives arrived, the Chilkats had a strong entrepreneurial hold on the travel route into the Interior, controlling passage through the pass. In the late 1800s, there were more than 500 residents of Klukwan. Today, there are less than 150.

Prospectors were drawn to the Chilkat Valley with the discovery of gold in Porcupine Creek in 1898. As with so many strikes in the north at the turn of the century, as news spread, a town appeared almost overnight. By 1899 there were over a thousand people prospecting on the Porcupine and adjacent creeks. But most used the valley as a travel corridor to the Yukon gold fields, finding it longer but less harrowing than the Chilkoot or White Pass routes. In 1903, Fort William H. Seward was built in Port Chilkoot to provide law and order in an isolated area experiencing a major gold-rush boom. The fort is now a national landmark.

Rating: Swift Class I.

Cautions: Brown bears along river; shallow gravel bars.

Trip length: About 20 miles; 1 day.

Season: June to early September.

Watercraft: All.

Access: In—Take the Alaska Marine Highway from Juneau to Haines, or fly from Juneau to Haines. Drive to Mile 19 on the Haines Highway and put in on the Chilkat River, or drive to Mile 26.3 and put in on the Klehini River. To float the lower Tsirku River, drive to Mile 25 and take the turnoff to the river. Out—Take out on the road just outside of Haines.

Land manager: Chilkat Bald Eagle Preserve, Alaska Division of Parks, Juneau. (See Land Managers section at back of book for address and phone information.)

Maps: Skagway A–2, B–2, B–3, B–4.

Fish: Dolly Varden, eulachon; king, coho, sockeye, chum, and pink salmon. **Wildlife:** Brown and black bear, moose, wolf, river otter, coyote, bald eagle, trumpeter swan, waterfowl.

76 MENDENHALL RIVER

The Mendenhall is a popular spot for Juneau residents to hone their whitewater technique in the spring and summer and for cruise ship passengers visiting Juneau, with incredible views of the Mendenhall Glacier and the Juneau Icefield. Originating in Mendenhall Lake about 10 miles west of Juneau, the Mendenhall River flows southward about 5 miles, emptying into the Gastineau Channel. Mendenhall Glacier sits at the head of the lake and, with a 7,000-foot-high spine of mountains and the Juneau Icefield rising steeply above, offers a dramatic backdrop to the lake and river.

The Mendenhall is cold, swift, and dangerous. It has Class II drop-pool rapids and sharp bends, requiring lots of technical maneuvering. The longer, more technical rapids, like Pinball Alley, may approach Class III and require scouting in order to choose the best route. At the end of a long technical section there is a large standing wave that has capsized many a boat. Another short stretch of rapids follows and then the river takes a sharp 90-degree turn to the right; the bend is plugged with rocks and requires skillful boat handling to run.

The valleys in which Juneau lies were originally Tlingit Indian territory. The Tlingit Nation had one of the most highly developed aboriginal cultures in North America, with a prosperous economy based on the abundant resources of Southeast Alaska.

When John Muir first described the large glacier he observed in the area, he referred to it as Auke Glacier. In 1892 it was renamed for the Superintendent of the U.S. Coast and Geodetic Survey, Thomas Corwin Mendenhall.

Hudson's Bay Company operated a fur trading post south of Juneau on Taku Bay from 1841 to 1843, but non-Natives did not permanently settle in the area until 1880. Joe Juneau and Richard Harris discovered gold in 1879, and the settlement of Harrisburg, later called Juneau, sprang up. Until the gold rushes in Alaska's Interior were well under way in the early 20th century, Juneau was the gold mining center for Alaska. Fishing, lumbering, and farming became important industries, and Juneau incorporated and became the capital of the territory in 1900.

Rating: Class II, with a couple tricky rapids, approaching Class

III, at certain water levels.

Cautions: Rocky rapids; cold, swift glacial water.

Trip length: 5 miles; 1 to 2 hours.

Season: April to October.

Watercraft: Canoe, raft, or white-water kayak.

Access: In—Drive from downtown Juneau to Mendenhall Loop Road. Turn right and follow the road toward the U.S. Forest Service's Mendenhall Visitors Center. Put in at the outlet from the campground. Out—Take out at Backloop bridge. Because much of the land along the river is private, access is difficult, especially for scouting rapids. The Forest Service should be encouraged to provide adequate put-ins and take-outs.

Land manager: Tongass National Forest; private. (See Land Managers section at back of book for address and phone information.)

Maps: Juneau B–2 (SW), B–2 (NW).

Wildlife: Waterfowl, bald eagle.

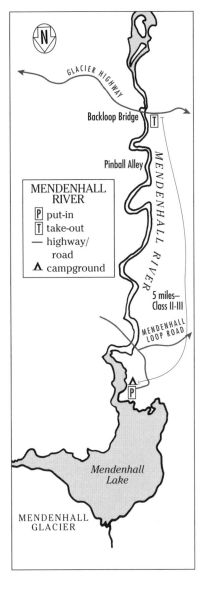

77   SITUK RIVER

Beginning in Situk Lake, the Situk River flows southwesterly for 19 miles, ending in the Gulf of Alaska. The Situk is a small, braided, clearwater stream containing many tributaries and cross-channels characteristic of streams flowing across glacial outwash deposits. The gradient is slight, so the current is gentle.

From Situk Lake, situated in an open meadow in the spruce forest, there are excellent views of the Brabazon Mountains and the St. Elias Range. A 5.5-mile maintained trail leads from the gravel Forest Highway 10 to Situk Lake. Once on the river itself, the view is largely restricted to the narrow river corridor, due to dense forests and alder thickets along the banks. About 7 miles below Situk Lake, the West Fork Situk River enters the Situk, and a quarter mile below, the Situk highway bridge crosses. Below the bridge, the river meanders through the spruce-covered forelands to the ocean.

At the mouth of the Situk lies an estuary with saltwater beaches and breaking surf. Hiking is excellent along the beaches, affording views of the Fairweather Range to the south. The Yakutat Forelands, across which the Situk flows, has been free of glacial ice for about 8,000 years. The first inhabitants of the area are believed to have been Ahtna Athapaskans from the Copper River area and Eyaks from the Cordova/lower Copper River area. The Tlingit influence is now dominant.

A Tlingit fisherman with his catch of coho salmon at the mouth of the Situk River.

Rating: Class I.

Cautions: Bears, sweepers, log-jams.

Trip length: 19 miles from Situk Lake to the mouth of the river; allow 2 days. Lower Situk, from Situk bridge to mouth, is 12 miles; allow 8 hours.

Season: April to November.

Watercraft: Canoe, kayak, or raft.

Access: In—Scheduled airline to Yakutat. From Yakukat, fly by charter floatplane to Situk Lake, approximately 12 miles from Yakutat. To float lower half of the river, drive out Forest Highway 10, about 9 miles from Yakutat. Put in at Situk bridge. Or put in by wheelplane at a primitive landing strip on the middle Situk River, between Mile 9 and 10 of the river. Out—Take out at mouth of Situk, where there is a boat launching area and Lost River Road leads 9 miles back into Yakutat.

Land manager: Tongass National Forest; Russell Fiord Wilderness (Situk Lake and the first mile of the Situk River); Yak-Tat Kwaan village corporation; private. (See Land Managers section at back of book for address and phone information.)

Maps: Yakutat B–5, C–4, C–5.

Fish: Dolly Varden, steelhead, and cutthroat trout; king, coho, sockeye, pink, and chum salmon. **Wildlife:** Brown and black bear, moose, lynx, river otter, marten, bald eagle, waterfowl, shorebirds.

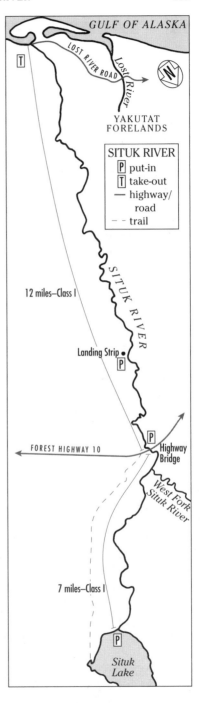

78 TATSHENSHINI-ALSEK RIVER

With origins in the mountains of Canada's Yukon Territory, the Tatshenshini and Alsek rivers slice through the massive St. Elias and Fairweather mountain ranges, the largest nonpolar glaciated mountain system in the world. The Tatshenshini flows northwest and then bends southwest through the 6,000- to 8,000-foot-high Alsek Range, a subrange of the St. Elias. The Tat meets the Alsek in the Fairweather Range, and the combined river, now called the Alsek, flows southwesterly within a 1- to 3-mile-wide valley surrounded by the Fairweather Range.

At the point in British Columbia where the rivers meet, the water is more than a mile wide. Not far downstream from this point, you can count 14 glaciers by just looking around in all directions. In Alsek Bay, 15,300-foot Mount Fairweather towers above the 3-mile-wide Alsek Glacier. The glacier calves into the bay constantly, transforming it into a lagoon filled with spectacular giant icebergs. The river then breaches the Brabazon Range, the subrange of the St. Elias Mountains closest to Yakutat, and empties into the Gulf of Alaska from an ever-changing slough and broad river delta.

The Tatshenshini-Alsek, a large-volume glacial river about 160 miles long, is considered by many to offer one of the world's premier river trips for its sheer grandeur and scenery. Traversing the subarctic tundra and Interior forests of the Yukon Territory, cutting through the Fairweather and St. Elias ranges, and emerging to the salmon-rich, spruce-and-alder-clothed Gulf of Alaska coast, the Tatshenshini courses through 2.8 million acres of some of the world's most spectacular wilderness.

The river is contained partly within Canada's Kluane National Park in the Yukon Territory and partly within the U.S. Glacier Bay National Park and Preserve, and is bordered by Tongass National Forest in its lower reaches. Much of the Tatshenshini also is in British Columbia, but the river has yet to receive official protection by the government of that province.

From the Canadian site of Dalton Post, the Tatshenshini River drops 2,000 feet to sea level for an average gradient of 13.3 feet per mile. The upper river travels at a speed of 10 miles per hour. (On the lower river, below Alsek Glacier, the river moves at 4 to 5 miles per hour.) At normal water levels, the Tat is rated Class I–IV. Class V

A sunny day on Alsek Bay, Glacier Bay National Park and Preserve.

whitewater occurs in the Tatshenshini's lower canyon during high water.

The significant whitewater on the Tatshenshini lies in the Yukon within the steep, rocky walls of the lower canyon. Directly below Dalton Post, there are a few miles of Class I–II rock-dodging to give you about 45 minutes to prepare for the big rapids. The canyon itself is 8 miles long, and has only one or two spots to eddy out at low water. At high water, no eddies exist at all. Scouting is not possible due to high canyon walls. A rapid at Pirate Creek marks the end of the canyon. Boaters usually pull out at Silver Creek to bail out, dry out, and regroup after the canyon.

From Silver Creek to about 3 miles above Sediments Creek is Class II. The river then flows through a slow-moving canyon where the water seems to deepen, with little hydraulics and eddies that pop up here and there. Huge holes appear unexpectedly, along with big standing waves and a huge ledge on the right. Just above O'Connor River, a landslide sent part of a ridge into the river in the spring of 1990. The landslide dammed the river, which finally pushed through, but now there is a narrow chute with big standing waves that approach Class IV.

The rest of the river is basically fast Class II, with large rollers (2 to 4 feet high), large rocks, logjams, and sweepers. From the confluence of the Alsek and Tatshenshini, the river flows another 54 miles to the sea.

The Tatshenshini Valley was used as a trading corridor by the coastal Tlingit and southern Tutchone Indians long before non-Natives ever discovered it. During the Klondike gold rush, a trail that avoided the arduous Chilkoot Pass went from Haines to the Interior partially along the upper Tatshenshini. Jack Dalton, an American entrepreneur, guided *cheechakos* (newcomers to Alaska) up a Tlingit trail from Haines to the Klondike gold fields. Soon the route and a stopover on the route bore his name.

A journey down the Tatshenshini was reported in 1890, in *Frank Leslie's Illustrated Newspaper,* by adventurer Edward James Glave. He and a partner hired two Natives with a dugout canoe to guide them down the river. Shank, a medicine man, and his companion Koona Ack Sai took them down safely, all the way describing previous trips full of accidents and drownings. Glave reported:

> This stream is the wildest I have ever seen; there is scarcely a one hundred yard stretch of fair water anywhere along its course. Running with an eight to ten knot current, and aggravated by rocky points, sharp bends and immense boulders, the stream is also rendered dangerous by the innumerable rapids and eddies which disturb its surface.

Some prospectors decided that the two routes that existed at that time into the Yukon (Chilkoot Pass and the Dalton Trail) were much too long, and a group of 300 set out from the Gulf of Alaska to find an easier route to the Yukon via the Tatshenshini Valley. Beginning near the head of Disenchantment Bay, outside of Yakutat, the men hauled their gear and boats 50 miles across Hubbard Glacier to the Alsek River. Many casualties and abandoned dreams later—after 18 months of struggle up the Tatshenshini and Alsek valleys, encountering glaciers, raging glacial rivers, and steep canyons—the survivors staggered into Dalton Post, only to learn that the point at which they had arrived could be reached from the coast at Haines in a few days' travel.

Rating: Class I–V. Wild and remote roadless wilderness. Only experienced boaters with excellent wilderness skills should attempt this trip.
Cautions: Big water, tricky canyon, weird currents on the Alsek, and cold, wet weather.
Trip length: 129 miles from Dalton Post to the mouth of the river at Dry Bay; river can be floated in 5 days; allow 10 days to fully

experience the river.

Season: June to mid-September. River flow fluctuates throughout the summer season, depending on snowmelt or rain.

Watercraft: Medium to large (13-foot and above) raft is best; hard-shell kayaks are possible, but difficult and costly to fly out from the river. Some boaters have used canoes with spray decks, with mixed results. Folding boats are not recommended.

Access: In—Drive Haines Highway to put-in on the Tatshenshini at Dalton Post off the highway, Mile 99.5. If traveling from Haines, it is necessary to check in with Canadian Customs. Customs may require store receipts for groceries and supplies purchased in the United States or Canada to be used on river trips through Canada. Carry identification (driver's license or equivalent). A steep, winding, graveled 4-wheel-drive road leads off the Haines Highway to Dalton Post. Several historic buildings still exist at Dalton Post; a fishing weir operates during the summer. Out— Take out on the lower Alsek River at Dry Bay (National Park Service campground and ranger station). When approaching Dry Bay, after the last set of rapids, stay on the left side of the river so that you can pull into the Dry

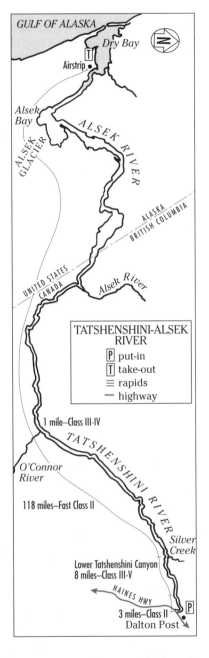

Bay Slough, which leads to the fish processing plant, campground, and closest access point to the airstrip. The slough is slow-moving, with little current. Fly by charter wheelplane to Haines or to Yakutat for scheduled airline to Juneau or Anchorage.

Land manager: Glacier Bay National Park and Preserve (contact park for restrictions on size of parties and commercial trips); United Nations World Heritage Site; Kluane National Park; British Columbia Provincial Government. (See Land Managers section at back of book for address and phone information.)

Maps: Skagway 1:250,000; Skagway B–8; Yakutat A–1, A–2, B–1. Canadian map: Dezadeash 115A.

Fish: King, silver, and sockeye salmon. **Wildlife:** Brown and black bear, moose, wolf, mountain goat, fox, beaver, muskrat, bald eagle, gyrfalcon, waterfowl. British Columbia's only winter range for Dall Sheep is here. The region has one of the highest brown bear populations in the world. The area has Canada's only population of the glacier bear, a rare silver-blue phase of the black bear found only in a narrow coastal region between Cape Fairweather and Cape Yakataga.

Glacier-walking in the Tatshenshini-Alsek River Valley.

GLOSSARY

aufeis: overflow ice that forms as a river freezes in the winter.

back-ferry: to move sideways while going downstream by back-paddling with the boat at an angle to the current.

baidarka: Aleut or Eskimo kayak with a light wood frame and sea mammal skin covering.

barabara: Aleut or Eskimo pit house built partially underground, with wood structural members and sod or skin covering.

beam: width of a boat at its widest point.

boil: an upwelling in the river caused by underwater obstructions or constrictions.

boreal forest: northernmost limit of woodlands; also referred to as taiga; in Alaska, vast, open conifer/birch/aspen/poplar forests throughout the Interior and up to the foothills of the Brooks Range.

boulder garden: a section of rapids with rocks that boaters must weave around and between.

boulder sieve: a jumble of large rocks that allows the passage of water but not of boats.

braided: split into many river channels that keep joining and dividing and joining again.

breakup: the annual Alaskan spring phenomenon in which winter ice on the rivers breaks apart with the arrival of warmer weather.

broach: to turn broadside to wind and waves.

calving: the action of ice breaking free from a glacier or from a wall of aufeis and falling into the water; hazardous to small boats.

chute: a tongue of current caused by a constriction in the stream or a sudden increase in river gradient.

commercial recreation: recreational use of land, water, and natural resources for financial gain, such as water taxi services or guided fishing, hunting, or river rafting.

draft: the depth at which a boat is riding in the water, measured on the side of the boat from the water's surface (waterline) to the point at which the boat is deepest in the water.

eddy: a place of flatwater where the current stops or flows upstream; found along shorelines, inside bends, or behind rocks and other obstructions.

Eskimo roll: a kayak maneuver in which a paddler rolls the boat upside down and then flips it back to an upright position while remaining in the boat.

falls: a vertical drop in the river of 6 or more feet.

feather: to turn a paddle so that it moves through the air or water edgeways, providing the least possible resistance.

ferry: to move a boat laterally across the current by use of a back-paddling technique.

flatwater: a lake or slow water with no rapids.

freeboard: distance from the surface of the water on the side of the boat (waterline) to the top of the gunwale.

giardia: intestinal parasite found in streams worldwide, spread by fecal/oral transmission (usually from drinking unpurified water); microscopic cysts develop in the intestine, causing explosive diarrhea and cramps.

gunwale: the part of a boat that runs from end to end along the top edge of the hull; usually a finishing strip of wood or aluminum on a canoe or folding kayak.

haystack: a pileup of water that is formed as fast-moving water meets still water; usually found at the apex of a downstream V-shaped section of water.

hole: a depression formed when the river flows abruptly over a rock, ledge, or other drop.

hydraulics: holes, whirlpools, boils, and other water phenomena that are associated with whitewater.

ledge: a ridge of rock that acts as a natural dam; difficult to see from water level.

leeward: the area of water or land that is sheltered from the wind (as opposed to windward, the area that takes the brunt of the wind's force).

lining: to use a rope to guide a boat downstream from shore; the technique of lining is used to get around rapids that cannot be safely navigated; lines (usually 30 feet long) are attached to a boat's bow and stern, and boaters on shore walk the boat at the edge of the rapids, using the lines to guide the boat.

oxbow: a wide loop in a river's course, created when a slow-moving river tears away the bank on the outside of a curve; also referred to as a meander.

permafrost: the layer of perennially frozen ground below the surface ground and vegetative layer; a phenomenon of high latitudes and altitudes, especially throughout Interior and northern Alaska.

pillow: a mound of water surging back after hitting an obstruction.

portage: to carry a boat to or between bodies of water; to take a boat out of the water and carry it around a rapid or other hazard.

pourover: a condition in which a river flows over a rock just beneath the water's surface, creating a hole behind it.

put-in: a place along a river where it is possible to launch boats and begin a river trip.

riffle: a shallow area extending across the bed of a stream over which the current flows swiftly, creating short, choppy waves, or baby rapids.

scout: to check out rapids or other parts of the river from shore before floating the river.

shoal: shallows.

sleeper: a submerged rock or obstacle hidden below the surface of the water.

spray cover: a removable fabric cover on open canoes and kayaks.

standing wave: a wave of water that stays in position as water passes through; caused when fast-moving water meets still water.

strainer: a submerged tree with branches that allows water to flow through but can entrap boats.

sweeper: a tree, stump, or log that is hanging over a riverbank or has fallen into a river, often at the outside of a river bend where strong current undercuts the bank.

take-out: a logical place to end a river trip, where it is possible to take boats out and get transportation by road or air.

tracking: to use a rope to tow a boat upstream, usually from shore.

tundra: the land beyond the limit of trees, where sedges, herbs, wildflowers, and dwarf shrubs flourish; a phenomenon of high latitudes and altitudes. Arctic tundra lies north of the tree limit throughout circumpolar regions of the world; alpine tundra lies above treeline and below the perennial snowline in mountain regions.

umiak: an open Eskimo or Aleut boat constructed of wood ribs and sea mammal skins, used on rivers and the open sea; often large enough to carry a dozen or more people.

washed out: description of a river in which the water level is so high that holes and rocks are covered.

whitewater: fast-moving frothy water; rapids.

williwaw: a sudden gust of wind that can reach speeds in excess of 100 miles per hour.

windward: the area of water or land that takes the brunt of the wind's force (as opposed to leeward, the area that is sheltered from the wind).

RIVERS GROUPED BY LEVEL OF DIFFICULTY

Class I
Alexander Creek
Andreafsky River
East Fork Andreafsky River
Anvik River
Beaver Creek
Black River
Chena River
Chilkat River
Lower Copper River (Iliamna Lake)
Deshka River
Eagle River (Visitor center to Briggs bridge)
Goodnews River
Holitna River
Lower John River
Kantishna River
Lower Kenai River
Knik River
Kobuk River
Middle Fork Koyukuk River
Kroto Creek
Kuskokwim River
Lower Little Susitna River
Moose Creek
Middle and Lower Mulchatna River
Nonvianuk River
Nowitna River
Nushagak River
Nuyakuk River
Porcupine River
Portage Creek
Selawik River
Situk River
Squirrel River
Talachulitna Creek
Lower Talachulitna River
Togiak River
Tyone River
Unalakleet River
Wild River

Class I–II
Alagnak River
Alatna River
Ambler River
Campbell Creek
Chatanika River
Colville River
Mosquito Fork Fortymile River
Ivishak River
Kanektok River
Killik River
Koyuk River
North Fork Koyukuk River
Melozitna River
Nabesna River
Upper Newhalen River
Noatak River
Savonoski River
Sheenjek River
Stony River
Lower Susitna River
Tlikakila River
Wood River Lakes System
Yukon River

Class II
Aniuk River
Birch Creek

Chilikadrotna River
Chitina River
Delta River
Dennison Fork Fortymile River
Middle John River
Upper Kenai River
Nenana River (except Nenana
  Gorge)
Tokositna River

Class II–III
American Creek
Middle Fork Bremner River
Charley River
Copper River (Wrangell
  Mountains)
Eagle River (Briggs bridge to
  above Campground Rapids)
Fortymile River
Middle Fork Fortymile River
North Fork Fortymile River
South Fork Fortymile River
Gulkana River
Upper John River
Kenai Canyon
Kennicott River
Kisaralik River
South Fork Kuskokwim River
Mendenhall River
Upper Mulchatna River
Nizina River
Upper Susitna River
Talachulitna River
Tinayguk River

Class III–IV
Aniakchak River
Delta River, Black Rapids
Gulkana River, Canyon Rapids
Kobuk River canyons
Lake Creek
Talkeetna River

Class IV–V
North Fork Bremner River
South Fork Bremner River
Delta River, second and third
  falls
Upper Little Susitna River
Nenana Gorge
Lower Newhalen River
Upper Nuyakuk River
Tatshenshini-Alsek River

Class VI
Upper Susitna River, Devils
  Canyon

NATIONAL WILD AND SCENIC RIVERS AND STATE RECREATION RIVERS

Twenty-five rivers in Alaska were designated for protection by Congress under the National Wild and Scenic Rivers Act (1980). Each river and a corridor of land averaging half a mile on each side of the river are protected under the act, which is designed to keep the rivers free-flowing and to guard water quality, scenery, fisheries, wildlife, history, culture, geology, and recreation. (Most of these 25 Wild and Scenic Rivers are among the rivers featured in this book.)

Three categories of designation were established: wild, scenic, and recreational. Wild rivers have no roads or impoundments, are unpolluted, and are generally recognized for their primitive character. Scenic rivers may have an occasional road and mining or other activities within their corridor. Recreational rivers may flow through developed areas, but development must demonstrate concern for protecting and enhancing the features for which the river was set aside. Hundreds of other rivers await consideration for protection designation.

WILD AND SCENIC RIVERS

Alagnak Wild River, including Nonvianuk River (60 miles); Katmai National Park and Preserve

Alatna Wild River (83 miles); Gates of the Arctic National Park and Preserve

Andreafsky Wild River, including East Fork Andreafsky River (220 miles); Yukon Delta National Wildlife Refuge

Aniakchak Wild River (63 miles); Aniakchak National Monument

Beaver Creek Wild and Scenic River (127 miles); White Mountains National Recreation Area

Birch Creek Wild and Scenic River (126 miles); Steese National Conservation Area

Charley Wild River, including tributaries (203 miles); Yukon–Charley Rivers National Preserve

Chilikadrotna Wild River (11 miles); Lake Clark National Park and Preserve

Delta Wild, Scenic, and Recreational River (51 miles); Bureau of Land Management

Fortymile Wild, Scenic, and Recreational River, including tributaries

(375 miles); Bureau of Land Management

Gulkana Wild and Scenic River, including portions of Middle and West Forks (181 miles); Bureau of Land Management

Ivishak Wild River (60 miles); Arctic National Wildlife Refuge

John Wild River (53 miles); Gates of the Arctic National Park and Preserve

Kobuk Wild River (upper 110 miles); Gates of the Arctic National Park and Preserve

North Fork Koyukuk Wild River (102 miles); Gates of the Arctic National Park and Preserve

Mulchatna Wild River (upper 24 miles); Lake Clark National Park and Preserve

Noatak Wild River (330 miles); Gates of the Arctic National Park and Preserve and Noatak National Preserve

Nowitna Wild River (223 miles); Nowitna National Wildlife Refuge

Salmon Wild River (70 miles); Kobuk Valley National Park

Selawik Wild River (168 miles); Selawik National Wildlife Refuge

Sheenjek Wild River (127 miles); Arctic National Wildlife Refuge

Tinayguk Wild River (47 miles); Arctic National Wildlife Refuge

Tlikakila Wild River (51 miles); Lake Clark National Park and Preserve

Unalakleet Wild and Scenic River (65 miles); Bureau of Land Management

Wind Wild River (98 miles); Arctic National Wildlife Refuge

In addition to 25 designated rivers, 12 others were selected for study for possible inclusion in the National Wild and Scenic Rivers system. These rivers were found eligible, but recommendations have not been sent to Congress. Others await consideration.

Colville River
Kanektok River
Kisaralik River
Koyuk River
Melozitna River
Nigu-Etivluk River
Porcupine River
Lower Sheenjek River
Situk River
Squirrel River
Utukok River
Yukon River (Ramparts section)

STATE RECREATION RIVERS

The Alaska Recreation Rivers Act (1988) was passed by the Alaska Legislature to maintain and enhance certain river areas for recreation while ensuring their scenic and natural integrity. The Susitna Basin Recreation Rivers Management Plan, adopted in 1991, addressed the issues of crowding, littering, campsites, access, and motorized versus nonmotorized use, and designated six state recreation rivers.

Alexander Creek State Recreation River
Kroto Creek and Moose Creek State Recreation River (including Deshka River)
Lake Creek State Recreation River
Little Susitna State Recreation River
Talachulitna State Recreation River (including Talachulitna Creek)
Talkeetna State Recreation River

LAND MANAGERS

Listed below is information on how to contact the land managers named with the river trips in this book. The postal abbreviation for Alaska is AK, and the area code for all telephone numbers is 907.

STATE PARKS, RECREATION AREAS, AND RECREATION RIVERS

Alaska Department of Natural Resources, 3601 C Street, Suite 1080, P.O. Box 107005, Anchorage 99510-7005. 762-2251

Alaska State Parks, 400 Willoughby Avenue, Juneau 99801. 766-2292

Alaska State Parks, Chugach/Southwest Area Office, 3601 C Street, Suite 1280, P.O. Box 107001, Anchorage 99510-7001. 762-2617

Alaska State Parks, Mat-Su Area Office, HC32, P.O. Box 6706, Wasilla 99687. 745-3975

Alaska State Parks, Northern Region Office, 3700 Airport Way, Fairbanks 99709. 452-2695

Wood-Tikchik State Park, P.O. Box 3022, Dillingham 99576. 345-5014

NATIONAL PARKS, MONUMENTS, AND PRESERVES

National Park Service, Alaska Regional Office, 2525 Gambell Street, Anchorage 99503. 257-2696

Aniakchak National Monument and Preserve, P.O. Box 7, King Salmon 99613. 246-3305

Bering Land Bridge National Preserve, P.O. Box 220, Nome 99762. 443-2522

Denali National Park and Preserve, P.O. Box 9, Denali Park 99755. 683-2686

Gates of the Arctic National Park and Preserve, P.O. Box 74680, Fairbanks 99707. 456-0281

Glacier Bay National Park and Preserve, Gustavus 99826. 697-2230

Katmai National Park and Preserve, P.O. Box 7, King Salmon 99613. 246-3305

Kobuk Valley National Park, P.O. Box 1029, Kotzebue 99752. 442-3890

Lake Clark National Park and Preserve, 4230 University Drive, Suite 311, Anchorage 99508. 271-3751

Noatak National Preserve, P.O. Box 1029, Kotzebue 99752. 442-3890

Wrangell-St. Elias National Park and Preserve, P.O. Box 29, Glennallen 99588. 822-5234

Yukon-Charley Rivers National Preserve, P.O. Box 64, Eagle 99738. 547-2233

NATIONAL WILDLIFE REFUGES

Arctic National Wildlife Refuge, 101 Twelfth Avenue, P.O. Box 20, Fairbanks 99701. 456-0250

Kanuti National Wildlife Refuge, 101 Twelfth Avenue, P.O. Box 11, Fairbanks 99701. 456-0329

Kenai National Wildlife Refuge, 2139 Ski Hill Road, Soldotna 99669-2139. 262-7021

Koyukuk/Nowitna National Wildlife Refuge, P.O. Box 287, Galena 99741. 656-1231

Selawik National Wildlife Refuge, P.O. Box 270, Kotzebue 99752. 442-3799

Tetlin National Wildlife Refuge, P.O. Box 155, Tok 99780. 883-5312

Togiak National Wildlife Refuge, P.O. Box 270, Dillingham 99576. 842-1063

U.S. Fish and Wildlife Service, Alaska Regional Office, 1011 East Tudor Road, Anchorage 99503. 786-3487

Yukon Delta National Wildlife Refuge, P.O. Box 346, Bethel 99559. 543-3151

Yukon Flats National Wildlife Refuge, 101 Twelfth Avenue, P.O. Box 14, Fairbanks 99701. 456-0440

NATIONAL FORESTS

Chugach National Forest, 201 East Ninth Avenue, Suite 206, Anchorage 99501; 271-2500; cabin reservations 271-2599

Tongass National Forest, P.O. Box 1980, Sitka 99835. 774-6671

Yakutat Ranger District, P.O. Box 327, Yakutat 99689. 784-3359

BUREAU OF LAND MANAGEMENT

Alaska State Office, 222 West Seventh Avenue, P.O. Box 13, Anchorage 99513; 271-5555 for recreation information; 271-5960 for land information

Anchorage District Office, 6881 Abbott Loop Road, Anchorage 99507; 267-1225 for information on National Wild, Scenic, and Recreational Rivers.

Bureau of Land Management, 1150 University Avenue, Fairbanks 99709: Steese/White Mountains District 474-2350; Arctic District 474-2301; Kobuk District 474-2343

Glennallen District Office, P.O. Box 147, Glennallen 99588. 822-3217
Tok Field Office, P.O. Box 307, Tok 99780. 883-5121.

CANADIAN PARKLANDS
British Columbia Provincial Government, Committee on Resources
and the Environment, 1802 Douglas, Seventh Floor, Victoria, B.C.,
Canada Y8V 1X4
Kluane National Park, P.O. Box 5495, Haines Junction, Yukon
Territory, Canada Y0B 1L0
Northern Yukon National Park, Environment Canada—Parks, Haines
Junction, Yukon Territory, Canada Y0B 1L0

ALASKA REGIONAL NATIVE CORPORATIONS
Ahtna Inc., P.O. Box 649, Copper Center 99573. 822-3476
Bering Straits Native Corporation, P.O. Box 1008, Nome 99762.
443-5252
Bristol Bay Native Corporation, P.O. Box 198, Dillingham 99576. Toll
free 800-478-3602
Calista Corporation, 601 West Fifth Avenue, Suite 200, Anchorage
99501-2225. 279-5516
Chugach Alaska Corporation, 3000 A Street, Suite 400, Anchorage
99503. 563-8866
Cook Inlet Regional Corporation, 2525 C Street, Suite 500, Anchorage
99509. 274-8638
Doyon Ltd., Doyon Building, 201 First Avenue, Suite 200, Fairbanks
99701. 452-4755
NANA Regional Corporation, P.O. Box 49, Kotzebue 99752. 442-3301

ALASKA VILLAGE NATIVE CORPORATIONS
Alaska Peninsula Corporation, P.O. Box 104360, Anchorage 99510.
274-2433
Aleknagik Natives Ltd., P.O. Box 1630, Aleknagik 99555. 842-2385
Chalkyitsik Native Corporation, General Delivery, Chalkyitsik 99788.
848-8212
Choggiung Ltd., P.O. Box 889, Dillingham 99576. 842-5218
Dineega Corporation, P.O. Box 28, Ruby 99768. 468-4405.
Ekwok Natives Ltd., P.O. Box 10064, Dillingham 99576. 464-3317
Gana-A'yoo Ltd., P.O. Box 38, Galena 99741. 656-1606
Gwitchyaa Zhee Corporation, P.O. Box 329, Fort Yukon 99740.
662-2325

Iliamna Natives Ltd., P.O. Box 267, Iliamna 99606. 571-1256
Ingalik Native Corporation, General Delivery, Anvik 99558
Koliganek Natives Ltd., General Delivery, Koliganek 99576. 596-3430
Koyuk Native Corporation, P.O. Box 50, Koyuk 99753. 963-3551
Kuitsarak Inc., P.O. Box 10, Goodnews Bay 99589. 967-8520
Kuskokwim Corporation, 645 G Street, Suite 300, Anchorage 99501.
    276-2101
Northway Natives Inc., P.O. Box 401, Northway 99764. 778-2298
Nunamiut Corporation, P.O. Box 21009, Anaktuvuk Pass 99721
Qanirtuuq Inc., General Delivery, Quinhagak 99655. 556-8814
Stuyahok Ltd., P.O. Box 50, New Stuyahok 99636. 693-3122
Togiak Natives Ltd. Corporation, P.O. Box 169, Togiak 99678.
    493-5520
Twin Hills Native Corporation, General Delivery, Twin Hills 99576
Unalakleet Native Corporation, P.O. Box 100, Unalakleet 99684.
    624-3411
Yak-Tat Kwaan, P.O. Box 416, Yakutat 99689. 784-3335

OTHER HELPFUL SOURCES OF INFORMATION

Alaska Conservation Foundation, 430 West Seventh Avenue,
    Anchorage 99501; 276-1917; information on environmentally
    responsible guide operations
Alaska Tourism Marketing Council, P.O. Box E-701, Juneau 99811;
    465-2010; publishes Alaska Travel Directory of visitor services
Alaska Wilderness Recreation and Tourism Association, P.O. Box
    1353, Valdez 99686; promotes recognition and protection of
    Alaska's natural resources and ecologically responsible recre-
    ation and tourism; composed of recreation and tourism operators

PUBLIC LANDS INFORMATION CENTERS

Anchorage Public Lands Information Center, 605 West Fourth
    Avenue, Anchorage 99501. 258-7275
Fairbanks Public Lands Information Center, 250 Cushman Street,
    Suite 1A, Fairbanks 99701. 451-7352
Tok Public Lands Information Center, Mile 1314, Alaska Highway,
    P.O. Box 359, Tok 99780. 883-5667

TOWN SERVICES

This listing details services available at principal towns and villages within the areas described in the river trips.

Akiachak: Limited groceries, scheduled air service.

Aleknagik: Groceries, general merchandise, landing strip.

Allakaket: Groceries, general merchandise, scheduled air service. Possession of alcohol is illegal.

Ambler: Lodging, meals, groceries, hardware, gas, auto and boat rental, scheduled and charter air service. Sale and importation of alcohol is illegal.

Anchorage: All services. Commercial center for the state.

Aniak: Lodging, meals, groceries, hardware, scheduled and charter air service.

Anvik: Lodging, meals, groceries, scheduled and charter air service.

Bethel: All services. Visitor center for Yukon Delta National Wildlife Refuge. Sale of alcohol is illegal. Bethel is administrative and transportation hub for 57 villages in the Yukon-Kuskokwim Delta.

Bettles: Lodging, meals, groceries, general merchandise, scheduled and charter air service. Headquarters for Gates of the Arctic National Park and Preserve.

Big Delta: Lodging, meals, gas.

Chalkyitsik: Groceries, general merchandise, gas. Sale and importation of alcohol is illegal.

Chitina: Lodging, meals, groceries, gas, charter air service, National Park Service ranger station.

Chuathbaluk: Limited groceries, scheduled air service.

Circle: Campground, meals, groceries, general store, gas, fishing licenses, charter helicopter service.

Copper Center: Lodging, meals, groceries, gas. Headquarters for Wrangell-St. Elias National Park and Preserve.

Cordova: Lodging, meals, groceries, gas, car rental, taxi, ferry, scheduled and charter air service.

Dawson: All services.

Deadhorse: Lodging, meals, scheduled and charter air service.

Delta Junction: Lodging, meals, groceries, gas.

Denali National Park (just outside entrance): Lodging, meals, groceries, gas.

Dillingham: All services. Office for Togiak National Wildlife Refuge.

Eagle: Campgrounds, limited lodging, groceries, gas, charter boat service, scheduled and charter air service, Yukon-Charley Rivers National Preserve headquarters.

Eagle River: Lodging, meals, groceries, gas.

Ekwok: Lodge (open summer only), groceries, sporting goods, clothing, fishing licenses, charter boat service, scheduled and charter air service.

Fairbanks: All services.

Fort Yukon: Lodging, meals, groceries, general merchandise, gas, fishing licenses, boat charter and rental, scheduled and charter air service. Hub of the Yukon Flats; largest village in the region.

Galena: Groceries, general merchandise, auto and boat rental, scheduled and charter air service, offices of the Alaska Department of Fish and Game and the U.S. Fish and Wildlife Service. Lodging and meals available through the village corporation, Gana-A'yoo Ltd.

Goodnews Bay: Groceries, hardware, general merchandise, fishing licenses. Sale and importation of alcohol is illegal.

Grayling: Groceries, general merchandise, scheduled and charter air service. Sale and importation of alcohol is illegal.

Gulkana: Groceries, gas, charter air service.

Haines: Campgrounds, youth hostel, lodging, meals, groceries, gas, auto service, car rental, commercial float trips and jet-boat tours on Chilkat River. Alaska Marine Highway has a stop in Haines.

Healy: Lodging, meals, groceries, gas.

Iliamna: Lodging, meals, groceries, fishing supplies, taxi, scheduled and charter air service.

Juneau: All services. Commercial raft trips on the Mendenhall River. U.S. Forest Service/Interagency Information Center (in Centennial Hall).

Kalstag: Scheduled air service. (Lodging, meals, and groceries limited or unavailable.)

Kashwitna Lake: Charter floatplane service.

Katmai National Park: Brooks Camp—Campground, lodging, meals, charter boat and air service. Grosvenor Lake—fishing lodge.

Kiana: Meals, groceries, scheduled air service. Sale and importation of alcohol is illegal.

King Salmon: Lodging, meals, groceries, sporting goods, clothing, first-aid supplies, film, gas, fishing licenses, charter boat and air service. Offices of the Alaska Department of Fish and Game, National Park Service, and U.S. Fish and Wildlife Service;

Interagency Visitor Center at airport.

Kobuk: Scheduled and charter air service. Sale and importation of alcohol is illegal.

Koliganek: Scheduled air service. (Food and lodging may not be available because many villagers may be gone to fish camps in the summer.)

Kotzebue: All services. Scheduled air service to Noorvik, Noatak, Selawik, Kiana, Kobuk, Shungnak, and Ambler.

Koyuk: Groceries, sporting goods, first-aid supplies, film, gas, fishing licenses, scheduled air service. Boats may be available for rent or charter. Ask locally for transportation to upper river. Sale and importation of alcohol is illegal.

Kwethluk: Groceries, general merchandise, scheduled air service. Sale and importation of alcohol is illegal.

Lake Minchumina: Lodging, meals, groceries, general merchandise.

Lime Village: Scheduled air service.

Manley Hot Springs: Lodging, meals, gas.

McCarthy: Lodging, meals, charter air service.

McGrath: Lodging, meals, groceries, hardware, charter air service.

Medfra: Landing strip.

Nenana: Lodging, meals, groceries, gas.

Newhalen: Lodging, meals, groceries, fishing supplies, charter air service.

New Stuyahok: Lodging, meals, groceries, general merchandise, gas, scheduled air service.

Nikolai: Lodging, meals, groceries, scheduled air service.

Noatak: Groceries, general merchandise, scheduled air service. Sale and importation of alcohol is illegal.

Nome: All services. Commercial center for the Seward Peninsula. Offices of the National Park Service and the federal Bureau of Land Management.

Nondalton: Lodging, meals, groceries, fishing supplies, taxi, scheduled air service.

Noorvik: Lodging, meals, groceries, general merchandise, scheduled air service. Sale and importation of alcohol is illegal.

Northway: Lodging, meals, groceries, gas, charter air service.

Nuiqsut: Groceries, hardware, sporting goods, film. Scheduled and charter air service to Barrow and Deadhorse. Possession of alcohol is illegal.

Old Crow: Limited supplies.

Paxson Lake: Campground, lodging, meals, groceries, gas.

Port Alsworth: Lodging, meals, boat rental, scheduled and charter air service, Lake Clark National Park ranger station.

Port Heiden: Lodging, meals, limited groceries, charter air service.

Quinhagak: Groceries, hardware, sporting goods, film. Sale or possession of alcohol is illegal.

Red Devil: Scheduled air service. (Lodging, meals, and groceries limited or unavailable.)

Ruby: Lodging, meals, groceries, hardware, clothing, film, fishing licenses, auto rental, scheduled and charter air service.

St. Marys: Lodging, meals, groceries, hardware, sporting goods, fishing licenses, scheduled and charter air service.

Selawik: Groceries, hardware, scheduled air service.

Shungnak: Lodging, groceries, general merchandise, scheduled air service. Sale and importation of alcohol is illegal.

Skwentna: Lodging, meals, groceries, boat taxi, scheduled and charter air service.

Slana: National Park Service ranger station.

Sleetmute: Groceries, general merchandise, scheduled air service. Sale and importation of alcohol is illegal.

Stony River: Limited groceries, scheduled air service.

Talkeetna: Lodging, meals, groceries, hardware, clothing, film, gas, charter boat and air service. The Alaska Railroad passes through Talkeetna.

Tanacross: Lodging, meals, groceries, gas, charter air service.

Togiak: Lodging, meals, groceries, scheduled and charter air service. (Through arrangements made with its manager, you may be able to camp at the Togiak Fisheries processing plant, across the neck of the bay from Togiak.) Sale, importation, and possession of alcohol is illegal.

Tok: Lodging, meals, groceries, hardware, gas, charter air service.

Tuluksak: Scheduled air service. (Lodging, meals, and groceries limited or unavailable.)

Umiat: Lodging, meals, charter air service.

Unalakleet: Lodging, meals, groceries, hardware, fishing licenses, charter boat and air service.

Whitehorse: All services.

Willow: Charter air service.

Wiseman: Camping, general store.

Yakutat: Lodging, meals, groceries, general merchandise, fishing licenses, car and boat rental, scheduled and charter air service. Offices of U.S. Forest Service and National Park Service.

CONSERVATION GROUPS

The area code for all telephone numbers in Alaska is 907.

Alaska Center for the Environment, 519 West Eighth Avenue, Anchorage 99501. 274-3621

Alaska Conservation Foundation, 430 West Seventh Avenue, Suite 215, Anchorage 99501. 276-1917

American Rivers, 801 Pennsylvania Avenue SE, Suite 400, Washington, DC 20003-2167. (202) 547-6900

Anchorage Waterways Council, P.O. Box 241774, Anchorage 99524-1774. 277-9287

Knik Canoers and Kayakers, P.O. Box 101935, Anchorage 99510. 272-9351

National Audubon Society, 308 G Street, Anchorage 99501. 276-7034

National Parks and Conservation Association, Box 202045, Anchorage 99520. 258-9154

Northern Alaska Environmental Center, 218 Driveway, Fairbanks 99701. 452-5021

Sierra Club, 241 East Fifth Avenue, Suite 205, Anchorage 99501. 276-4048

Southeast Alaska Conservation Council, 419 Sixth Street, Suite 328, Juneau 99801. 586-6942

Tatshenshini Wild, Western Canada Wilderness Committee, 20 Water Street, Vancouver, B.C., Canada V6B 1A4

The Wilderness Society, 430 West Seventh Avenue, Suite 205, Anchorage 99501. 272-9453

RELATED READING

Alaska Trees and Shrubs, by Les Viereck. Fairbanks: University of Alaska Press, 1986. The trees and shrubs of Alaska are described, illustrated, and mapped in this informative book.

Alaska Wilderness: Exploring the Central Brooks Range, by Robert Marshall. Berkeley: University of California Press, 1956. A classic in North American wilderness writing, this book explores some of the last of the blank spaces on the map and proposes a vast protected wilderness area north of the Arctic Circle.

The Alaska-Yukon Wild Flowers Guide Bothell, Wash.: Alaska Northwest Books, 1990. A handy reference guide, with large color photos to assist in learning the many fascinating plants of Alaska and the Yukon.

Arctic Village, by Robert Marshall (1933). Fairbanks: University of Alaska Press, 1991. An early account of life on the Koyukuk River during the gold rush days of the 1920s and 1930s.

Baby Animals of the North, by Katy Main. Bothell, Wash.: Alaska Northwest Books, 1992. A charming illustrated book that introduces children to the creatures of the North Country.

Basic River Canoeing, by Robert E. McNair. Newington, Va.: American Canoeing Association, 1987. Excellent basic instructional text on river canoeing and proper canoeing technique, useful for both students and teachers.

Born on Snowshoes, by Evelyn Berglund Shore. Boston: Houghton Mifflin, 1954. A woman's account of growing up on the Black River in the 1930s.

A Dena'ina Legacy—K'tl'egh'i Sukdu: The Collected Writings of Peter Kalifornsky. Fairbanks: Alaska Native Language Center, 1991. A collection of 147 bilingual Dena'ina-English stories, poems, and language lessons by a self-taught Dena'ina writer and scholar, born in 1911 in Kenai.

Discovering Wild Plants: Alaska, Western Canada, the Northwest, by Janice J. Schofield. Bothell, Wash.: Alaska Northwest Books, 1989. Information about wild plants in the North and Northwest and how to prepare them for eating and medicinal use, with excellent photographs, drawings, and habitat descriptions.

The Family Canoe Trip: A Unique Approach to Canoeing, by Carl Shepardson. Merrillville, Ind.: ICS Books, 1985. A narrative describing the canoe trip of a couple and their two young children from New Hampshire to Fort Yukon over the course of three summers.

The Great Bear: Contemporary Writings on the Grizzly, edited by John A. Murray. Bothell, Wash.: Alaska Northwest Books, 1992. This collection of thoughtful essays by distinguished nature writers on one of the most revered and feared inhabitants of the North Country is a perfect companion for traveling in grizzly country.

Grizzly Cub: Five Years in the Life of a Bear, by Rick McIntyre. Bothell, Wash.: Alaska Northwest Books, 1990. The story of a young bear's first five summers, told through wonderful color photos and descriptive prose, make this a thoughtful book for readers of all ages.

Guide to the Birds of Alaska, by Robert H. Armstrong. Bothell, Wash.: Alaska Northwest Books, 1991. Authoritative guide to Alaska's bird life, with color photos and detailed information on 437 species found in the state, plus a list of accidentals from Asia.

Make Prayers to the Raven, by Richard K. Nelson. Chicago: University of Chicago Press, 1983. Insightful reflections on the modern spirit/subsistence world of the Koyukon Athapaskans.

Medicine for Mountaineering, edited by James A. Wilkerson, M.D. Seattle: The Mountaineers Books, 1985. An excellent text on wilderness emergency medicine.

Path of the Paddle, by Bill Mason (1980). Minocqua, Wis.: NorthWord Press, 1984. An illustrated guide covering basic paddling strokes and maneuvers for solo and double canoeing.

People of the Noatak, by Claire Fejes. New York: Alfred Knopf, 1966. The author, an artist and writer, shares vignettes of her life among the Inupiaq Eskimos in Northwest Alaska.

The Roots of Ticasuk: An Eskimo Woman's Family Story, by Ticasuk (Emily Ivanoff Brown). Bothell, Wash.: Alaska Northwest Books, 1981. An Eskimo woman tells the history of her Inupiaq family at Unalakleet.

Two in the Far North, by Margaret Murie (1956). Bothell, Wash.: Alaska Northwest Books, 1978. In this Northern classic, Murie describes her adventures on the Alaskan frontier in the gold-mining, dog-team era, with an emphasis on the preservation of wilderness and an account of her summer on the Sheenjek River.

The Wake of the Unseen Object: Among the Native Cultures of Bush Alaska, by Tom Kizzia. New York: Henry Holt, 1991. A journalist's enlightening narrative about the people who live off the land and waterways of Alaska—and how they cope with the modern world.

"A World Inside a Mountain," by Bernard R. Hubbard. *National Geographic*, September 1931. Report on a visit to Aniakchak Crater in the Aleutian Range.

Yukon Wild: The Adventure of Four Texas Women Who Paddled 2,000 Miles through America's Last Frontier, by Beth Johnson. Stockbridge, Mass.: Berkshire Traveller Press, 1984. From dream to completed reality, the author details the logistics of their journey and provides a description of the region and insight into the history of the Yukon. Entertaining as well as informative.

INDEX

Boldface numbers indicate pages on which photographs appear.

A young Karen Jettmar at the helm, with her brother.

ABOUT THE AUTHOR

Karen Jettmar learned to paddle and row on the placid waters of the Severn River in Maryland, over 30 years ago. In the intervening years, she has discovered the joys of kayaking and river running from Alaska to South America. Alaska has been her home for 20 years, where she has combined a passion for the earth's wild places with writing, photography, and a life in the outdoors. She worked as a backcountry ranger in several of Alaska's premier national parks, taught school in rural Native communities, and was Assistant Regional Director for The Wilderness Society.

Karen Jettmar is the founder of EQUINOX, a wilderness travel business that specializes in taking small groups to explore Alaska's wild rivers, coasts, and mountains. Also an award-winning writer/photographer, she has published feature articles and photos in many books and periodicals, including *National Geographic, USA Today, Newsweek, National Parks and Conservation,* and *National Wildlife.* She lives in Anchorage.

Look to **Alaska Northwest Books**™ for other fascinating guides to the North Country, including:

GUIDE TO THE BIRDS OF ALASKA, by Robert H. Armstrong.
With the addition of 38 species, this guide offers detailed information on all 443 species of birds found in Alaska, with color photos and paintings, and a useful map of the state's biogeographic regions. This revised edition is the only book exclusively on Alaska's birds.
Softbound, 324 pages, $24.95, ISBN 0-88240-462-8

THE NATURE OF SOUTHEAST ALASKA: A Guide to Plants, Animals, and Habitats, by Robert H. Armstrong, Richard Carstensen, and Rita O'Clair; illustrations by Richard Carstensen.
This intimate guide to southeastern Alaska's plants, animals, and habitats was written by authors who know the area's most guarded secrets. With 64 color photos, 130 black-and-white illustrations, 1 map.
Softbound, 256 pages, $17.95, ISBN 0-88240-488-1

ALASKA'S WILD PLANTS: A Guide to Alaska's Edible Harvest, by Janice J. Schofield.
For hikers, foragers, and plant lovers, *Alaska's Wild Plants* is an introduction to more than 70 common edible plants. One of the first in the "Alaska Pocket Guide" series published by Alaska Northwest Books™, this easy-to-use book has color photographs of each plant, information on habitat and medicinal uses, recipes, and much more.
Softbound, 96 pages, $12.95, ISBN 0-88240-433-4

CHILKOOT PASS: The Most Famous Trail in the North, by Archie Satterfield.
A hiker's guide to the Klondike Gold Rush National Historical Park, *Chilkoot Pass* provides all you need to experience the famous Chilkoot Trail, called "the meanest 32 miles in history." With 97 photographs, 2 maps.
Softbound, 224 pages, $12.95, ISBN 0-88240-109-2

Ask for these books at your favorite bookstore, or contact Alaska Northwest Books™.

ALASKA NORTHWEST BOOKS™
An imprint of Graphic Arts Center Publishing Company
Catalog and Order Department
P.O. Box 10306
Portland, OR 97210
800-452-3032